MOSCOW IN MOVEMENT

MOSCOW IN MOVEMENT

Power and Opposition in Putin's Russia

SAMUEL A. GREENE

STANFORD UNIVERSITY PRESS

Stanford, California

Stanford University Press
Stanford, California

Printed in the United States of America on acid-free, archival-quality paper

Library of Congress Cataloging-in-Publication Data has been requested.

ISBN: 978-0-8047-9078-9 (cloth)
ISBN: 978-0-8047-9214-1 (paper)
ISBN: 978-0-8047-9244-8 (electronic)

Typeset by Thompson Type in 9.75/15 Sabon

To Russia

За Россию

Contents

List of Illustrations

Acknowledgments

This project has benefited from the support, guidance, and insight of innumerable people, not all of whom I can name here. It goes without saying that I am forever indebted to the Russian citizens, activists, experts, and well-wishers who informed this endeavor, including, but not limited to, all of those quoted in this volume.

At the LSE, I would like to thank first and foremost Abby Innes, without whom this project never would have begun. Tremendous thanks go to Sarah Ashwin, whose patient, tireless, and skilled guidance shepherded me through a long and convoluted process. Likewise, Jennifer Jackson-Preece's last-minute addition to the team was invaluable in keeping the project on track. Terhi Rantanen and Chris Binns worked closely with this project in its early phases and provided solid criticism. And, of course, my colleagues at the School—especially Natalia Leshchenko, Tome Sandevski, and Stacy Closson, as well as the inhabitants of J14—offered the ideas, conversations, and motivation that got me out of endless methodological, bibliographical, and empirical labyrinths. My enduring appreciation goes to the European Institute of the London School of Economics and Political Science.

Tremendous thanks go to Geoffrey Burn, James Holt, and the team at Stanford University Press, as well as to two anonymous reviewers.

Elsewhere in the academic world, I have benefited immeasurably from the advice, criticism, and friendship of numerous scholars, including Michael Bernhard, Yitzhak Brudny, Tim Colton, Bob Conrad, Inna Deviatko, Vladimir Gel'man, Leah Gilbert, Henry Hale, Steve Hanson, Charles Kurzman, Mary MacAuley, Andrei Makarychev, Ellen Mickiewicz, Natalia Mirovitskaia, Sarah Oates, Graeme Robertson, Gulnaz Sharafutdinova, Marat Shterin, Guillermo Trejo, Josh Tucker, Tatiana Vorozheikina, Stephen White, and David Woodruff.

Special thanks go to my students in the Sociology Department of the Higher School of Economics in Moscow, whose open minds and fresh approaches challenged me to keep my own mind open and my approaches fresh. I am equally endebted to my colleagues at the Center for the Study of New Media and Society at the New Economic School in Moscow, particularly Sergei Chernov, Ruben Enikolopov, Floriana Fossato, Sergei Guriev, Ivan Klimov and Masha Petrova, and to my new colleagues at King's College London, including Marc Berenson, Gulnaz Sharafutdinova (again), and Adnan Vatansever.

Early on in this project, I benefited tremendously from a workshop at Harvard University, organized and funded by the U.S. Social Sciences Research Council; particular thanks go to the SSRC and to Cynthia Buckley and Tim Colton (again) for their critiques and encouragement.

My fieldwork was made possible by two organizations that gave me a desk, a salary, and the freedom to pursue my interests in Moscow. In the first instance, I must thank the Independent Media Program of the New Eurasia Foundation and my colleagues there, including Masha Eismont, Dima Surnin, Zhenya Antonov, and Anna Averina, who tolerated me for an entire year. Even more patient were my colleagues at the Carnegie Moscow Center, including Masha Lipman, Lilia Shevtsova, Nikolay Petrov, Andrey Ryabov, Alexei Malashenko, and the three directors under whom I had the pleasure to serve, Andrew Kuchins, Rose Gottemoeller, and Dmitri Trenin; tremendous thanks as well to Mary Frances Lindstrom and the Open Society Foundations, who funded my position at Carnegie and thus made my fieldwork possible. In Russia, numerous activists, journalists, and experts generously gave of their time and insight, including Lyuba Alenicheva, Lyudmila Alexeeva, Vyacheslav Bakhmin, Vasily Gatov, Elena Kovalevskaya, Boris Makarenko, Oleg Novikov, Tonya Samsonova, Natalia Taubina, and Natalia Zubarevich.

If I have gotten anything right in this project, it is because of the help of these and other wonderful people; if I have gotten anything wrong, it is entirely my own fault.

Finally, I owe the deepest gratitude to my wife, Anya, for keeping me grounded; to our daughter, Elyana, for keeping me inspired; and to my parents, for everything else.

MOSCOW IN MOVEMENT

1   The Puzzle of Russian Civil Society
An Introduction

On Saturday, July 15, 2006, as the leaders of the Group of Eight industrialized democracies gathered in St. Petersburg for their annual summit, attended by aides and throngs of journalists, the city itself was disturbingly quiet. Along the city's elegant main avenue, Nevsky Prospekt, squadrons of riot police in full battle gear stood on every second street corner. Police buses and armored personnel carriers idled on the side streets. There was not a hint of the antiglobalization riots that had plagued other cities unlucky enough to host G8 summits, but the police were ready nonetheless.

On that same morning, three metro stops to the north of Nevsky Prospekt, Petersburgers lazily spilled out of the underground onto Krestovsky Island, one of the city's most beloved parks, occupying almost an entire island in the delta where the Neva River flows into the Gulf of Finland. Jugglers, clowns, and balloon twisters amused children; a small marching band played Strauss; teenagers lounged on benches or skated down the alleyways; and everyone went about the business of enjoying St. Petersburg's short but glorious summer.

Some of those leaving the metro, however, walked straight through the park, the entire length of the island, until they reached the city's old football stadium at the far end. They made their way into a small tent, received a green name tag, and filed through a metal detector to get into the stadium complex. There, they joined several hundred protestors—almost all Russian—who had gathered to show the world that they were not part of the show the Kremlin was putting on for the G8. They wanted nothing to do with a regime that fixed elections, shuttered independent media outlets, jailed political opponents, and continued to call itself a democracy. The Russia that President Vladimir Putin was showing his colleagues from the vantage of a lavishly restored tsarist palace was not their Russia. Theirs was an "Other Russia," a concept born only days earlier at a meeting in an equally lavish Moscow hotel, bringing together opposition leaders from across the political spectrum.

Of those who had been present in Moscow, only one—the longtime human rights activist Lev Ponomarev—came to St. Petersburg. Many of the activists from around the country who had planned to come never made it, having been pulled from planes, trains, and buses along the way. Some had their internal passports confiscated. Others were barricaded in their apartments. Those who did make it to the stadium found themselves surrounded by the Gulf of Finland on three sides and a long, high fence guarded by riot police on the other, with only one gate. The city authorities had banned a planned march from the stadium through the city to the cruiser *Aurora*, the ship that had launched the 1917 Revolution when it fired on the Winter Palace. Small groups of participants attempted to stage running protests in the city center but were followed by the police as they left the stadium and detained as soon as they emerged from the metro anywhere near Nevsky Prospekt. They would not be a part of the Kremlin's show, but the Kremlin ensured there would be no other.

As the day wore on, the organizers in the stadium gathered the remaining participants to discuss what to do. A few television cameras—all of them foreign—were present and ready to report on whatever the protestors did, if only they could decide on a plan of action. Holding an unsanctioned march was clearly impossible; the police would never let them out of the stadium. Eventually, two proposals were put up for a vote. The first was to march in circles around the stadium track ten times, in a symbolic show of futility. The second was to stage a sit-in at the gates of the stadium in the hopes that the image of sitting protestors behind the iron bars of the fence and surrounded by police would garner at least some publicity. In the end, the protestors selected the second option, climbed out of the stadium, and made their way to the fence. There, they sat down, placards in hand, and began shouting, "Rights aren't given; rights are taken!" and "We need another Russia!"[1]

Bit by bit, the crowd began to dissipate, protestors filing back through the metal detector, pulling off their green name tags, and heading back through the park to the metro. Many of those who forgot to remove the name tags were detained when they reemerged elsewhere in the city, just as a precaution. Pictures of the protest were broadcast in Germany, France, and Italy. In Russia, however, no one noticed. In the park on Krestovsky Island, where the band was still playing Strauss when the last protesters left, a boy asked his father why there were so many police down by the stadium.

"Must be a football game," the father answered. "The police have to keep an eye on the hooligans."[2]

⁓

Until tens and then hundreds of thousands of Russians poured onto the streets of Moscow in December 2011 to protest what they perceived to be a rigged parliamentary election, the foregoing picture was the predominant view of Russian social and political mobilization. Indeed, the idea of the weakness of Russian civil society remains well established and widely accepted. Russians, on the whole, do not organize and are difficult to mobilize, and they do not tend to join movements or participate in public protests (see, for example, Fish 1995; Domrin 2003; McFaul and Treyger 2004). Understanding why something does not occur, however, is perhaps the most difficult task in the social sciences. Some attempts have been made to explain the void of civic mobilization in Russia, predominantly by pointing either to macrolevel social phenomena (low levels of trust and social capital, for example) or macrolevel political phenomena (the resource curse or repression).

When nonlinear events occur—events that our prior conceptions did not allow us to predict, events that seem to be "out of the blue"—the natural tendency is to focus our analysis entirely on the future, to assume that at the moment of the departure from the norm something inherently unforeseeable happened to shift the narrative, and to seek to understand the "new world" in which we have evidently arrived. Indeed, much of what has been written about the Russian protest wave of 2011 and 2012 pointed to purportedly new phenomena—new communication media, new leaders, new wealth, a new global context—as the proximate cause of what prior wisdom had failed to envisage.

Truly understanding where we are, however, requires correcting our understanding of where we were. Even as we look to the future and try to understand what it holds in store, we must ask what recent events tell us about the past. Before we accept the idea that the present condition is entirely novel, we should at least consider the notion that it has roots in what came before, roots which we, for whatever reason, failed as social scientists to notice, or at least to deem important. Such a reevaluation may, we can hope, reduce the magnitude of the analytical mistakes we will make in the future.

As with all rules, there are and always were exceptions to the blanket explanations put forward for the failure of civil society in Russia. Along the margins, in unexpected corners and pockets of society, there has been throughout Putin's rule activism and engagement, and it was often sustained and sometimes fruitful. These exceptions are the focus of this volume, which asks whether the rare instances in which Russian civil society does succeed can shed some light on the question of why, in the vast majority of cases, it does not.

Russia, by most accounts, has spent most of the twenty-first century to date institutionalizing the middle ground between democratic and authoritarian governance. In that respect, Russia resembles what Marina Ottaway (2003) termed a "semi-authoritarian regime," or what Steven Levitsky and Lucan Way (2010) called "competitive authoritarianism" and a "hybrid regime." There is a large degree of individual freedom in Russia, as well as significant (though diminishing) freedom of speech, association, and assembly—all of which are typically cited as the prerequisites of a "democratic" civil society. There has also been significant (though diminishing) funding available for a large (though shrinking) number of initiatives, likewise a widely recognized pillar of organized civic activity. However, whereas Soviet dissident groups relied on networks of dedicated volunteers, who were able to exert pinpointed pressure on the government and frequently achieved their goals (whether freedom of emigration, tighter ecological controls, or the clandestine distribution of articles), civil society in twenty-first-century Russia has broadly failed to match up in all of these categories. Thus, if we judge by the ability to mobilize public opinion and support and achieve defined goals (other than the attraction of grant money), civil society in Putin's Russia has in some ways been *less* effective at achieving its aims than it was during the Soviet Union, when none of the previously mentioned freedoms existed. That, surely, appears to be a paradox.

From the perspective of the social scientist, this paradox is exacerbated by the lack of useful theory. The broadest studies of democracy, in order to achieve generalized relevance, take their definitions and categorizations to a level of abstraction that is scarcely useful to someone trying to understand why a particular country falters. Given its narrower focus and emphasis on dynamic processes, the specific study of democratic transition is often more useful. Transitology, however, also has its limits, a common criticism being that it "may be too 'political' a framework, in the sense that it ignores how underlying economic and social structures may persist despite 'democratic change' and thus subvert political outcomes" (Kubicek 2000). And yet even the most recent political economy studies of democratization have been unable to identify causal variables that go beyond the traditional triumvirate of economic modernization, political history, and culture/religion, none of which is particularly helpful in applied analysis of country cases or small-N comparisons (Borooah and Paldam 2007).

The even narrower field of postcommunist studies has yielded some valuable insights, particularly regarding the development of formal institutions, including political parties and infrastructure underpinning privatized economies. It is argued with increasing force and frequency that Russian citizens suffer from a postcommunist syndrome, of which all of the previously mentioned pathologies are common symptoms. Public initiative of the kind generally associated with civil society is seen to be considerably lower in the former Soviet Union and Central and Eastern Europe than in other regions of the world (see, most prominently, Howard 2003). More broadly put, the entire postcommunist space—even in those countries that have created the most open political systems—appears to suffer from a deficit of democratic participation (see, for example, Anderson, Fish, et al. 2001; Grzymala-Busse and Luong 2002; Innes 2002). The most common explanation put forward for this generally centers on the problem of trust: Russians and other postcommunist denizens are inclined to distrust both their neighbors and themselves (Rose 1994; Sztompka 1998; Lovell 2001).

But the identification of postcommunist commonalities also has the unfortunate effect of obscuring important differences. And nowhere has this been more the case than in the study of civil society, where supposedly low levels of trust and social capital are cited as a blanket explanation for the regionwide weakness of civic initiative (Howard 2003). The issue of trust notwithstanding, there is significant variation in the level and nature of civil–societal activity both within countries and from one postcommunist country to another that cannot be easily accounted for by discrepancies in the degree of trust.

While the bulk of the literature on civil society tends to focus on broad, society-based explanations such as trust, some of the literature on transition—both within and outside the transitology tradition—has begun to focus more attention on the behavior of elites as the source of civic weakness and atomization, with particular reference to Russia. Thus, both McFaul and Treyger (2004) and Kitschelt and Smyth (2002)[3] suggest that the withdrawn and self-centered nature of elite competition in many postcommunist countries, driven by the peculiarities of their political economies, effectively pulls the rug out from under potential civic initiatives. Indeed, while contemporary civil society theory tends to look in other directions, there is significant support for such considerations in social movement theory, where Tarrow places the behavior of elites as a central element in forming the opportunity structure of potential civic initiative (Tarrow 1998). What is missing from these arguments, however, is a detailed study of the specific processes and mechanisms that link one to the other.[4]

What We Know about Russian Civil Society

Beyond the general categorizations mentioned earlier of Russian civil society as weak, what do we really know about the processes that weaken it? By now, most analysts have abandoned notions that the political changes occurring since 1991 have constituted a democratizing revolution. The views on why democratization has failed are varied, and although they are dealt with more fully in Chapter 3, they can be generally summed up as follows. In one camp, Peter Reddaway and Dmitri Glinski, joined by Marshall Goldman, blame undemocratic elites for capturing and perverting a process of reform, subjugating political democratization to economic liberalization (Reddaway and Glinski 2001; Goldman 2003a). To this, others add structural elements, such as the "resource curse" of oil, gas, and mineral wealth, which stymied true economic liberalization and discouraged the development of parliamentary democracy (Fish 2005). Still others blame Russia's democrats themselves for being insufficiently determined, organized, and unified (Garcelon 2005).

All regimes need a power base, which is simultaneously the source of its support, the object of its control, and the group with which it will most intensely interact. In a Soviet Communist regime, although the classical conception has been that the regime's power base was the Party, the desire of the regime to maintain comprehensive control over all aspects of economic, political, and social life means effectively that its power base was the entire population. Support for the regime did not have to be active; the way things were arranged, the mundane acts of participation in everyday life were all that was required. In the words of Vaclav Havel, the Soviet state "occupies and swallows everyone, so that all should become integrated within it, at least through their silence" (Havel 1988: 390). As the Kadarists said in Hungary, *if you're not against us, you're with us.* This engagement with the whole of the population—which is the hallmark of any truly totalitarian regime—leaves open the possibility that the population at large can become a source of opposition, embodied in civil society; this is, arguably, what occurred in 1989 throughout much of Central and Eastern Europe.

In Putin's Russia, political competition exists, but it is closed, not so much in the sense of barriers to entry (though these obtain) as in the sense that the state organizes politics in such a way as to prevent competitors from creating a power base that draws support from outside the limited sphere of "administrative resources." Thus, in a limited authoritarian regime like post-Soviet Russia, the regime's power base is considerably narrower than it was during the Soviet period. It derives its support not from the broad participation of the population in a highly centralized economic system but from the subordination (through regulatory, forceful, or clientelistic relations) of crucial groups, such as the oligarchy, regional strongmen, or the security establishment. The population remains a resource, but one on which the state depends only indirectly, insofar as the oligarchy, for example, may depend on it for labor. One result is a dispersal of the potential targets of blame and protest for mass dissatisfaction. In the Russian context, this arrangement is particularly effective at insulating elites from the public and thus creating room for state autonomy, because the primary resources on which the oligarchy depends are natural, and thus even they depend on the population only indirectly. Civil society, then, finds itself doubly removed from access to power. A fundamental result of this arrangement is that the contemporary Russian state does not engage society at large. Indeed, it actively works to exclude the public from the processes of government, not so much to control the public as to prevent uncontrollable elements—such as a mass-based movement—from entering the political arena. Thus, if we conceive of civil society as a mediator between state and individual, the almost total disregard of one for the other might seem to obviate this function.

The result has been the dismantling of layers upon layers of institutions governing much of social life in Russia, including the ways people work, study, communicate, participate in political and economic life, procreate, and die. This has been replaced primarily by pervasive uncertainty—uncertainty as to the future of the country, as to how much a ruble will be worth tomorrow, as to whether the rights a citizen had yesterday will be respected today. As constantly changing rules of the game prevent the consolidation of the formal institutions that constitute the state, so do the intermediary institutions fall away. There has been a general devolution—what Michael Burawoy, Pavel Krotov, and Tatyana Lytkina call "involution"—of the center of life activity from collective institutions to the family. As Burawoy and coauthors write, "As industry and agriculture have disintegrated, the fulcrum of production and redistribution has moved from factory to household" (Burawoy, Krotov, et al. 2000: 43). They point to two "involuted" strategies, one defensive and the other entrepreneurial; in either case, however, the strategy is individualistic and highly suspicious of the collective.

This is borne out, meanwhile, by what we know about various sectors of civil society. The environmental "movement," for example, is dominated by particularistic interests. As a whole, "green" groups fail to serve as state–society intermediaries in the classic civil–society sense. As Laura Henry writes: "Instead, [their] activities represent efforts to provide services related to environmental protection or recreation that were once the responsibility of the state. Grassroots groups in particular have leapt in to fill the loss of recreation opportunities for children and public maintenance of city parks" (Henry 2006: 223). Likewise, migrants' evident preference for informal networks instead of formal organizations suggests a similar particularistic logic:

> Many migrants choose not to engage with nongovernmental organizations at the site of settlement. This choice may well be rooted in a mistrust of formal organization inherited from the Soviet period. However, the choice is also a positive one and a rational one, made in favor of a better option at the time. The trust and support offered by more informal networks of family and friends points to a thriving, responsible, and moral community that provides very real assistance to its members, rather than to isolated, atomized individuals and households, which would more likely impede the building of civil society. (Flynn 2006: 260)

Stephen Wegren (2003) suggests that this increase in self-reliance, rather than contributing to the sort of atomization that is seen as the antithesis of civil society, creates new assets for the development of civil society. He writes:

> Increased independence by rural households limits future state incursions against individuals' rights. For example, expanded land holdings, land lease relations, and the utilization of market-based channels of food trade create significant political, economic, legal and psychological barriers that the political leadership most likely would be reluctant to breach. (Wegren 2003: 24)

Likewise, James Gibson follows a similar notion to dispute the widespread argument that Russians suffer from a deficit of trust and are atomized:

> Russian social networks may well have emerged primarily as a response to the repressive state. Unable to organize publicly, Russians have substituted private social networks for formal organizations. But Russians are not atomized, and as a con-

sequence, Russian social networks have a variety of characteristics that may allow them to serve as important building blocks for the development of a vibrant civil society. In addition to carrying considerable political content, these networks are characterized by a relatively high degree of trust. Because the networks are not closed (strong), they link Russians together to an extent not often recognized by most analysts. (Gibson 2001: 60)

It would be easy to accept this as the end of the story—the state divorces itself from the public, the public say "good riddance," and the two go their separate ways—were it not for the fact that states and societies cannot simply go their separate ways. They are bound to share a common territory and common resources, and although they may do their best not to notice each other, they will inevitably come into contact and, thus, conflict. If we accept that broad-spectrum political engagement and civic activism are effectively suppressed by the state's disengagement from society, then we should be particularly interested in the content and meaning of the exceptions, the points at which conflict occurs and engagement ensues.

Two of the most remarkable recent works on Russian politics and society—Andrew Wilson's *Virtual Politics* (2005) and Ellen Mickiewicz's *Television, Power, and the Public in Russia* (2008)—frame this situation quite clearly. Wilson describes the Russian regime as an "edifice kept standing . . . [by] . . . four key conditions . . . : a powerful but amoral elite; a passive electorate; a culture of information control; and the lack of an external counterpoint, i.e., foreign intervention" (2005: 43). In later chapters we will examine how this is achieved; suffice it for now to confirm that it is achieved, though with Wilson's own caveat: "The post-Soviet states are not totalitarian. Other versions of reality creep in at the margins. The main priority of the powers-that-be is that their version of reality should predominate—they know that it can never exclusively dominate. They want the majority to believe something like their version of events. . . . But more crudely, they are happy simply to get away with it; not every loose end needs to be tied up" (2005: 45).

Loose ends do accumulate, however, and therein lies the potential for the sorts of cases this volume examines. In her study of Russians' reception of television news, Mickiewicz finds not only that viewers are deeply dissatisfied with what they receive but that the ruling elite should be equally dissatisfied with the work of its media proxies. Particularly when it comes to political news and election coverage, she writes,

9

The Kremlin's appropriation and suppression of televised diversity has not resulted in the expected acceptance of the broadcasters' desired frame. The election story has become an expensive article of faith for its producers; for viewers, it is a confusing phenomenon that occurs with considerable regularity (since such stories form a single genre) and exists outside their own lives—lives from which under other circumstances they derive the cognitive shortcuts so necessary for processing information." (2008: 87–88)

The issue Mickiewicz identified is not one of cognitive dissonance; Russians are perfectly able to interpret political information. The problem is that coverage of elections is unsatisfactory and off-putting because elections are deeply irrelevant to Russian citizens. They very clearly understand all of the virtuality of politics Wilson describes. What they do not understand is why so many in the West expect them to take part in political actions that are so obviously and thoroughly virtual. Faced with a disengaged elite, civic disengagement is a rational response. But we should understand that disengagement to be circumstantial and contingent, rather than cultural and absolute. Exceptions can and do occur, presenting themselves as instances in which citizenship and participation take on real content and meaning. It is important that we understand why.

In seeking to determine why Russian workers put up with privations in the 1990s, amid the almost total collapse of heavy industry, Sarah Ashwin argued that the key to understanding Russians' "endless patience" is in "linking the political behaviour of workers to the form and content of their lives"; in particular, "workers' reaction to the pressures of reform has exhibited both an attachment to the collective institutions of the past, and the active development of individual survival strategies" (Ashwin 1998: 195). Given that the collective institutions have been deprived of any useful function, the individual strategies naturally gain in preeminence. If we look into the example of the Soldiers' Mothers' committees, one of Russia's strongest grassroots movements (see, for example, Sundstrom 2006b), we might thus hypothesize that collective action reemerges in those instances, when individual strategies can be channeled through "involved" groups such as traditional familial and gender networks into effective modes of interaction with the state. To find these instances, though, it is not simply enough to run down the list of standard "causes" and look for the relevant nongovernmental organizations (NGOs). This is a highly specific process, contingent, as Ashwin writes, on the "content of people's lives." It requires a careful and unprejudiced approach.

The Morphology of Governance

The Place of Civil Society

In their seminal text on democratization, Juan Linz and Alfred Stepan identified "five arenas of a consolidated democracy": (1) civil society (defined as "that arena of the polity where self-organizing groups, movements, and individuals, relatively autonomous from the state, attempt to articulate values . . . and advance their interests"); (2) political society (defined as "that arena in which the polity specifically arranges itself to contest the legitimate right to exercise control over public power and the state apparatus"); (3) rule of law; (4) a usable state bureaucracy; and (5) a stable economic structure (Linz and Stepan 1996: 7). Bucking the dominant tendency to place civil and political society in inherent opposition to one another, Linz and Stepan wrote: "For modern democratic theory, especially for questions about how to consolidate democracy, it is important to stress not only the *distinctiveness* of civil society and political society, but also their *complementarity*. This complementarity is not always recognized" (Linz and Stepan 1996: 7–8; italics in the original).

Some points of view, largely hinging on differences of definition, would no doubt dispute this assertion. I do not intend, however, to spend time debating definitions—particularly the always problematic definition of civil society—here; I will address definitional issues in full detail in Chapter 2. It will suffice for now to note that most prominent definitions of civil society include at least some reference to the political (see, for example, Gellner 1994; Ehrenberg 1999; Kaldor 2003). Indeed, this tradition has strong historical roots. Locke, Rousseau, and the philosophers of the Scottish Enlightenment all emphasized the role played by civil society in maintaining the subjugation of the power of the state to the democratic sovereignty of the public (Locke [1681] 1993; Rousseau [1762] 1968; Ferguson [1767] 1966; Hume [1772] 1994b).

Further developments in political philosophy would more clearly elucidate the location and role of civil society. Hegel famously defined civil society as "the realm of difference, intermediate between the family and the state" (Hegel [1820] 1896: 185). In this view, civil society consists primarily of the organization of individual wants and their satisfaction into a corporatized economy, the "protection of property by the administration of justice," and "provision against possible mischances, and care for the particular interest as a common interest" (Hegel [1820] 1896: 192). De Tocqueville ([1835] 1994) and Mill ([1848]

1970), meanwhile, both wrote that civil society is strongest when the public is included in the political process through open institutions.

The development of Marxist thought (Fromm 1963; Bobbio 1988; Marx [1844] 1970) and the rise of political sociology (Moore 1967; Duverger 1972; Giddens 1984; Polanyi [1944] 2001) together reinforced the notion that civil society reflects the surrounding institutions in a given state—both the deep, historically informed institutions of social relations and the surface institutions of political and economic life. Indeed, if civil society's role is to serve as an intermediary between the state and society, it seems only logical that it would take on the contours of its two interlocutors, much like molten metal poured into a mold.

The implication that civil society is contingent at least in part on political institutions, although unpopular with some normative theorists, is not overly controversial. However, the question remains as to how that contingency operates. The immediate suggestion from historical political philosophy is that political openness is key; indeed, civil society is clearly stronger in democratic states than in totalitarian ones. This, too, seems logical: For civil society to mediate a conversation between two parties, both parties have to be interested in talking; if the state balks, civil society is left with not much to do (except start a revolution, which calls into question the designation "civil") and could be expected to wither away.

Democracy and Authoritarianism

The necessity of studying authoritarianism alongside democracy came into sharp focus as what Michael McFaul called the "fourth wave" of transition wore on: If the "third wave" had been a story of democratization, then the fourth was more ambiguous, as former members of the Soviet bloc embarked on processes of political, economic, and social transformation with highly uncertain outcomes. This was a disheartening prospect, both for those who believe in democracy and for those who study it. It was the third wave, after all, that had yielded modernization theory, as well as ideas on elite pacts, constitutionalism, and other institutional aspects that seemed to play predictable and reliable roles in the development of democracy. But unlike in the "third wave" of democratization, in which precarious balances of power encouraged democratic competition, democracy in post-Communism emerged only in those cases when ideologically committed democrats enjoyed sufficient political hegemony to impose their favored system of governance (McFaul 2002). Where dominant elites had other ideas, obviously, they took their countries in other directions.

At the same time this was happening, the geopolitical recognition that democracy had become "the only game in town" meant that even dictators began holding elections, revising constitutions, and ridding themselves of the formal institutions of autocracy that could make them seem less than honorable on the international scene. In theorizing semiauthoritarianism, Marina Ottaway (2003) describes regimes that combine formal democratic institutions—many of which to a great degree outwardly resemble those described by Linz and Stepan—but that nonetheless remain essentially authoritarian. To do this, she writes, they "rely" on four key deficiencies: (1) "mechanisms that effectively prevent the transfer of power through elections"; (2) noninstitutional power structures; (3) "the lack of positive synergy between political and economic reform"; and (4) repression of politically oriented civil society.

Similarly, in theorizing "defective democracies," Wolfgang Merkel begins with the concept of embedded democracies, which he sees as grounded in five "interdependent partial regimes" that in some aspects resemble Linz and Stepan's "five arenas": "[the] electoral regime, political rights, civil rights, horizontal accountability, [and] effective power to govern" (Merkel 2004: 36). He writes: "Defective democracies are by no means necessarily transitional regimes. They are able to form stable links to their environment and are seen by considerable parts of the elites and the population as adequate solutions to the extreme accumulation of problems in post-autocratic democracies" (Merkel 2004: 55).

These outwardly stable, seemingly sustainable regimes—whether referred to as semiauthoritarian, as defectively democratic, or by any number of other "adjectival democracies"—have been able to develop systems that allow them to govern with little or no regard for the consent of the governed; this is the outcome of the configurations that Ottaway and Merkel described. These are most often painted as the choices of elites, who are assumed to desire maximum autonomy and to have a penchant for rent seeking, unless, perhaps, they are ideologically committed to more open rule or bound by conditionality such as that imposed by the European Union. Often, but not always, this system is supported by the presence of abundant natural resources, as the so-called resource curse discourages elites from allowing competition and allows them to buy their way out of accountability (Ross 1999; Herb 2005).

And yet, occasionally, societies appear to be able to break through. A series of "colored revolutions"—starting in Serbia, then in Georgia and Ukraine—saw publics rise up to protest rigged elections, removing one set of political leaders and installing others through extraconstitutional but peaceful means. If the regimes in Belgrade, Tbilisi, and Kiev had developed the equilibrium needed to sustain nondemocratic rule over more than a decade, why did they so suddenly become so fragile?

Looking at the regimes themselves, Henry Hale categorized them as "patronal presidencies," in which extremely powerful executives maintain control by simultaneously monopolizing and reinforcing the rent-seeking abilities of the elite (Hale 2006). The competing necessities in these semiauthoritarian regimes of maintaining outward democratic legitimacy and the security of the elite means that, at certain points in the political cycle, they are subject to catastrophic uncertainty, creating opportunities that were capitalized on in the "colored revolutions," Hale argues.

In a somewhat wider-ranging analysis, Michael McFaul identifies seven factors that underpinned the success of the antiauthoritarian opposition movements in Serbia, Georgia, and Ukraine, including "(1) a semi-autocratic rather than autocratic regime; (2) an unpopular incumbent; (3) a united and organized opposition; (4) an ability to drive home the point that voting results were falsified; (5) enough independent media to inform citizens about the falsified vote; (6) a political opposition capable of mobilizing tens of thousands or more demonstrators to protest electoral fraud; and (7) divisions among the regime's coercive forces" (McFaul 2005: 7).

Neither of these explanations includes any real reference to democracy or democratization. Rather, they view the "colored revolutions"—and in this are followed by the bulk of the literature—as having been (more or less unique) political opportunities that allowed for an opening in the system of elite competition. There is nothing inevitably democratic about a change in rulers, nor does the ability of an opposition candidate to win a presidential election guarantee that all or even any future elections will be free and fair. Indeed, if we focus on the question of why these regimes were vulnerable, then democracy seems to have very little to do with the answer.

However, if we approach the question from a point of view that sees civil society as an integral part of any democratic system, then a different question arises: Why were publics in Serbia, Georgia, and Ukraine moved to defend their political rights in ways that citizens of other countries—Russia, for example—

were not? Prior to the protests of 2011–2012, Russians, by all accounts, were under no illusions that their elections had been free and fair, and, although they professed support for their president, they were manifestly unhappy with many of the policies that the regime pursued (Colton and Hale 2009).

My suggestion stems from the supposition that citizens form their relationships to political regimes based not on formal institutional arrangements but on the real products that these regimes deliver. In this view, normative expectations that elections should not be stolen are of little value. Rather, rights will be demanded and defended when they are perceived as useful, when the time and resources expended in the context of protest action or a social movement can be expected to bring commensurate dividends. This is, moreover, more than a problem of collective action or social capital: It gets to the very core of the nature of a political regime, a reality, I contend, that citizens feel and understand very well.

Civil Society in Movement

Civil society, in theory, exists at the nexus between the state and society, but the civil society literature finds the link between civil society and politics to be particularly problematic. Civil society, it is frequently argued, must be inherently apolitical, so as to be differentiated from political society (much in the same way that it is not profit oriented, so as to be differentiated from economic society). This approach has led to two dominant trends in the civil society literature—one dealing with NGOs and the formalized "third sector," the other dealing with less formal concepts of social capital—both of which tend to eschew politics.

Unlike more normatively guided civil society theorists, social movement theorists have generally recognized the importance of the political context. As Sidney Tarrow writes:

> Whatever the source of contentious claims, it is political opportunities and constraints that translate them into action. They produce social movements by accessing known and flexible repertoires of contention; by developing collective action frames and collective identities; and by building mobilizing structures around social networks and organizations. (Tarrow 1998: 141)

Likewise, Dietrich Reuschemeyer, Evelyne Huber Stephens, and John Stephens write:

The state has many ways of shaping the development of civil society. It can ease or obstruct the organization of different class interests; it can empower or marginalize existing organizations; it may succeed in co-optation and, in the extreme, use whole organizational networks as conduits of hegemonic influence. The complex interdependence of state and civil society creates a wide variety of possible relations between the state and different social classes and, consequently, of conditions conducive or hostile to democracy. (Rueschemeyer, Stephens, et al. 1992: 67)

Broadening out from social movement theory to civil society and reflecting back on social capital, Helmut Anheier and Jeremy Kendall start from Keane's view of civil society as "permanently in tension with each other and with the state" (Keane 1988: 6), writing:

This tension-ridden and conflictual associational infrastructure creates opportunities and mechanisms for the generation of trust among citizens as either individuals or by virtue of their membership in organizations. These opportunities in the form of social inclusion and participation in extra-familial networks, in turn, create social capital, which becomes a major factor in social mobility at the individual level and for economic advancement of entire population segments more generally. Such opportunities may lead to the creation and maintenance of trust under two circumstances: first, if forms of social inclusion, participation and capital formation enforce beliefs in the basic legitimacy of the social order and the political system as rightful expressions of fundamental values; and second, if they strengthen confidence in the operation of society as [a] reliable and predictable system. Confidence can refer to either equity or efficiency considerations. The central point is that the relationship between trust and social capital is highly conditional, i.e., dependent on the structure of civil society and the legitimacy of the political system, and indirect, i.e., mediated through processes like social inclusion and participation. (Anheier and Kendall 2000: 15)

This, then, places significant emphasis on the political regime, its ability to generate legitimacy, and the ways in which it manages power. If we define a regime as "the basic pattern by which government decision-making power is organized, exercised, and transferred in a society" (Dogan and Higley 1998: 20), and if we take this "pattern" in the sense of a socially constructed institution, then the importance of how elites behave is clear. This is all the more true in transition, when regimes may be unconsolidated and the room for maneuver open to elites greater. Thus, this project operates with a model of civil society in which a crucial role is seen to be played by the political elite, by virtue of their nearly exclusive ability to determine the extent and character of the state's interaction with society. That said, this is not a project about states and regimes. Rather, it centers on civil society, asking what the requirements are for its emergence and consolidation.

This approach, tying up civil society with the behavior of the political elite, takes direct inspiration from the literature on social movements. Social movements are self-referential, reflexive processes, in which "actions affect other actions: actions are not just isolated, independent responses to external economic or political conditions—rather, one action changes the likelihood of subsequent actions" (Oliver and Myers 2003: 1). Thus, while an actor-centered view sees social movements as an iterative process of interaction between challengers and the state, it may also be useful to conceive of a social movement

> as a distribution of events across a population of actors. Social movements rise when the overall frequency of protest events rises in a population, they become violent when the ratio of violent events to non-violent events rises, and so forth. . . . The term "event" here is used very generally, so that adopting a belief or writing a document may be thought of as events, as can resource flows from one group to another. (Oliver and Myers 2003: 3)

Two aspects of this point of view are particularly useful in the present investigation. First, it further frees us from the need to be too closely tied to organizations, allowing us to see movements more clearly in various stages of their development. And, second, it allows us to see "framing events" as an integral part of social movements, on a par with a protest or a negotiation, rather than as an ephemeral artifact of social psychology.

Social movement theory and the sociological study of protest are particularly well suited to the task of this volume because, by investigating opposition in Russia, we are interested in exceptions to rules. Charles Kurzman writes:

> The more unexpected the event, the greater the effort needed to make sense of it. Protest movements pose particular difficulties because they intentionally challenge the expectations of routine social behavior. Predicting these movements retroactively is thus one of the greatest quests in social science: to discover the regularities underlying irregularity—the rules underlying behavior that flouts the rules. (Kurzman 2004: 340)

Thus, to recap the theory briefly, we begin from the position that, in the study of civil society, it is crucial not to confuse the means with the ends. The ends of civil society are not achieved in the simple presence of the means; the existence of NGOs and the like may be a necessary condition for civil society (though this is highly debatable), but it is clearly not sufficient. Rather, the "public good" at the heart of the concept of civil society is generated by an iterative process of action and interaction between the state (as represented by the ruling elite and/or more consolidated institutions of power) and society (as represented by civic initiatives). The process begins with the nature of the state's intervention in the sphere of private interests. Following social movement theory, exactly what these interests are is secondary and contingent on the specific political economy of a given state. Intervention that is concerted and coherent (as opposed to haphazard and individualistic) may be expected to generate a collective response. The state may then be expected to react, this reaction engendering a further civic reaction. As iterations continue, there should ideally emerge a stable pattern of interactions, in which civic and state actors may reasonably judge the effectiveness of one or another course of action; this may be considered the consolidation of civil society.

As a corollary, two things may occur in this process to inhibit the consolidation of civil society. First, the state's intervention may be incoherent and haphazard, engendering a one-on-one relationship between individual citizens and individual officers of the state. In this case, collective action may not occur; the relationship between state and citizen (as opposed to state and society) is unstable and uninstitutionalized. (It would seem that the institution of state–citizen relations must be consolidated before the state–society relationship may experience meaningful development.)[5] Second, in its reaction to collective civic action the state may fail to adhere to a coherent strategy, in turn preventing civic actors from settling into predictable patterns of action. In this case, civic initiative will fail to consolidate into civil society. This insistence on coherence in both the first and second instance should not be taken as redundancy: Institutions are consolidated through iteration and reiteration; for civil society to engage effectively with the state, the state must be consistent both in how it intrudes into private life and in how it responds to civil society's reaction.

It has already been said that the genesis of civil society begins with the intrusion of the state into the private interests of its citizens. In the classical conception, as described by de Tocqueville, this occurs when the workings of the state affect the interests of the owners of private property. (This, incidentally, may occur through both state action and inaction, that is, the failure to defend.) This is the same as the "middle-class" model of civil society, in which the existence of private property is considered a necessary condition. This model, however, should not be taken as universal. Rather, the mobilizational interests are more properly seen as contingent on the specific political economy of the state in question. There is no sound theoretical reason to believe that the state's intrusion into other spheres of private interest—so long as those interests are sufficiently dear—may not provoke a civil–social reaction. Indeed, we observe in the West so-called postindustrial civil society, organizing around interests that amount to little more than moral indignation; likewise, civil society in the communist world mobilized primarily on moral grounds. In even more recent experience, we have seen some post-Soviet societies organize against the infringement of their political rights. This, then, raises the operative questions: In what contexts may we expect civil–social mobilization around political interests? What determines the triggers and cleavages of such mobilization? What is the distribution of causation between structure and agency?

This theory, then, consists of two elements, one concerning the emergence of civil society and the other concerning its consolidation. In the view presented here, civil society emerges in response to a concerted and coherent intrusion by the state into the lives of its citizens, and the form and content of that response will broadly reflect the stimulus and the political-economic context. It is crucial that this intrusion be concerted and coherent; haphazard intrusion, such as bribe seeking by corrupt bureaucrats, will elicit individualistic coping strategies. Thus, collective action arises in response to collective affliction, so to speak. The consolidation of civil society likewise requires coherence on the part of the state. As with any institution, the consolidation of civil society needs stable rules of play; if the ruling elite cannot or will not settle on a coherent strategy of engagement with civic initiative, civil society will face the need to continuously adjust, and no institutional consolidation will occur.

About the Book

This book begins with a question about civic mobilization and engagement in Russia, asking whether it is possible to determine patterns according to which we might expect Russian citizens to organize for the collective defense of their rights—as they did in December 2011 and the months thereafter, but also as they had done, on closer inspection, throughout Putin's earlier rule. When talking about civil society, this volume refers primarily to the phenomenon of grassroots activism, which in turn involves at least some recognition of an overall political goal (without breaching the divide between civil and political society). The focus is on the genesis, consolidation, and (when applicable) dissipation of civic initiative. In this view, the specific organizational form that is taken is only of secondary importance and is contingent on a number of factors, including the political, legal, and economic environment and the specific history and traditions of the society in which these institutions are grounded. The research agenda reformulates the question as follows: What are the causes of civic discouragement in Russia? What are the specific obstacles that cause grassroots activism to struggle and fall? More importantly, what are the limitations of these obstacles—in other words, under what conditions is civil society able to overcome them? Thus, if Ashwin asked why Russians appear to be so patient, this project begins by asking specifically in which circumstances they tend to lose their patience.

In seeking to address this question, I start from a theoretical assertion that the emergence of civil society requires concerted intrusion by the state into the private interest of citizens and that the sustainability of civil society requires stable (institutionalized) patterns of interaction between state and nonstate actors, then—at least in the context of transition—political elites should have the upper hand in determining the relationship between civil society and the state. To test this hypothesis, however, I look down, rather than up.

The most enlightening modern work on civil society—such as that by Chris Hann (1996) and Marc Morjé Howard (2002)—has started from the notion that homogenized, normatively determined conceptions of civil society are unhelpful, seeking instead to study the detail of state–society relations. In a recent review of such developments in the study of civil society, Jan Kubik wrote (with specific reference to Howard and Hann):

> [The] next generation of studies on civil society must not concentrate merely on the levels of participation and the quantity of civil society associations and organizations . . . but rather on their *quality* and *connectedness* with other domains of the polity and the international arena. To operationalize these features, we will have to find comparative empirical measures for the . . . attributes and . . . linkages of civil society. . . . We also need to heed Chris Hann's warning that these attributes and linkages do and indeed must take specific forms, congruent with their cultural and political contexts. The project of civil anthropology—proposed by Hann and supported by Howard—needs to specify "functional equivalents" of civil society in detail and offer proper tools for "measuring" them. (Kubik 2005: 119–120)

In keeping with this spirit and in seeking to understand the phenomenon of civil society, this volume has begun from concepts originating in political science and philosophy. For the purposes of field research, however, I take my inspiration from sociologists and anthropologists. In the next several paragraphs, I will attempt to explain why this is so, as well as to justify the methodology that underpins the research presented in the following chapters.

In turning for inspiration to the social movement literature, this volume takes certain methodological cues from sociology more broadly. Thus, Charles Kurzman, writing about the study of political change, quotes Mario Bunge to remind us that "social relations pass through the heads of people," as well as that "all forms of explanation must plausibly account for the inner states of the individuals who enact causation" (Kurzman 2004: 329–330).

Given, however, that movements can be both more and less than organizations, and that "demarcating the boundaries of a movement . . . is extremely difficult," Doug McAdam asks: How do we study them? "The only way," he writes, answering his own question, " . . . is to shift the focus of analysis from these unwieldy abstractions known as movements to specific demonstrations, actions, campaigns, or other bounded forms of activism. We *can* study the process by which an individual comes to participate in a particular instance of activism" (McAdam 1986: 67).

The core argument of this book is that political elites, by structuring the political arena, exert a decisive influence on the patterns of collective behavior that make up civil society. Moreover, it seeks to test this theory by applying it to observable facts in historical and comparative perspective. Thus, the proof of the pudding, to botch a metaphor, is to be found in the shifting details of life. It is difficult to conceive of a viable quantitative study that would be adequate to the task at hand; the changes we are looking for will not be captured by voting patterns, membership statistics, or quantifiable answers to formal questionnaires. What is needed is not a formal methodology, applied rigidly and in identical fashion across all cases, but a methodology that allows flexibility in the field in order to uncover results that can be compared in rigorous analysis.

The ensuing chapters delve deeply into the stories of organizations, events and, in some cases, individuals. In every case, what I am interested in is a self-conscious evaluation of behavior. Certainly, it is important to know as exactly as possible what happened and when. It is just as crucial, however, to reach an understanding of why decisions were made and actions undertaken, based not on theoretical assertion but on close observation. In so doing, I do not limit myself to one or another method of field research. To draw as full and accurate a picture as possible, I rely on a broad range of sources, including documentary and archival records, interviews (structured, semistructured, and informal), participant observation, credible media reports, and, of course, the work of numerous other scholars in the field.

Three case studies form the core of this project. The first is of a "traditional" human rights NGO of interest because it is simultaneously successful at defending rights in individual cases and unsuccessful at addressing more systemic issues. The second explores Russia's various housing-rights "movements," focusing in part on a high-profile conflict between residents and city authorities, asking why the protesters are able to generate "heat" but not sustain the movement. Finally, the third case follows the development of a protest movement of motorists, which grew into the only grassroots organization capable of exerting consistent policy pressure on the state. Each case study explores a different configuration of the independent variable identified in this project: incoherent state intrusion in the first instance, coherent intrusion but incoherent reaction in the second, and coherent intrusion and reaction in the third.

2   Perspectives on Civil Society

> The only security against political slavery, is the check maintained over governors, by the diffusion of intelligence, activity and public spirit among the governed.
>
> —John Stuart Mill ([1848] 1970, 313)

Political Philosophy and the Concept of the Civil Society

The idea of civil society, relating to society in general and its *civil*ized aspect in particular, begins in the classical era of political philosophy. Thus, Cicero linked the *societas civilis* to *res publica* and described it as "an assemblage of people in large numbers associated in an agreement with respect to justice and a partnership for the common good."[1] This concept proved remarkably long lived and indeed remained the standard understanding of the term *civil society* from its publication in the first century before the common era well into the nineteenth century.

However, the reality of civil society, so defined, began to recede in Europe with the fall of the Roman Empire and the rise of Christian ideology, which saw society as organized for the service of a higher power, rather than for the improvement of the human condition. Indeed, in an era where states (or at least their borders) were transient, and under the institutions of feudalism, which prevent the coalescence of an encompassing common interest, society was anything but civil. Thus, it was only with the development of Europe's monarchies, and the ensuing regimentation of increasingly stable states, that the idea of civil society began to regain currency.

And so it was with an eye to the ancients that Locke, in the second half of the seventeenth century, began to ruminate on the nature of civil society. It is not, he argued, organized for the pursuit of liberty, because absolute liberty is found in the state of nature. Natural liberty, however, he saw as imperfect, as it left a constant threat to people's livelihoods, if not their lives. Thus, Locke's civil society consists in the voluntary abdication of liberty in return for a measure of justice, and that justice in turn is based on the preservation of property through equitable laws and their impartial enforcement. Thus, in his *Second Treatise on Government*, Locke wrote:

> And so whoever has the legislative or supreme power of any commonwealth is bound to govern by established standing laws, promulgated and known to the people, and not by extemporary decrees; by indifferent and upright judges, who are to decide controversies by those laws; and to employ the force of the community at home only in the execution of such laws, or abroad to prevent or redress foreign injuries, and secure the community from inroads and invasion. And all this to be directed to no other end, but the peace, safety, and public good of the people. (Locke [1681] 1993: 327)

This is a model based on interaction between state and society to achieve an overarching end: justice. If justice consists in the preservation of property, no society is to be considered civil in which property can be arbitrarily seized, be it by a neighbor, a brigand, or a sovereign. The corollary of this is that no society can be civil that is ruled by an absolute monarch, "For he being supposed to have all . . . power in himself alone, . . . no appeal lies open to anyone who may fairly and indifferently, and with authority, decide, and from whose decision relief and redress may be expected of any injury or inconveniency that may be suffered from the prince or by his order" (Locke [1681] 1993: 306). This combination of law with the subjugation of authority to common accountability—accountability that, Locke argues, may justifiably be enforced through violent rebellion—is the beginning of the modern recognition that civil society involves the participation of the governed in the production of the common good. This was, of course, a conclusion that would have seemed quite logical to Cicero; to most of the monarchs following the assassination of Julius Caesar, however, it would have been anathema.

It is notable that Europe rediscovered this notion at a time when monarchs, already comfortable in their thrones, were seeking to define and extend the role of the state inwardly, by "formalizing" its relationship with the church and other social institutions (Islamoglu 2001: 1892). This effort effectively opened up at least the philosophical possibility of an alternative order, one in which civil society itself could conceivably be sovereign. This was not the order Locke was proposing. Rather than the public, he saw the common good as sovereign and an extremely powerful (although not absolute) monarch as its surest guarantor. Society was the source of the state's legitimacy, and thus people were to be given freedom, he argued, but not to the extent that they might interfere in the conduct of affairs of state or even in the general governance of society. In his *Essay Concerning Toleration*, he wrote:

> There are some opinions and actions that are wholly separate from the concernment of the state, and have no direct influence on men's lives in society, and these are all speculative opinions and religious worship, and these have a clear title to universal toleration which the magistrate ought not to entrench on. . . . [All other opinions and actions] have a right to toleration so far only as they do not interfere with the advantages of the public or serve any way to disturb the government. (Locke [1667] 1993: 201)

Nearly a century later, Rousseau began with Locke's conceptions of civil society and asked, essentially, the following question: If people sacrifice their liberty only to increase justice, why did he observe in Europe so little liberty and so little justice? Unlike Locke, however, he sought the answer not only in government but in the human character as well. Exploring the differences between the subjects of an uncivil society and the citizens of a civil one, Rousseau wrote:

> Subjects prize public tranquility; citizens the freedom of the individual—the former prefer security of possessions, the latter security of the person; subjects think the best government is the most severe, citizens that it is the mildest; the former want crimes to be punished, the latter want them to be prevented; subjects think it is a good thing to be feared by their neighbours, citizens prefer to be ignored by them; the former are satisfied so long as money circulates, the latter demand that the people shall have bread. (Rousseau [1762] 1968: 129–130)

This dichotomy between subject and citizen, Rousseau argued in *The Social Contract*, was due to the way in which different forms of government organized relations both among residents and between residents and the state. Whereas Locke argued that the failure of a state to deliver justice should lead to a rebellion or a reversion to a state of nature, Rousseau observed that, in the absence of both justice and liberty—in other words, under an illegitimate social contract—societies behaved as though in a partial state of nature, with individuals guided exclusively by self-interest, and the "collective" in evidence only to the extent that the sovereign is able to exploit it.

Rousseau, then, goes beyond Locke's conception of a sovereign accountable for the public good and argues that, under a true social contract, the public itself is sovereign. Sovereignty, he writes, is "a covenant of the body with each of its members" (Rousseau [1762] 1968: 77). Thus, Rousseau's "prince" or "government" properly derives authority from the general will, and any attempt to wield authority independent of that will is a breach of contract, resulting in the dissolution of the state. Although not a departure from Locke's conception, Rousseau's assertion here goes farther in mandating direct accountability of the government to the people and thus a significant role for the people in the conduct, or at least oversight, of government. Civil society, then, was not simply to legitimate government; it was to manage it.

Indeed, *accountability* is too soft a word; Rousseau uses the word *subordination* to describe the relationship between society and government and argues that the entire arrangement of government institutions must be engineered to enforce this subordination. His theory thus lays the groundwork for later institutional thinking and particularly the sociology of government and bureaucracy that would eventually arise in Weber. This view arises also out of the increasing tendency of European monarchies at the time to recruit a corps of professional bureaucrats, although the term had yet to be invented (Torstendahl 2001: 1411). The government apparatus, Rousseau writes:

> . . . must have a particular *ego*, a consciousness common to its members, a force, a will of its own tending to its preservation. . . . The difficulty is to find a method of ordering this subordinate whole within the greater whole, so that it does not weaken the general constitution while strengthening its own, and so that its private force, designed for its own preservation, shall always be distinct from the public force, designed for the preservation of the state; in short, so that it will always be ready to sacrifice the government to the people and not the people to the government. (Rousseau [1762] 1968, 106)

Civil society, then, can be taken to mean not just the sovereignty of the public within the state but also the institutional arrangements necessary to achieve the subjugation of the government to the public. Coupled with Rousseau's earlier thoughts on the way that the nature of the state influences the behavior of its citizens/subjects, we have the makings of an institutionalist theory to explain various constellations of state and civil-society organization, all informed by the goal of subordinating the state to society.

Meanwhile, as Rousseau was writing about government, the thinkers of the Scottish Enlightenment were exploring changes in society writ large, specifically as regards increasing specialization and thus differentiation of tasks. Locke, in his historical theorizing, had identified the opportunity for a more efficient allocation of labor, and thus the creation of wealth, as one of the primary drivers of humanity's decision to abandon the state of nature for "civilization." Later, Ricardo picked up on the same theme in his economic theory of competitive advantage. In the context of Britain's industrial revolution, however, a number of thinkers in Scotland—particularly Adam Smith, Adam Ferguson, and David Hume—returned to an issue that seemed to be gaining ever-greater currency.

Still within the realm of the political, Hume argued that the greatest liberty was to be found in systems that balanced monarchy with republic, such that the potential excesses of each are held in check. Like Locke and Rousseau before him, Hume identified the public as the guarantor of this balance, but, unlike Rousseau in his reliance on a public bureaucracy, Hume looked to an institution wholly independent of government: the press. Public opinion, he wrote in "Of the First Principles of Government," is the foundation of all governance, no matter how democratic or despotic (Hume [1772] 1994b: 16). Thus, in his "Of the Liberty of the Press," he writes:

> It is apprehended, that arbitrary power would steal in upon us, were we not careful to prevent its progress, and were there not an easy method of conveying the alarm from one end of the kingdom to another. The spirit of the people must be frequently rouzed, in order to curb the ambition of the court; and the dread of rouzing this spirit must be employed to prevent that ambition. Nothing [is] so effectual to this purpose as the liberty of the press, by which all the learning, wit and genius of the nation may be employed on the side of freedom, and everyone be animated to its defence. (Hume [1772] 1994c: 3)

Hume's close colleagues, meanwhile, looked more closely at the bearers of this opinion. In *The Wealth of Nations*, Smith observed that, unlike other animals, consigned to self-sufficiency, "In civilized society [a human being] stands at all times in need of the co-operation and assistance of great multitudes, while his whole life is scarce sufficient to gain the friendship of a few persons" (Smith [1776] 1970: 118). Rather than friendship or altruism, he wrote, we rely on the logic of the exchange:

> As it is by treaty, by barter, and by purchase that we obtain from one another the greater part of those mutual good offices which we stand in need of, so it is this same trucking disposition which originally gives occasion to the division of labour. (Smith [1776] 1970: 119)

Smith expands this argument to make two assertions. First, presaging Ricardo, that we are better off when we specialize, as specialization leads to an increase in our talents and thus in our ability to satisfy our wants. This logic, meanwhile, should hold not only for economic actors, but for all in society, as the performance of any task is necessarily made less efficient by the introduction of unrelated concerns. And second, following Locke, the role of government is no more and no less than the preservation of property, by which Smith means the enforcement of the rules of exchange, such that force (or potential force) should not enter the equation.

Although writing somewhat earlier than Smith, Ferguson had foreseen this development and was troubled by its implications. He agreed with the prevailing argument that "the commercial and political arts have advanced together," such that "a people, possessed of wealth, and become jealous of their properties, have formed the project of emancipation, and have proceeded, under favour of an importance recently gained, still farther to enlarge their pretensions, and to dispute the prerogatives which their sovereign had been in use to employ" (Ferguson [1767] 1966: 261–262). However, the growing propensity to guard politics and economics from one another and the discouragement of participation in both simultaneously by one person—in short, Smith's and Ricardo's very exhortation to specialize—Ferguson saw as fatal to the liberal project. It is precisely the broadest possible participation of individuals in public affairs that Ferguson argued was the guarantor of freedom. He wrote:

> The sovereign may dazzle with his heroic qualities; he may protect his subjects in the enjoyment of every animal advantage or pleasure: but the benefits arising from liberty are of a different sort; they are not the fruits of a virtue, and of a goodness, which operate in the breast of one man, but of the communication of virtue itself to many; and such a distribution of functions in civil society, as gives to members the exercises and occupations which pertain to their nature. (Ferguson [1767] 1966: 270)

Thus, in Ferguson's view, exactly a century after Locke's *Essay Concerning Toleration*, civil society consists not simply in Locke's hegemony of the public good, or in Rousseau's institutionalized subjugation of the government, or even in Smith's self-perpetuating prosperity, but also in the institutionalization of broad participation in public affairs. Central among these institutions, as we have seen, have arisen Rousseau's neutral public bureaucracy, Hume's vigorous free press, and Ferguson's activist civic sphere. But these ideas did not arise in a vacuum. Rather, they came about at a time when government in Europe was changing—modernizing, if you will—and taking philosophy along with it. Urbanizing societies, with growing mercantile classes independent of feudal loyalties, began to develop ever more complex systems of interests, along with new institutions to mediate them. This led to changes both in the way society related to government and in the way that government itself was practiced. In the words of a contemporary observer:

> But though all kinds of government be improved in modern times, yet monarchical government seems to have made the greatest advances towards perfection. It may now be affirmed of civilized monarchies, what was formerly used in praise of republics alone, that they are a government of Law, not of Men. They are found susceptible of order, method, and constancy, to a surprising degree. (Hume [1772] 1994a: 56)

The *Philosophy of Right, Democracy in America,* and the Triumph of Empiricism

As the eighteenth century waned, two events—one spectacular, one more subtle—brought several of these philosophical questions into sharper focus. One was the American War of Independence, which, as Ernest Gellner would later write, represented the triumph of civil society over government and the state (Gellner 1994). It appeared to be the vindication of Locke and Rousseau and even of Ferguson. It proved the potential force of the collective will.

The second—lasting into the nineteenth century—was the deepening of the Industrial Revolution in Europe, which again seemed to vindicate Ferguson's fears of social atomization. It was in this context that Hegel wrote his *Philosophy of Right*, less as a reaction to earlier writers than to what he saw around him in Germany. Industrialization, in addition to the routinization of economic activity, had brought the professionalization and routinization of government, which was becoming increasingly geared toward management of the economy. Far from Smith's vision of efficient separation, this was a government that Hegel observed to be deeply intertwined with the dominant economic interests, an aspect that would later be picked up on by Karl Marx.

Modifying Rousseau's argument that the state is the embodiment of the public will, Hegel redefined civil society—in the earliest prominent usage of the term in a way resembling our contemporary understanding—as "the realm of difference, intermediate between the family and the state" (Hegel [1820] 1896: 185). In this definition, civil society consists primarily of the organization of individual wants and their satisfaction into a corporatized economy, the "protection of property by the administration of justice," and "provision against possible mischances, and care for the particular interest as a common interest" (Hegel [1820] 1896: 192).

This, then, makes civil society the scene of conflict to set the priorities of the state and to control government or at least influence its agenda. Rather than being the governor of civil society, as Locke wrote, or the opponent of civil society, as later writers would suggest, Hegel saw government as an integral part of civil society, together with corporations, public organizations and whatever other institutions individuals might create to advance their interests. Although the hierarchy is redrawn, the *Philosophy of Right* presents essentially an elucidation of prior theory—with clear links to Rousseau and Ferguson—based generally on contemporary empirical observation. Moreover, Hegel's conclusion was not optimistic. Though he noted the broad participation that Ferguson argued was crucial to liberty, Hegel said it did not appear to be sufficient. Rather, those forces in civil society that were strong enough—and here he foreshadowed Marx—could gain enough influence to shut broader but less well represented interests out of the process of government. In these conditions, he wrote, "the civic community affords a spectacle of excess, misery, and physical and social corruption" (Hegel [1820] 1896: 188).

At fault, Hegel argues, is the grounding of the "universal interests" of civil society in the "particular interests" of its members, and thus there is no "universal interest" at all, only a cacophony of competing wants. This, in turn, stems from nominal equality of political rights of participation and representation, regardless of status—still, at that point in history, a fairly novel development in Europe. As counterintuitive as it might sound to the modern reader, the dangers of equality to liberty—particularly, the prospect that the sin of envy, given political enfranchisement in the context of economic inequality, might lead to unrest and even repression—was a common theme in political thought at the time. It was also a major concern of Alexis de Tocqueville when he traveled, famously, to the United States.

It should be noted that the publication of the second volume of *Democracy in America*, in 1840, preceded only by approximately four years the start of Darwin's work on the *Origin of the Species*. Both were written in the growing spirit of scientific empiricism, in which the proof of theory, unlike in Locke's day, lay not in the eloquence of reason but in the presentation of evidence. Certainly, Hegel had begun in this direction, although he was still first and foremost a philosopher. Tocqueville, however, remained unconvinced by the gloominess of views from Europe. These, he reasoned, could be conditioned by any number of factors peculiar to the history of the continent. Much as Darwin sought to study evolution in the isolation of the Galapagos, Tocqueville wondered whether democracy might not be better explored in the relative isolation of America.

Like Rousseau before him, Tocqueville was most concerned with the character of citizens and citizenship. Following the prevailing logic in Europe—which saw equality at the root of social disharmony—Tocqueville wondered why the unprecedented equality among Americans failed to engender the sort of strife Old World writers would have expected. The answer he found in public associations:

> Americans of all ages, all conditions, and all dispositions constantly form associations. They have not only commercial and manufacturing companies, in which all take part, but associations of a thousand other kinds. . . . Wherever at the head of some new undertaking you see the government in France, or a man of rank in England, in the United States you will be sure to find an association. . . . Thus, the most democratic country on the face of the earth is that in which men have, in our time, carried to the highest perfection the art of pursuing in common the object of their common desires and have applied this new science to the greatest number of purposes. (de Tocqueville [1840] 1994: 106–107)

Meanwhile, in an argument owing much to Hume, de Tocqueville singles out the press as crucial among all other civil institutions and argues for its near-complete freedom. "Nothing but a newspaper," he wrote, "can drop the same thought into a thousand minds at the same moment" (de Tocqueville [1840] 1994: 111). Moreover, the very freedom and diversity of the press—and thus the opportunity it affords readers to participate in the formation of their own worldview—helps to strengthen the conviction with which opinions are held (de Tocqueville [1835] 1994: 188).

None of this is theoretically different from Hegel. De Tocqueville's definition of an association—as "the public assent which a number of individuals give to certain doctrines and in the engagement with which they contract to promote . . . those doctrines" (de Tocqueville [1835] 1994: 192)—is essentially the same as Hegel's universalization of the particular. But de Tocqueville's observation of the phenomenon in the American context allowed him to highlight an aspect that Hegel missed, namely the role of ownership. "Civic zeal," he argued, "seems to be inseparable from the exercise of political rights" (de Tocqueville [1835] 1994: 243). This interest in the public welfare, in turn, appears best achieved by institutionalizing individual participation in the good of smaller groups, in other words, by making politics local. He wrote:

> It is difficult to draw a man out of his own circle to interest him in the destiny of the
> state, because he does not clearly understand what influence the destiny of the state
> can have upon his own lot. But if it is proposed to make a road cross the end of his
> estate, he will see at a glance that there is a connection between this small public
> affair and his greatest private affairs; and he will discover, without its being shown
> to him, the close tie that unites private to general interest. (de Tocqueville [1840]
> 1994: 104)

Thus, in Tocqueville's view, ownership of private property, in conditions of
political liberty and freedom to associate, allows individuals not only to feel
part of a political community but to feel that their livelihood is part of the
collective livelihood, or the *common weal*, and to recognize that interests are
most fruitfully defended in concert with others. Seen in the American context, then, "Life, Liberty and the Pursuit of Happiness" becomes not simply a
statement of principles but a system of social, political, and economic organization. Its success as described by Tocqueville is, in effect, the empirical proof
of Locke's initial assertion that the just society is the one that best preserves
property.

In 1848, eight years after the publication of the second part of *Democracy in
America*, John Stuart Mill wrote his *Principles of Political Economy*, which was
to stand for generations as a seminal text at Oxford and elsewhere. While not as
famous as *On Liberty*, published eleven years later, *Principles* marks the turning
point of attention in political science away from the character of government
and toward the character of public participation in government. At a time of
increasing social dislocation and controversy over the extent of the franchise—
Charles Dickens published *Hard Times* in 1854, while the young Karl Marx was
grappling with the same issues politically on the continent—Mill argued that it
was the spirit of the public, rather than the virtue of the government, that was
crucial to justice. Drawing from de Tocqueville, he wrote:

> This discussion and management of collective interests is the great school of that
> public spirit, and the great source of that intelligence of public affairs, which are al-
> ways regarded as the distinctive character of the public of free societies. (Mill [1848]
> 1970: 313)

Taking that empirical lesson and reapplying it to the nearly two centuries of
"modern" political theory that preceded him, Mill drew the conclusion that the
crux of just government lies in the public institutions that surround it. He set
out this assertion in a passage so remarkable in its foresight—and, in my view,

unimproved by the ensuing 150 years of political thought—that I present it almost in its entirety:

> A democratic constitution, not supported by democratic institutions in detail, but confined to the central government, not only is not political freedom, but often creates a spirit precisely the reverse, carrying down to the lowest grade in society the desire and ambition of political domination. . . . In proportion as the people are accustomed to manage their affairs by their own active intervention, instead of leaving them to the government, their desires will turn to repelling tyranny, rather than to tyrannizing: while in proportion as all real initiative and direction resides in the government, and individuals habitually feel and act as under its perpetual tutelage, popular institutions develop in them not the desire of freedom, but an unmeasured appetite for place and power: diverting the intelligence and activity of the country from its principal business, to a wretched competition for the selfish prizes and the petty vanities of office. (Mill [1848] 1970: 313–314)

On first glance, this may not read so differently from the writings of Locke or Rousseau. However, in the context of social processes about which earlier writers could only postulate, and given the empirical backing of writers such as de Tocqueville, Mill's revision of the theory carries much greater weight. And at the center of the theory—where once stood bare concepts of justice and efficiency, of virtue and right—there are now institutions and actors, with specific, well-defined roles, involved in the maintenance of the public interest and the "containment" of government.

Marx, Weber, and the Sociological Revolution

Powerful as it was, Mill's revision of the theory left open important questions about the relationships between individuals and institutions and how those relationships inform and are informed by the character of the state. Broadly put, it was de Tocqueville who had first pointed out the importance of these relationships and Hegel who first attempted to theorize them. But it was Karl Marx who would first develop a dynamic, encompassing model.

Marx explicitly began with Hegel, critiquing the *Philosophy of Right* while still a student. He saw in Hegel a key insight that seemingly eluded earlier writers (although it was not foreign to de Tocqueville), namely that civil and political society are indeed one (Marx [1844] 1970: 76). In Marx's view, however, Hegel failed to take this assertion far enough. Having shown the possibility for civic institutions to be captured, and arguing that civil society sets the direction of the state, Hegel nonetheless placed the state and civil society in conflict. Although Marx saw this as an accurate reflection of the current state of affairs, he believed that the broader relationship was one of collusion to the point of a unity of interests. In other words, because each depends on the other for its existence, the conflict between civil society and the state is illusory, as is the independence of civil society—consisting of all of those "intermediate" institutions between the individual and the state—itself. (Note, already, the beginning of the conflation of civil society with the institutions that represent it.)

This conclusion was a product of Marx's effort to reexamine history with an empiricist's eye, developing the theory of historical materialism to identify and trace those factors that seemed to be crucial in determining individual and institutional behavior and change over time. Central to this theory was the assertion that individual behavior in capitalism is conditioned overwhelmingly by economic imperatives, imperatives that would necessarily overcome any other intervening factors. This was, in essence, a classical economist's argument, postulating the dominance of rational choice, with the assumption that preferences are determined by class consciousness.

It was here that Marx departed from Hegel, who had written that offices of the state and civil society are carried out by individuals, whose behavior may be conditioned by the character of that office itself. This would mean that institutions could take on logics of their own, capable of overwhelming whatever motivations individuals might face on their own. Marx, on the other hand, wrote:

> It is ridiculous to say, as Hegel does, that "it is in an external and contingent way that these offices are linked with particular persons." On the contrary, they are linked with them by a *vinculum substantiale*, by reason of an essential quality of particular persons. These offices are the natural action of this essential quality. Hence the absurdity of Hegel's conceiving the activities and agencies of the state in abstract, and particular individuality in opposition to it. He forgets that particular individuality is a human individual, and that the activities and agencies of the state are human activities. . . . Thus it is evident that individuals, in so far as they are the bearers of the state's activities and powers, are to be considered according their social and not their private quality. (Marx [1844] 1970: 21–22)

Owing to the alienation of the laborer from his product—the same alienation of which Ferguson warned—Marx argued that individuals are dominated by their socioeconomic circumstances, broadly regardless of their particular experiences or the social and institutional context in which they operate

(Fromm 1963: 25–26). Institutions, then, to the extent that they have discernible egos, are to be seen as determined by the interests of whatever group of individuals comes to dominate them. As a result, justice "is not a question of the possibility of every citizen to dedicate himself to the universal in the form of a particular class, but of the capability of the universal class to be truly universal, i.e., to be the class of every citizen" (Marx [1844] 1970: 50). Lenin would later take this argument to its logical conclusion, writing that the revolution that would capture the state would, in so doing, transform civil society and eventually obviate the need for both (Lenin [1917] 1962).

Beyond narrowing the spectrum of human motivations to a startling degree, Marx's placement of capital and economic imperatives at the center of his model negates the role of institutional frameworks and eliminates the possibility that institutions, including civil society actors, might take on the sort of independent ego that both Rousseau and Hegel had ascribed to them. He had come to this conclusion scientifically, by expanding the scope of his research from the study of the contemporary (which had been de Tocqueville's realm) to a systematic reevaluation of history. Other writers, however, also looked to history, and the answers they found were quite different.

The essential question facing Max Weber was the same one that had concerned Marx: Why and how do societies and states change? Weber, however, was unconvinced by an answer that assumed a universal logic across time, geography, and culture. Historical materialism might be useful in describing certain aspects of observed history, he reasoned, but it could not explain why group and individual priorities seemed to differ according to circumstances. Weber noticed that societies, and subgroups within those societies, displayed "mentalities" or "ethos" that seemed to be more or less well suited to different modes of economic and political behavior (Parsons 1947: 32–33). By examining the development of belief systems over time, Weber famously deduced that the success of certain European nations at modern capitalism seemed to derive from aspects of Protestant philosophy. Put more broadly, this would mean that states and societies were not the product of inexorable economic processes but rather that those processes and the contexts in which they occur were themselves the products of complex combinations of social institutions—some tangible, others not. This, Weber reasoned, should hold true on all levels, from the state itself down to the smallest community.

Thus, whereas Hegel defined a *corporation*—taken to mean any combination of individuals, for commercial, political, governmental or social purposes—as the attempt to universalize the particular, and although Marx saw corporations as tools of the particular interests of those who control them, Weber saw much more room for the corporation to take on a life of its own. He wrote:

> [A corporate group] exists so far as there is a probability that certain designated persons will act in such a way as to express the true meaning of the laws governing the group; in other words, that there are persons who are determined to act in that sense and in no other when the occasion demands it. What causes such orientation, whether it is a case of emotional, traditional or value-related devotion to duty, any one of which may be involved in feudal fealty, loyalty to an office or to service, or whether it is due to expediency, as, for instance, a pecuniary interest in the accompanying salary, is conceptually of no consequence (Weber 1962: 108).

An understanding of how ethos may be formed, meanwhile, allows a clearer view of what institutional frameworks might be most conducive to normative expectations of justice and efficiency. In Weber's typology, he posited that the increasingly common mode of operation for corporate groups, states included, based on "rational-legal authority" could create an ethos that would be rule-bound, regimented, and devoid of subjective motivations such as personal favoritism (Weber 1947: 330–332). This, of course, is based on the bureaucratic systems Weber observed to be working most perfectly in Europe, and he was not the first to observe it. Indeed, Hegel had earlier made the argument that a civil service ethos could be bred through a combination of education, recruitment, and proper encouragement, an argument that Weber would later develop in much greater detail.

If this were true—if life were becoming increasingly regimented and professional—then one would expect the role of "civil society" as the realm of difference and conflict to shrink. This had been Ferguson's fear, and it was a major concern of early sociologists. One pioneer, however, came to a different conclusion. Examining the development of legal canons, Emile Durkheim found no proof that the public sphere was shrinking; to the contrary, the growing body of positivistic law to enable it strongly suggested that civil society was gaining strength and importance (Durkheim [1893] 1984: 152–153).

Clearly, then, both the Marxist and the liberal schools were mistaken in their predictions of the demise of civil society. Weber recognized this and developed detailed responses. I will deal with Weber's specific thoughts a bit later. Suffice it for now to say that his sociological approach had two important effects. The first was to provide a powerful alternative to Marxist conceptions of sociopolitical development. And the second was to leave open the suggestion that institutions could, at least in some respects, be engineered to deliver normatively desirable outcomes. As we will see, both results would turn out to be both useful and damaging, but the rise of sociology saved the study of civil society actors—and institutions in general—from the Marxist challenge.

The Babelization of the Social Sciences

Max Weber provided two profound opportunities to those social scientists who remained unconvinced by the simplicity of Marxian historical material- ism. First, in positing the Protestant origins of Western capitalism, he offered a lucid and robust alternative to a model of historical development dominated by the role of capital. Second, in blazing a trail for organizational sociology, he brought scientific rigor to the hypothesis that individuals may indeed act on motivations other than the basest necessities of survival. It is not appropriate here to go into great detail on the specifics of Weber's theories. Instead, I will identify what I believe to be the key advances relevant to our discussion.

As mentioned earlier, Marx ridiculed Hegel's contention that the structures of an hierarchical institution—in particular, standardized aspects of recruit- ment, training, and interaction—could in any meaningful manner condition the way individual actors within that institution behaved. Weber disagreed, noting the regularity with which members of certain institutions, particularly what he called rational-legal bureaucracies, acted in ways contrary to their best personal interests. Whereas Marx saw institutions as the embodiment of the interests of the individuals who control them, Weber demonstrated the exist- ence of an "impersonal order" within organizations capable of producing and reproducing a specific "ethos" of office independent of the social, economic, or class status of the officeholder (Parsons 1947: 58). Indeed, Weber made that factor the definition of corporate groups, the very significance of which Marx sought to negate (Weber 1962: 108).

This assertion had two important implications for the subsequent study of civil society and, in particular, of what I will call "enabling actors"—actors such as the press, advocates, or even the public bureaucracy, that, through nor- matively "positive" behavior, "enable" the functioning of democratic systems. First, it refuted both the claims of Marxists that class identification guides in- dividual behavior and the claims of classicists and moralists that normatively "good" behavior results from culturally ingrained ethical conceptions. And secondly, with its emphasis on the specific subinstitutional underpinnings of the rational-legal bureaucracy (Crozier 2001: 1408), it opened the door for several subsequent generations of social scientists to explore the internal logics of institutional actors.

The first of these effects dealt a mortal blow to classical Marxist doctrine, which eventually responded with an institutionalist approach of its own (Islamoglu 2001: 1895). But the second, ironically, has also been nearly fatal to the study of civil society. This endeavor has, throughout the second half of the twentieth century and beyond, been dominated by investigations of the minutiae of the Weberian paradigm. Decades of research have elucidated ever more intricate chains of causality in the effort to understand institutional behavior, applying new methods such as rational choice and game theory; at their most useful, these studies have attempted to link these relationships to the aggregate output of these institutions, but even this is not always the case. The result has been more information but not necessarily more understanding (for particularly good critiques, see Gellner [1994] on civil society, Splichal [2001] on the press, and Subramaniam [2000] on public administration). All too often, this has resulted in a "babelization" of the vocabulary of increasingly distinct subsciences, a dismaying result for anyone who believes that the issues involved are all intrinsically part of the same fundamental question: Namely, how do people, in society, come together to improve their lives and manage their governance?

A more constructive result of the growing body of sociological literature, however, was to illustrate the degree to which modern capitalist democracies rested on institutional behavior, rather than the "elites seeking votes" conception advanced by Joseph Schumpeter (1942). It also made possible truly important developments, foremost among which was the elucidation by Mancur Olson of the "logic of collective action" (1982). Here too, though, there arose a dilemma: The refutation of Schumpeter seemed to show that the capacity of institutions to create a constructive ethos—what would eventually come to be called the civic culture—was important to democracy, but Olson's work equally convincingly argued that demands of institutions would often trump this ethos.

This tension found an outlet in a growing debate among political theorists, comparative political scientists, and comparative political economists over the place of civil society in modern states. Those who saw civil society as the realm of charity posited that growing welfare states would eventually obviate it; those partial to Jurgen Habermas's idea of the "public sphere" saw civil society as the realm of discourse, often about the state itself, and thus inherently separate from and often in opposition to the state (Habermas [1962] 1995). Perhaps it was inevitable, given the debilitating theoretical deadlock in the study of civil society, but the debate led to a fracture in the conventional understanding of civil society, assigning away many groups, such as journalists, bureaucrats, political activists, and even alms-givers, to other, more narrowly defined categories of society and leaving civil society as the arena for debate on those issues seen (accurately or otherwise) as peculiar to postindustrial societies; in other words, civil society came to be seen as the stomping ground of movements and causes, whether on behalf of women, homosexuals, or spotted owls. Definitions began to become increasingly formalistic; thus USAID's equation of civil society to NGOs (USAID 1999), or even Larry Diamond's oft-quoted "realm of organized social life that is voluntary, self-generating, (largely) self-supporting, autonomous from the state, and bound by a legal order or set of shared rules" (Diamond 1994: 5). Gone are considerations of function, whether in the form of Habermas's public sphere, or de Tocqueville's creation of public interest, or Hume's aggregation, dissemination, and mobilization of public opinion. By the end of the twentieth century, the academic conception of civil society had devolved from an institution critical to the functioning of democracy to a theoretically contentious gaggle of interest groups most rigorously studied in the narrow context of those interests than in aggregate.

Social Capital and New Thinking about Institutions

The growing difficulties involved with discussing civil society as a unified concept coincided with a tendency in the late twentieth century toward increasing abstraction in social thought. In many ways, these two trends complemented each other; thus, scholars of the practice of journalism and students of the media's role in Habermas's "public sphere" frequently recognized, at least on some level, that they were studying different aspects of the same basic question. In other ways, however, the result was a growing gap in vocabulary. Ideas on "social capital" and "trust" gradually lost their link to practical research and were reappropriated by the realm of normative theory. Brilliant ideas arose, but they became increasingly difficult to operationalize. My goal in the remainder of this chapter is to propose an approach that will bring some of these ideas back down to earth in such a way that they might inform useful empirical research.

Writing on the development of bourgeois society in industrializing Europe, Jürgen Habermas observed:

> In this stratum, which more than any other was affected *and* called upon by mer-cantilist policies, the state authorities evoked a resonance leading to the *publicum*, the abstract counterpart of public authority, into an awareness of itself as the latter's opponent, that is, as the public of the now emerging *public sphere of civil society*. For the latter developed to the extent to which the public concern regarding the private sphere of civil society was no longer confined to the authorities but was considered by the subjects as one that was properly theirs. (Habermas [1962] 1995: 23)

Note particularly how Habermas uses the idea of *the public*. In a departure from classical political theory, which saw the public as the progenitor and owner of the apparatus of state, the Habermasian public is the counterpart of authority within a larger whole. Together, the public and authority comprise the state. The implication is that, to the extent that one changes in form or con-tent, the other is transformed in response.

Theorists of democracy, meanwhile, began picking up on this notion of a reactive (or constituent) public sphere as a new way of exploring the impor-tance of civil society to democracy that had been taken for granted since at least the eighteenth century. Evaluating the institutional makeup of liberal de-mocracy, Maurice Duverger wrote, "The political organization and structure of liberal democracy forms a well-patterned whole. It comprises popular sov-ereignty, popular elections, legislative assemblies, the independence of the ju-diciary, civil liberties, and political parties, all of which are complimentary to each other and derive from the same fundamental principles" (Duverger 1974: 50). And this cohesiveness is based, he argued, not as much on the design of institutions (though these are important, especially if incongruent) so much as on the patterns of social relationships that inform institutional arrangements (Duverger 1972: 69–70).

In the early 1960s, Gabriel Almond and Sidney Verba revisited Rousseau's observation on the differences in behavior between "subjects" and "citizens" and began reopening questions about what they called "civic culture" (Almond and Verba 1963). Democracy, they wrote, seemed to be underpinned by more than just formal institutions, and certainly more than Schumpeter's simple "elites seeking votes" formula. Expanding on Rousseau, Almond and Verba elaborated three categories of political culture—the parochial, the subject, and the participant—differentiated by patterns of individual orientation toward political "input" and "output" mechanisms. Identifying the participant culture with democracy, they wrote, "The participant culture . . . is one in which the members of the society tend to be explicitly oriented to the system as a whole and to both the political and administrative structures and processes: in other words, to both the input and output aspects of the political system. . . . They tend to be oriented toward an 'activist' role of the self in the polity" (Almond and Verba 1963: 19). Their research consisted of interviewing 5,000 citizens of five Western democracies to evaluate attitudes toward their political environment and participation in that environment. Methodological issues aside, the key point for our discussion is that the questions asked in large part centered on issues of trust.

Ideas on social capital have been built on the centrality of trust in conceptions of civic culture. Although its roots are older, the concept of social capital was popularized by Robert Putnam and his coauthors, who defined the term as "features of social organization, such as trust, norms, and networks, that can improve the efficiency of society by facilitating coordinated actions" (Putnam, Leonardi, et al. 1993: 167). Particular emphasis is placed by Putnam on "networks of civic engagement," which lower the risks of opportunism and free-riding, reinforce "norms of reciprocity," increase perceptions of trustworthiness and transmit the experience of "success at collaboration" (Putnam, Leonardi, et al. 1993: 4).

Like Habermas and others before, Putnam and his colleagues argued that "success in overcoming dilemmas of collective action . . . depends on the broader social context within which any particular game is played," but unlike conceptions of the public sphere, for example, this "broader social context" does not include the political (Putnam, Leonardi, et al. 1993: 167). James Coleman's somewhat broader conception of social capital—which he sees as the aggregate product of any and all forms of social organization—leaves open the possibility for the political environment to shape incentives but remains, in essence, apolitical (Coleman 1990: 300–312). Francis Fukuyama similarly broadly defines social capital as "an instantiated informal norm that promotes cooperation between two or more individuals. . . . By this definition, trust, networks, civil society, and the like, which have been associated with social capital, are all epiphenomenal, arising because of social capital but not constituting social capital itself" (Fukuyama 2000: 3); here, too, politics is absent. Indeed, all prevailing conceptions of social capital, for all definitional differences, share one thing in common: "They locate social capital in a pre-economic and pre-political civil society" (Gamarnikow and Green 2005: 97).

And yet Robert Putnam posits social capital as the element essential to maintaining the legitimacy of elite rule in democracies (Putnam 1976: 137–138, 156–157; Putnam, Leonardi, et al. 1993: 171). Social capital is thus somehow simultaneously prepolitical and essentially political. The tension in that conceptualization—indeed, I would argue, the untenability of that conceit—becomes clearer in empirical application and is addressed later in this volume. Suffice it for now to note the following: Prepolitical conceptions of social capital assume either that the value of cooperation itself—that is, the reason that people seek to cooperate and thus place a value on social capital—is either constant from one context to another or else irrelevant (that is, people will always seek to cooperate, regardless of context). But everything we know about political behavior—and particularly the institutional and political sociology discussed earlier—suggests exactly the opposite: The value of cooperation differs greatly from one political context to another. And if that is the case, then it would take a tremendous leap of faith to assume that the relative presence or absence of demand for social capital has no bearing on its production.

A more promising approach comes from the language of economics. Writing in 1957, Kenneth Arrow likened trust to a "public good," a good that is nonexcludable in provision, nonrivalrous in consumption, and thus nonprofitable in production, essentially because everyone can have it for free. Arrow wrote:

> Trust has a very important pragmatic value, if nothing else. Trust is an important lubricant of a social system. It is extremely efficient; it saves a lot of trouble to have a fair degree of reliance on other people's word. Unfortunately this is not a commodity which can be bought very easily. If you have to buy it, you already have some doubts about what you've bought. Trust and similar values, loyalty or truth-telling, are examples of what the economist would call "externalities." They are goods, they are commodities, they have real, practical, economic value; they increase the efficiency of the system, enable you to produce more goods or more of whatever values you hold in high esteem. But they are not commodities for which trade on the open market is technically possible or even meaningful. (Arrow 1974: 23)

Usually, public goods—such as roads, parks, and pollution controls—are provided by government. There is nothing inherent in public goods, however, that demands that they be produced exclusively by government; as Arrow points out, any sufficiently encompassing collective institution will do. Thus, trust—as one product of "produced" social capital, to continue the economic metaphor—can be produced by civil society as a collective institution, given the appropriate circumstances (an issue I will return to shortly). More recently, this idea has been revived in the context of the globalization debate (see, for example, Kaul, Conceicau, et al. 2003).

Fukuyama and other writers on social capital reject this argument. He writes: "This is clearly wrong. Since cooperation is necessary to virtually all individuals as a means of achieving their selfish ends, it stands to reason that they will produce it as a private good" (Fukuyama 2000: 3). This reasoning is flawed on two counts. First, it is an axiom of economics that cooperation is actually not necessary, and, although its absence makes transactions more costly, sufficiently strong contracting can be devised to make transactions possible nonetheless.

More importantly, however, Fukuyama misunderstands the nature of public goods. All public goods, at the end of the day, are produced by private actors, even those that are procured by government. It is the very definition of public goods that their producers have little or no classical "interest" in producing them. The builder of a public park is first and foremost a builder, who needs a contract and a paycheck. A public school teacher may be devoted emotionally and professionally to the betterment of future generations, but he or she also eats and votes, and those more immediate interests may frequently take precedence over the public good, should the two come into conflict. Thus, the "public good" of a municipal park is really achieved not by the contractor hired to build it but by the political and economic arrangement that allows public resources to be allocated to the contractor for that end. Similarly, it may be useful to separate the production of such "societal public goods" as trust from those actors that "enable" its production for the purpose of clarity. The enablers—whether teachers, journalists, activists, or civil servants, as individuals or collective institutions—perform political and economic activities no differently than anyone else. In this view, ideational considerations are secondary and contingent. What is of interest to us here is the institutional or relational framework that channels such mundane activity into the production of vital public goods.

It is this same misunderstanding that bedevils the contemporary study of civil society. By placing the fundamental individual economic and political functions of individual and corporate civil society actors in direct conflict with our normative expectations for the production of social capital, we thrust ourselves into an insoluble dilemma. Social scientists have tended to resolve this in their own minds by discarding one or the other, the political-economic or the normative. Neither conception, however, can lead to anything useful in the final analysis. A purely normatively constructed civil society can never exist, but an institution devoid of normative concepts ceases to be useful in any "civil" sense. The result is two schools of thought, one divorced from theory, the other from reality. The former, ignoring the entire conceptual evolution outlined in the preceding pages, picks up from the idea of social capital and travels to nondemocratic states to engineer its emergence. The second has absorbed the theory but despairs of ever applying it usefully.

The Prism of Transition

It was against this background that a dramatic sequence of events brought the idea of civil society back to the foreground of the social sciences. In 1989, as communist regimes across Eastern Europe, and later Eurasia, began giving way in what were seen as liberalizing revolutions, civil society was the hero of the day (see, for example, Taylor 1990). Given the history of the concept previously described, this fact should at the very least seem strange. Civil society, from Locke onward, was always seen as the attribute of a democratic society, something that arose after liberalizing revolutions had been accomplished. By definition, civil society could not exist under an undemocratic regime, nor could it be the force behind a revolution.

Such considerations, however, were of little consequence to the dissidents who adopted "civil society" as their battle flag. The concept itself—a sphere of collective activity inherently independent from the state—was powerful well beyond rhetoric. In the end, the growing popularity of such independent organizations as Solidarity in Poland, Charter 77 in Czechoslovakia, the Young Democrats in Hungary, and the various national, professional, and other groupings that arose in the USSR, and governments' inability to control them, undoubtedly played an important role in the dissolution of the old regimes.

From the perspective of social scientists, meanwhile, the concept of civil society was reintroduced via newspapers and television screens, with disastrous consequences for theory. The dissidents, who first began to pick up on the idea in the late 1970s, saw civil society "not merely as the rule of law and the institutions to check abuses of the state, but the emphasis was on self-organization, autonomy, solidarity and non-violence" (Kaldor 2003: 56). Thus, as the debate over form versus function festered, the revolutions effectively decided the contest in favor of the formalists. Moreover, history seemed to be invalidating theory. Throughout the communist space there were interest groups, labor unions, samizdat publication circles, and myriad other underground networks organized to serve an entire range of purposes, except those mandated by the state. These organizations, movements, and initiatives, which (appropriately or otherwise) had taken on the mantle of civil society, predated not only democracy but also the revolutionary moment, often by decades. The lesson here is that, even when the circumstances for civil-social behavior would seem to be missing, the desire remains; the corollary of this, meanwhile, is that where there's a will, there's a way. Thus, in the words of one observer, the civil society of Havel, Michnik, and Konrad was a "civil society in conspiracy" (Sztompka 1998: 193), a development unforeseen by all of the aforementioned theorists in this chapter.

Not only was civil society being observed in unexpected places, but it was doing unexpected things. Organizations were intended not to mediate between individuals and the state, as the classic definition goes, but to help individuals avoid the state. Thus, ideas such as "networks of sympathy," "antipolitics," "living in truth," and the "parallel polis" involved generating "a sphere of society that escapes the total hold of the overbearing state" (Kaldor 2003: 56). Although many acknowledged the ultimate aim of using pressure from below eventually to force changes above, the more immediate goal was simply to exploit as far as possible those opportunities and niches for independent action that were available (Kis 1989). Because civil society for Eastern Europeans came to be inextricably linked with democratic ideals (Quigley 2000: 194), this widened conception of civil society was in turn linked with a "wider concept of democracy," one that goes beyond simply the organization of the state to encompass broader issues of behavior (Arato 2000: 35).

As I will discuss shortly, this all points to a "morphological" definition of civil society, in which form is understood to follow function. Observers, however, interpreted it formalistically, redoubling their emphasis on the vaunted independence of the organizations involved, with little regard for the purposes they served. Most seemed to come to the conclusion that "civil society consists only of voluntary associations that directly foster democracy and promote democratic consolidation" (Carothers and Ottaway 2000: 11). One unfortunate result, meanwhile, was that international donor and aid organizations, caught up in the frenzy to pick up on this (supposedly) new buzzword of civil society, spent much of their money on initiatives that were formally ideal but functionally useless (see, for example, Ottaway and Carothers 2000; Henderson 2003).

Another is that many residents of the region, once so enamored with the idea of civil society, have begun questioning the utility of collective, independent initiative altogether (Averkiev 2003).

More generally, the issue of civil society and social capital in transition is well elaborated by the comparative politics literature in broad strokes, even if contentious and not well understood in its details. One line of thought, represented by authors including Seymour Martin Lipset and Samuel Huntington, sees democratization as resting on certain "social requisites," including adequate levels of economic development and the presence of conducive social institutions, the latter of which is generally construed to include civil society (Lipset 1994). Others, including Dankwart Rustow, reject this socioeconomic evolutionary approach, opting instead for a model based on institutional arrangements and patterns of conflict. In Rustow's model, among other things, democracy arises when there is "a sense of national unity," "entrenched and serious conflict," "a conscious adoption of democratic rules," and "politicians and [an] electorate . . . habituated to these rules" (Rustow 1970: 361). In the context of our earlier discussion, these four prerequisites clearly imply a role for civil society. Thus, there was a consensus, summed up by Alfred Stepan just three years prior to the wave of anticommunist revolutions: "The power of civil society to create and channel social pressures is extremely important" (Stepan 1986: 79).

In a robust early attempt to compare postcommunist transitions to those elsewhere, Juan Linz and Alfred Stepan (1996) noted an apparent trend: Civil society in Latin America, Southern Europe, and Central and Eastern Europe had been instrumental in bringing about cooperative political change. True, there were also discrepancies. In the first two regions, pretransition civil society was generally officially recognized, independent, and well organized. With some exceptions, pretransition civil society in Central and Eastern Europe (CEE) was officially banned, fragmented, and poorly organized. Nonetheless, "successful" transition to democracy seemed to be associated with the ability of civil society to help coordinate an "elite pact" that would achieve Rustow's requirements for conflict to be organized around democratic and accepted rules.

In theorizing this aspect of transition and democratic consolidation, Linz and Stepan argued that civil society itself must undergo a transition, from "ethical civil society in opposition" to "political civil society in a consolidated democracy"; among other things, this transition would involve a shift of emphasis from ideals to interests, a new willingness to cooperate with authority, and a new tolerance of internal dissent (Linz and Stepan 1996: 272). Similarly, Arato writes that civil society would eventually have to learn to be self-limiting and to "renounce the direct exercise of power" for democracy to be consolidated (Arato 2000: 78–80). This is, in effect, a simplification of an earlier model put forward by Marcia Weigle and Jim Butterfield, envisioning four stages of civil society development in transition: "defensive," "emergent," "mobilizational," and "institutional" (Weigle and Butterfield 1992). Both views relate directly to Adam Przeworski's conception of democracy as "institutionalized conflict," with participants' strategies determined by the surrounding institutional arrangements (Przeworski 1986). And they mesh with Claus Offe's conception of civil society as a state's "associational substructure," determining the formulation and implementation of policy goals (Offe 1996: 107, 113).

This strategy, meanwhile, generally manages to avoid equating the form and function of civil society actors, which, as discussed earlier, has been a critical error in other parts of the literature. Thus, when Weigle and Butterfield write that, when "formal channels of interest articulation are closed to independent social actors . . . groups utilize extrasystemic means of articulation, such as demonstrations, rallies and samizdat" (Weigle and Butterfield 1992: 17), what they are doing is concentrating on functional equivalents, rather than on formalistic categories.

Empiricists interested in civil society development in the region, however, reported a disturbing picture. In perhaps the most important such project, Richard Rose has overseen regular surveys to gauge public trust in and attitudes toward a variety of political and civil institutions, focusing on the same sorts of questions posed by Almond and Verba, and his findings have confirmed what any resident of the region would tell you outright: There's not much trust to go around. He found "widespread distrust in all of the institutions in the survey" (Mishler and Rose 1997: 424). This phenomenon he and others chalked up to "a legacy of distrust" holding over from the communist past (Rose 1994: 19). This and similar evidence has consistently been presented as evidence of the weakness of civil society in the region and thus of a dearth of social capital.

It is my view that the approach taken by Rose—although useful in the data that it provides about specific institutions—is severely limited in what it can actually tell us about civil society in the region. By using Almond and Verba and other work on Western "civic culture" as a starting point, Rose and the New Democracy Barometer project equate civil society with those institutions that embody it in the West, with no regard to the real history of these institutions either in the East or the West. If these institutions, such as newspapers or interest groups, are not trusted in the postcommunist East to the degree that they are in the West, the implication should be that they simply are not the functional equivalents of their counterparts in the West. Unfortunately, Rose's approach is typical of the dominant, formalistic model of analysis. If we are unsatisfied with the prevailing approach, however, it behooves us to propose something new.

Civil Society and Social Movements

While political scientists, theorists, and philosophers have had increasing difficulty with the concept of civil society, sociologists have had considerably more luck with the phenomenon of social movements. Social movements are the complex products of conflicts, perceptions, and resources. They begin with the transformation of a threat into an opportunity, giving rise to reiterative patterns of contention between groups of actors, most commonly a more or less broad segment of nonelite society on the one hand and the ruling elites, in whole or part, on the other. As such, Charles Tilly writes,

> It is a mistake to think of a social movement as a group of any kind. Instead, the term *social movement* applies most usefully to a sustained *interaction* between a specific set of authorities and various spokespersons for a given challenge to those authorities. The interaction is a coherent, bounded unit in roughly the same sense that a war or a political campaign is a unit. Such interactions have occurred from time to time ever since there were authorities of any kind. The broadest sense of the term *social movement* includes all such challenges. In a narrower sense, however, the national social movement draws its form and meaning from an interaction with the authorities who staff a national state. (Tilly 1984: 305; italics in the original)

For slightly more than a decade, a small group of analysts has posited the usefulness of social movement theory in revitalizing our understanding of civil society. Social movement theory, they argue, can help to move thinking on civil society out of the traditionalist, formalist trap of the strict literalist interpretations of social capital that have led others to write of the death of civil society. A formalist interpretation sees the breakdown of traditional forms of parochial and local organization as fatal to civil society. However, by moving the focus to the process-oriented analysis embodied in social movement theory, it becomes clear that other mobilizational forms—such as the often more geographically and structurally diffuse networks created by social movement organizations—

are equally capable of generating a vibrant civil society. Thus, Debra Minkoff argues that these organizations do four things worthy of note: They bear witness to "denser social networks and social infrastructures of the sort applauded by analysts of civil society"; they "contribute to an enduring opportunity structure for activism"; they "promote the diffusion of collective identities" by providing the infrastructure for mobilization by weak groups and linking otherwise isolated constituencies; and they "promote public discourse and debate, strengthening the public sphere" (Minkoff 1997).

Continuing the criticism of the dismal view of civil society most prominently represented by Putnam and, indeed, the debate that has centered around Putnam's writings, Robert Sampson and his coauthors write, "The positions of Putnam and his critics each have merit but tend to reinforce the way in which the debate on civil society has unfolded. Most of the data in dispute turn on trends in the individual-level backdrop to civil society—especially declines in group membership and social-psychological states of trust—rather than collective political action or public civic events. . . . The civil society debate has been waged on the potentially misleading perceptions, memberships, and behaviors of individuals as opposed to truly social, or collective, action" (Sampson, McAdam, et al. 2005: 674–675). Rather, Sampson and his coauthors propose a strategy of inquiry based on "an understanding of the social processes that give rise to and help sustain collective mobilization and action, an intellectual move that rejects the idea that collective action results simply from the aggregation of individual civic behavior" (Sampson, McAdam, et al. 2005: 676). This shift of emphasis is all the more important because it sees civil society as influenced in its development by its social and political context. Thus, Sampson and his coauthors write, "The main difference of note is that movements and related protest events are not just aggregations of individual participants; rather, they are social products born of complex interactive dynamics played out within established social settings" (Sampson, McAdam, et al. 2005: 678).

A social movement perspective recognizes that quantifiable "facts"—actions and voiced opinions by politicians and challengers, for example—must be seen in the context of their interpretation by the people in whose lives those facts exist. David Snow and his coauthors write, "What is at issue is not merely the presence or absence of grievances, but the manner in which grievances are interpreted and the generation and diffusion of those interpretations" (Snow, Rochford, et al. 1986: 466). Likewise, James Jasper writes that moral outrage depends on the interpretation of shocks in context, while "shocks depend on preexisting patterns of affect, which channel the interpretation of announcements and revelations"; thus, what people already know (or believe they know) about their contexts directly affects the meaning of what happens to them (Jasper 1998: 409). How people understand their grievances and their underlying causes, then, is as important as the presence of those grievances in the first place.

The interpretation of grievances is, Charles Kurzman writes, a potentially "confusing" process, particularly in contexts when individuals are unable to form reasonably certain expectations as to the actions and reactions of authorities. This "confusion," moreover, is different from uncertainty; Kurzman writes: "To the extent that the rules of the game stay relatively constant, we expect the unexpected. But when we sense that the rules of the game are suddenly changed, and we no longer know what to expect, that is confusion. To attempt a more formal definition, confusion is the recognition of deinstitutionalization" (Kurzman 2004: 335). It is here that the iterative nature of the development of social movements becomes particularly important, as the process of action, reaction, and interaction allows individuals to make estimations as to the contours and content of what Kurzman calls the "civic environment." When the contours are in flux, then confusion prevails, and collective action becomes less prevalent, potentially less purposeful, but also less predictable, Kurzman suggests. However, what might we expect in an environment in which deinstitutionalization is permanent, rather than transient, as it is in the revolutions Kurzman studies?

The answer begins by understanding how grievances are formed and perceived. In exploring the genesis of political opposition, Gamson begins by understanding the frame of reference employed by citizens when deciding to agree or oppose. Key here are two seemingly very basic and yet easily overlooked concepts: that of the decision that is binding and of the authorities whose position makes any given decision binding or not. The nature of authority here is also important, Gamson writes: "If authority is decentralized and diffuse, every member of the system may be an authority on at least some set of decisions, although these decisions may vary greatly in importance for the system" (Gamson 1968: 22). In this view, however, authority—even absolute authority—is never without consequences. By impinging on the lives of others in the system, any decision inevitably creates partisans, some of whom may be unhappy with the way a given decision affects their welfare. These partisans, in turn, seek to influence the decision-making authorities (Gamson 1968: 32–33).

Moreover, highly centralized, well-structured, and authoritarian states tend to run into a "large numbers problem" by creating masses of partisans all disaffected by the same blanket decisions (Jenkins 1995: 25).

It is, however, insufficient for citizens to formulate and "correctly" target grievances vis-à-vis the state. For the purposes of mobilization, those grievances must not only be shared but also understood to be shared. In an authoritarian context, this is particularly difficult. On the experience of dissent in the German Democratic Republic (GDR), Steven Pfaff and Hyojoung Kim write, "Even in repressive mono-organizational regimes, general knowledge of the state's poor performance is not difficult for citizens to obtain. What is often left secret is how widely grievances are *shared* among one's neighbors, particularly where extralocal communication is difficult and actors are clustered in localized, homophilous social niches. In the absence of such information, individual grievances remain too compartmentalized to fuel collective action" (Pfaff and Kim 2003: 408). Collective action, moreover, reaches its peak when grievances are sufficiently widely shared that dissenters can be assured of solidarity (Pfaff 1996).

Further, it is suggested that even an awareness of common grievance with properly directed blame is not sufficient for a movement to thrive. Francesca Polletta and James Japser write that movement participants are in need of a collective identity, which they define as "an individual's cognitive, moral, and emotional connection with a broader community, category, practice, or institution," and that this identity is often galvanized only through action (Polletta and Jasper 2001). Thus, the shared experience of protest solidifies perceptions of shared grievances and shores up expectations of solidarity while providing a common starting point for discussions of further action and organization.

The "resource mobilization" perspective on social movements likewise suggests that grievances are not enough and that politics has a role to play. Thus, John McCarthy and Mayer Zald write, "Grievances and discontent may be defined, created, and manipulated by issue entrepreneurs and organizations" (McCarthy and Zald 1977: 1215). Although this central thesis is not in dispute, it is unclear how many of the other tenets of the resource mobilization perspective are useful to our analysis. In large part, this is because the literature on the subject has been dominated by a heavily Western, and indeed a heavily American, perspective, in which movement organizations are accustomed to wooing donors, lobbying legislators, and interacting with a rich array of other organizations in a largely benign environment. This picture, needless to say, hardly resembles Russia. Thus, when McCarthy and Zald write, "Society provides the infrastructure which social movement industries and other industries utilize . . . [including] communication media and expense, levels of affluence, degree of access to institutional centers, preexisting networks and occupational structure and growth," one is left wondering whether they do not in fact mean that it is the political regime that provides (or fails to provide) the infrastructure they describe (McCarthy and Zald 1977: 1217).

The perspective provided by the social movement literature, when taken in the context of the historical debate on civil society, brings us back full circle to the initial insights of the political philosophers while rooting them in empirical investigation and analysis. By seeing civil society not as a formally defined category of actor but rather as the product of interaction between citizens and states, this perspective allows civil society to be simultaneously contingent in its form and content and purposeful in its action. It rids us of the necessity of determining what sorts of actors we may investigate because it is interested in processes rather than things. Although we must not assume an inherent link between actors and function, it reminds us that actions have purpose and meaning. And it gives us useful tools for understanding how those purposes and meanings are created.

Conclusions

This chapter has traced the remarkable evolution of a beleaguered idea. Indeed, it is sometimes tempting to surrender to despair and declare that the concept of civil society has been so stretched, contorted and abused over the last several centuries that it should simply be abandoned. Nonetheless, leading thinkers of almost every generation since Locke have found themselves returning to this territory, which one way or another finds itself implicated in the more robust theories of politics. In each case, definitions have been offered, and, though some degree of variation is to be expected, they often vary so widely that the associated theorists appear to be speaking different languages.

Recent history has both complicated matters further and suggested a solution. Despite the predominantly formalist approach taken to the study of civil society in transition, the way in which East European civil society defined itself up to and during the transition moment was essentially morphological. The goal they set out to achieve—the collective avoidance or circumvention of the state to achieve individual sovereignty—had not earlier been part of the civil society literature. It would thus be all too easy to forsake these activists as misguided and exclude them from consideration, as some observers have done (see, for example, Pelczynski 1988: 368). But that would be a mistake because it is precisely this development that allows us to see the common thread running through earlier conceptions—that of public sovereignty, or, more broadly put, the structure of state–society relations.

Further exploration of pretransition civil society in the communist space, meanwhile, warns us off of a formalist definition. Very few if any of the organizations active in Soviet-era civil society would meet the criteria mandated by the definitions that arose in their wake. Dissident movements, for example, generally put a premium on unanimity rather than pluralism and were less than democratic in their own decision-making processes (see, for example, Alekseeva 1984). Likewise, the publishers of samizdat failed miserably to achieve the standards of journalism demanded now from the press (see, for example, Feldbrugge 1975), and yet their success in the role Hume ascribed to newspapers is undisputed.

This excursion into history serves more than just a rhetorical purpose. Taken in the context of more than 300 years of political thought, the current vogue for conceptions of civil society that are either formalist (as in transitology) or prepolitical (as in social capital) appears an anomalous blip. Rather, the line of inquiry and analysis pursued in the literature on social movements is more solidly rooted both in theory and in empirical fact, for it conceives of civil society as a truly social institution, embedded in the context of political and economic institutions.

However, rereading the long literature on civil society also reminds us why a focus exclusively on social movement theory can be problematic. For all its strengths, the social movement "tool kit" deals primarily with isolated instances (if long and complex instances) of interaction, and this narrowness of view can sometimes obscure the importance of seeing civil society as being an encompassing environment. Here, the concept of social capital, with its emphasis on the aggregate of norms and relationships, finds its strength, even while it lacks explanatory power. Civil society is infinitely broader, larger, and more substantial; it is closer to the *societas civitas* than to the banal sum of NGOs. What is needed, then, is a definition of civil society that marries both of these observations, a definition that allows civil society to be discerned in the concrete facts of interaction between citizens and states but that also perceives civil society in the aggregate of those interactions.

Thus, I propose the following definition: Civil society is the nonviolent means by which individuals collectively seek sovereignty vis-à-vis the state. As such, its form is a reflection of the state with which it interacts. Where possible, it may indeed subjugate the state itself to the public. Where this is not possible (or desirable) it may create ways for the public to claim sovereignty by circumventing the state. In any case, the function we are interested in remains constant, even as the form it takes and the quantities in which it is produced are variable. The specific types of organizations that might be included in this definition will depend on the surrounding environment. Whether such organizations as NGOs, newspapers, labor unions, chess clubs, or political parties are included depends on the specific context.

This definition of civil society overlaps with other existing concepts, but is not concurrent with any of them. It involves social capital as the raw material with which civil society works but goes beyond it. Nor is it identical to the Habermasian public sphere, which is much too limited a realm to achieve true public sovereignty. It has linkages with political society, but in this view the dividing line is drawn at that point where organizations seek formal power for themselves or their constituents.

The concept of public sovereignty also requires definition. To an extent, it is present in Charles Taylor's three "senses" of civil society—"free associations, not under tutelage of state power"; "where society as a whole can structure itself and co-ordinate its actions through such associations which are free of state tutelage"; and "wherever the ensemble of associations can significantly determine or inflect the course of state policy" (Taylor 1990: 98). The sovereignty of people over the state is not something granted from above, as Locke would have it. In its most perfect form, when the state is subjugated to the degree that every individual is maximally autonomous (within the confines of Mill's maxim of no harm done to others), it is something continually achieved and maintained from below, much as Rousseau described. But the absence of democracy need not rule out a realm of public sovereignty. Even in a totalitarian regime, civil society creates corners of opportunity for people to be free, in part by redefining freedom itself, much as Havel and others did with their moral dissent in Czechoslovakia. In this case, to use the economic jargon, freedom or sovereignty is a private or at best a club good, available only to those who are in one way or another tied to its production. Democracy, then, results when civil society is able to convert this private good into a true public good, enforcing the sovereignty of each within a unity of all.

The collective nature of the action in question, too, requires explication. Although the fact of civil society, to the extent that it structures relations between citizens and their state, may enable individuals to exercise their sovereignty, it is not this individual exercise that interests us. While citizens no doubt seek sovereignty for the benefits it brings to them individually, what makes society *civil* is the fact of achieving that sovereignty collectively. Therein lies the creation and maintenance of a public in the sense expressed by Habermas and thus the potential for public sovereignty as expressed by Rousseau. And it is this combination of the "individual" and the "collective" in one definition that allows us to distinguish civil society from other phenomena, whether purely individual action or, to the contrary, collective action designed to subjugate rather than empower the individual.

The strength of this approach is that, without succumbing to eclecticism, it combines the approaches reviewed in this chapter and finds the common thread running through both those conceptions of civil society prior to 1989 and those that emerged from the transition literature. By focusing on the goal of sovereignty rather than on the act of mediation, this definition would be recognized by all of the major theorists, from Locke, Rousseau, and Hume through to Michnik.

Furthermore, it salvages the key realization of Hegelian-Marxist thought on the subject (though not necessarily its Leninist continuation), namely that civil society is contingent on the environment and patterns of interaction established by the state (defined here not simply as that entity that monopolizes legitimate violence but as the sum total of the institutions of coercive governance and their structured aspects). But, whereas Marx argued that civil society is captive, I argue that it is contingent.

This definition of *civil society* will allow me to make sense of the case studies that follow in this volume. Without a common conceptual thread, these studies might seem little more than disparate, passing glimpses into sociopolitical life in Russia. Informed by a definition of civil society in which individuals strive for the sovereignty of the public, however, they become part of a broader story, in which Russians are engaged in constant contact with their state. Without a definition to guide analysis, it would be difficult to recognize the significance of sporadic, low-level protests or the antagonistic state responses they generate, and the line between entrenched informal institutions and unstructured patterns of behavior would be blurred.

Still, a definition is not enough. Missing from all of this, as Hanson complains, is "a satisfying theory as to how 'civil societies' with high levels of trust get generated within some institutional contexts but not others" (Hanson 2001a: 137). One solution, I submit, is to remember the nature of public goods as "externalities," by-products of processes otherwise subject to their own logics. Civil society, like social capital, is always present in some quantity and form, a reflection, as Polanyi and Duverger wrote, of the political and economic institutions that surround it. As in the Habermasian public sphere, it mediates conflict and communication, but the end result—the production of the public good, in this case public sovereignty—depends not on the structure of the civil society so much as on the identities and interests of the participants in the communication and conflicts it mediates.

Finally, the application of the tools provided by the social movement literature, with their particular focus on the interpretation and reinterpretation of grievances and political contexts through an iterative and interactive process, allows us to operationalize the theory in a way that sees the production of civil society as a joint endeavor of both society and the state.

This, then, gives us the beginnings of the model Hanson seeks. As Chapter 1 suggested, and as subsequent chapters will illustrate, the key factor would seem to be the nature of elite competition. But we are getting ahead of ourselves. The crucial achievement thus far, I submit, is an operationalization of the concept of civil society that not only is encompassing but also allows for the application of analytical tools familiar to the social sciences, rather than the abstract reasoning of philosophy. That, I hope, will distinguish this book from many (though, of course, far from all) contemporary discussions on civil society, by relocating civil society squarely in the context of politics and contestation, identifying the institutional aspects of state–society interaction and telling a sociologically grounded story of how the nature of power in Russia influences the development of opposition.

In sum, if civil society is the realm of difference, then it is inherently defined by what surrounds it. As a mediator, it is conditioned by what actors want. As an enabler, it is constrained by what institutional frameworks allow. Civil society is not a force in and of itself. Rather, it is the means by which force is exerted, the tool with which aims are achieved, and the space in which conflicts are played out. Thus, the idea that a truly engaged civil society might somehow be engineered without concomitantly reengineering the state appears to me absurd. Civil society and the state inhabit the same territory and are always contiguous. One cannot change without altering the other.

The study of civil society, then, is most useful not as an end unto itself, but as a mirror held up to the state. By examining its successes and failures, we might learn much about how it works. But we learn much more about how states and citizens interact, about how they shape each other's desires and abilities.

3   Russia's Potemkin Revolution

On Tuesday, July 8, 2008, a dozen or so residents of the town of Protvino, about 100 km to the south of Moscow, gathered in a meeting room in city hall for a public hearing. At the front of the room stood a somewhat disheveled Nikolai Velichko, deputy mayor in charge of planning and investment for the city of around 40,000, who proceeded monotonously, quickly, and without particular enthusiasm to run through the details of the city's new short-, mid- and long-term development plans: x number of schools to be renovated, y amount of new homes to be built, and so forth.

Velichko was clearly not enjoying himself, but under federal law all such projects have to be presented at public hearings, and so there he was. A week before the hearing, the city posted flyers announcing the time and date—at 2 o'clock on a workday afternoon. As a result, almost all of those in attendance were retirees of the sort who made a habit of attending such meetings, predominantly in silence. One exception was a woman in her late twenties, Anna, on maternity leave at the time and thus the only member of a small group of local community activists able to attend the meeting.

"Is it true," Anna asked the deputy mayor, "that the new industrial zone will be home to a large bottle factory?"

"Yes," Velichko answered, and then proceeded to list the number of jobs the factory would create, the amount of money the city would get in new taxes, how that would help improve public services, and so on.

Anna had intended to raise a number of issues that she and her fellow activists found disturbing. Why, they wondered, would a city that was built around science—Protvino is home to the world's first particle accelerator and still has a number of important high-energy physics laboratories—need to invest so much in the low-tech business of turning sand into bottles? Who was the mysterious unnamed European investor behind the project? How much pollution would the factory create?

But it was not to be. The deputy mayor noticed Anna's pen and notepad and became agitated.

"You're taking notes," he said. "Are you a journalist?"

"No," she answered, "although I was thinking of writing a letter to the newspaper."

"Who told you that you could come in here and take notes?" Velichko demanded.

"I thought this was a public hearing?" she replied.

"It is a public hearing. But you can't just come in here without warning and start taking notes. Maybe you'd like to take pictures, too? How would you like it if I came into your bedroom at six in the morning and started taking pictures, just like that, without warning and without permission? You have to respect a person's privacy!"

With that, Velichko asked whether there were any further questions; noted that, other than from Anna, there were none; and declared the meeting adjourned.[1]

⌇

This is the environment in which Russian activists have found themselves throughout most of the post-Soviet period: one in which bureaucrats and public officials feel that public hearings are their private domain, one in which concepts of accountability and constituency seem foreign. Yuri Slezkine once wrote (albeit in a different context) that the Soviet Union resembled a communal apartment, in which ethnic communities, like families, were forced by circumstance and against their better judgment to live together and share resources (Slezkine 2000). Communal apartments are almost gone, and the various republics have gone their separate ways, but post-Soviet Russia continues to resemble an unnatural household that the elite and the governing apparatus are forced to share with the general public. Walls are erected, privacy is demanded, and mutual disdain all but rules out civilized dialogue.

In the rest of this volume, I will describe and analyze cases of civic mobilization, in which ordinary Russians attempt to seek collective redress of their grievances from the state. Throughout these cases, the state and its representatives will appear much as Vice-Mayor Velichko in the anecdote above: removed, callous, self-interested, and devoid of any of the ideal qualities embodied in the term *civil servant*. More than that, we will see a state in which the law neither binds officials nor empowers citizens but is instead a tool in the hands of the powerful, frequently used to afflict the powerless. Lines of accountability and control are contorted and perverted. Russian citizens are citizens in name only: They enjoy no real ownership of the state they inhabit.

Before launching into these cases, it is important to understand how the Russian regime works, and to do that we must understand how Russia evolved from a rigid totalitarian state, in which the government sought to control every significant aspect of public and private life, into an authoritarian but hyperflexible state, in which freedom coexists with disenfranchisement.

My purpose in this chapter is not to explain the demise of the Soviet Union but rather to demonstrate how processes of change and continuity shaped the practices of today's Russian elite. Because I hypothesize that elite behavior shapes civic mobilization, and because we are interested in institutions, we must understand that the patterns of state–society relations are ingrained; thus, some historical analysis is necessary. Moreover, none of the off-the-shelf regime types is adequate to describe Russia today. And we are in any case interested in the regime from the point of view of the incentives it creates for citizenship, and that is not the focus of most regime typologies.

Modern political science recognizes many more flavors of regime than simply democratic and totalitarian, open and closed. There is now a growing literature on the gradations of authoritarianism (most notably: Ottaway 2003; Levitsky and Way 2010), and since at least the 1960s researchers have explored differences in "political culture" among democracies (Almond and Verba 1963). In particular, Almond and Verba, as well as Robert Dahl (1971), suggest looking at orientations—of states toward societies and of societies toward states—as a way of understanding patterns of political and civic behavior. Indeed, many of those studying postcommunist civil society, particularly Richard Rose and his colleagues, have followed Almond and Verba's tack quite closely, tracking individuals' orientation toward the various input and output aspects of the state and then using the resulting data as an explanatory variable in the development of civil society (see, for example, Rose 1994; Rose and Mishler 1994; Mishler and Rose 1997). Clearly, as Rose and others have demonstrated, looking at the orientation of societies toward states does yield some explanatory power.

Much less, however, has been done to look at the orientation of states toward societies and the corresponding effect on civil society. This is despite the fact that a great deal has been written about the way states interact with constituents—that portion of the governed who enable the ruling elite's exercise of power. Clearly, just as constituents have choices in how to relate to the state, so too do states have choices in how to organize their relations with constituents. Whether or how to hold elections, the distribution of power and authority, the structure of taxation, and any number of other choices open to states continue to be thoroughly explored by social scientists. Indeed, the democratization and transition literatures are chock full of discussions of the implications of various choices political elites might make (to name just a few: Rustow 1970; Higley and Burton 1989; Horowitz 1990; Linz 1990; Przeworski 1991; Shugart and Carey 1992; Linz and Stepan 1996; Bunce 1999; Kitschelt 2000; Zielonka 2001). Unfortunately for our purposes, though, the vast majority of this literature focuses on constitutional choices and formal institutions. Only a small minority (for example: Bunce 1983; Innes 2002) look seriously at the less formal but nonetheless ingrained institutions governing the way elites identify and interact with their constituencies or at the sources of those institutions. And because formally democratic institutions are often systematically subverted by antidemocratic behavior, it may well turn out to be these less formal underlying institutions that truly inform state–society relations and thus give form to civil society.

What do we know, in broad terms, about the Russian political system? We know, for one, that it is seemingly powerful. During his first eight years as president, Vladimir Putin brought all major television channels under effective state control, disenfranchised the most uncooperative of the oligarchs and brought the others closer into line, effectively ended federalism, strengthened the military and the secret services, eviscerated the party system and the federal parliament, and made large-scale public protest nearly impossible.

At the same time, Russia's governing apparatus is not much of a system: Although an authoritarian ruling elite and bureaucracy dominate the country and have considerable coercive capabilities, theirs, as Valeri Ledyaev (2008) writes, is "power over" (the ability to control reactively) rather than "power to" (the ability to govern proactively). Meanwhile, the most recent analyses of the behavior of public officials in Russia have shown that laws and norms tend to be manipulated rather than obeyed (Solomon 2008), while those constraints that do exist on officials' opportunism are weak and loose, and laws and constraints "*enable* office-holders' pursuit of individual and group interests rather than *constraining* them" (Oleinik 2008: 184; italics in the original).

Establishing this behavioral portrait of the regime is essential because we hypothesize a link between the regime and strategies of civic mobilization (or the lack thereof). This chapter, then, seeks to understand the underlying institutions and practices that shape the Russian political regime and the behavior of bureaucrats and public officials from top to bottom. Because we see institutions as historically and socially ingrained patterns of behavior, I will begin with an analysis of the late Soviet period, in which power is transformed into a "club good" for the *nomenklatura* elite. From there, I suggest that the post-Soviet Russian elite inherited both this club good and many of the key habits of the old Soviet club that are required to maintain it, facilitated in large part by the country's natural resource wealth. Finally, I will complete the portrait of a regime that is driven in its interactions with the public by the necessity of maintaining "club" power behind a façade of democratic legitimacy.

The Club Good of Soviet Power

In 1994, the late Russian liberal economist and former prime minister Egor Gaidar looked back on the end of the Soviet Union and, in a volume titled *State and Evolution*, mocked Lenin and the entire Marxist tradition. He wrote:

A complete history of the relationship between the Soviet *nomenklatura* and the Soviet *nomenklatura* state, the history of their torturous conflicts and the eventual alienation of the former from the latter has yet to be written. But for the moment we can posit at least this: the Soviet system was devoured from within, by its own ruling class. Marx wrote that the bourgeoisie was digging its own grave. Well, the Communist oligarchy, too, may have dug its own grave, but this was a shrewd and mercenary gravedigger, and it aimed to profit from its own death. More accurately, it aimed to turn a funeral into a party, a celebration of liberation from the old system and the birth of a new one—which, by the way, it would also control. (Gaidar [1994] 2003: 60)

Gaidar went on to posit that his economic reforms—and his rapid privatization plan in particular—would thwart the *nomenklatura*'s aims. It is another question whether his dreams came true. Our immediate task is to explore how it is that Gaidar's initial observation came to pass.

In his landmark analysis of socialist political economy, Janos Kornai identified four main pillars on which the "classical" socialist system stood (1992: 42–43). These, in his view, were:

1. *Ideology*, which binds the Communist Party, together with the bureaucracy, into a more or less cohesive whole by providing a shared set of values, ideals, and philosophical landmarks;

2. *Power*, the aim and motivation behind the ideology, as the ruling elite seek to maintain, consolidate, and, in some cases, expand the control they exercise over society continually to reproduce the system;

3. *Prestige and privileges* that accrue to loyal members of the ruling elite more or less in accordance with their place in the bureaucratic hierarchy and, above and beyond ideology, constitute a powerful incentive for conformity, self-subjugation, and continued participation; and

4. *Coercion*, which is available to the elite as a means of enforcing adherence to rules and punishing deviation from bureaucratic group interests, with a wide range of options from the removal of privileges to internal exile and execution.

Notably missing from this list is total state ownership of the economy, the institution that most liberal theorists—including Gaidar—tend to see as the "original sin" of socialism. Kornai, however, disagreed, seeing state ownership as a tool for maintaining political control, rather than political control as a tool for maintaining state ownership. He wrote:

> It is not the property form—state ownership—that erects the political structure of classical socialism over itself. Quite the reverse: the given political structure brings about the property form it deems desirable. Although in this case the ideology plays a marked role in forming society, it is not the sole explanation for the direction of influence. The indivisibility of power and the concomitant totalitarianism are incompatible with the autonomy that private ownership entails. This kind of rule demands heavy curtailment of individual sovereignty. The further elimination of private ownership is taken, the more consistently can full subjection be imposed. (Kornai 1992: 362)

Meanwhile, increasing industrialization and the accompanying systematization of the Soviet government gave rise to a number of important trends in the Soviet elite. Most important, despite Stalin's purges, the elite by the late 1930s was becoming increasingly specialized, and by the 1950s education in the Higher Party School was becoming important to political advancement (Mawdsley and White 2000: 102, 116). This, in turn, helped give rise to the ambitious but disenfranchised elite to whom Khrushchev turned for support in the early years of his reign. Between 1956 and 1961, Khrushchev arranged the election of 458 new full and candidate members of the Central Committee, calculating that "expansion was a less painful means of renewal than turnover, and it was more profitable in terms of patronage" (Mawdsley and White 2000:

137–138). This, in effect, laid the groundwork for the creation of the *nomenklatura* club referred to earlier, by expanding the ranks of the elite, stabilizing elite membership, and deepening elites' collective ties.

Khrushchev, however, like Lenin and Stalin before him, perceived the need for systemwide reforms and a "leading role" more for himself than for the Party. Certainly, the fear and outright personal subjugation that accompanied Stalin's rule had faded, and the professionalization of the elite continued apace. Nonetheless, high-level turnover continued, including 77 percent of the voting members of the Central Committee between 1953 and 1961 (Hough 1976: 3). In a matter of a few years, the elite's initial gratitude for their physical security gave way to resentment of Khrushchev's reorganizations and interventions; as a result, the Central Committee that saved Khrushchev from a backlash in 1957 deposed him in 1964 (Hough 1976: 7; Mawdsley and White 2000: 137).

The 1964 putsch, then, represents the rejection of Khrushchev's autocratic control over the elite (even if his approach to society at large was relatively more liberal) and the coming together of an elite "club," organized to effect stable, collective rule over an industrialized state and its attending resources. This development was made inevitable by the opportunity Khrushchev provided to elites to pursue both individual and group interests, with privileges and well-being owed less to the leader than to the benefits of holding a particular office in a particular sector. Leadership was delegated to a quartet of largely uncharismatic functionaries—Brezhnev, Kosygin, Podgornyi, and Suslov—all of whom would remain in place for the bulk of what has become known as the "Brezhnev era" (Hough 1976: 3).

This collective government, as Jerry Hough wrote at the time (1976), recognized the *nomenklatura* and Party/state bureaucracy as its "electorate," in a way no previous Soviet regime had. An elite "club," initially formed to defend group interests against an autocratic leader, was now essentially sovereign and moved to consolidate its position. Aside from continuing to increase the size of the top elite (see Table 3.1) and instituting the famous "stability of cadres" policy, guaranteeing a large degree of job security, Brezhnev and his partners-in-power instituted a number of policies beneficial to elites both as individuals and as more or less formally organized groups. These included allowing the scientific and research-and-development institutes a degree of autonomy, guaranteeing virtually all enterprises regular increases in investment, keeping production requirements stable and predictable, and promising access to policy making and a minimum of central interference (Hough 1976; Bunce 1983). This "corporat-

TABLE 3.1. Size of the Central Committee.

	1927 expansion		1952 expansion		1986
	Before	After	Before	After	
Full Members	63	71	71	125	307
Candidate Members	43	50	68	111	170

Source: Mawdsley and White 2000, 103–104.

ist" arrangement, as Bunce termed it, gave elites unprecedented opportunities to satisfy their own personal goals, in exchange for adherence to a hierarchical system that would, in turn, guarantee and legitimize their positions and privileges. Brezhnev, as Robert Tucker wrote, "offered consensual leadership for order and stability. He has been content with, and may owe his longevity in power to, his willingness to be first among equals in a truly oligarchical regime in which the various power blocs, including the military and the police, wield a heavy influence on policy" (Tucker 1987: 127).

This newly empowered elite club faced all of the same systemic difficulties that had plagued their more autocratic predecessors. Returns on investment became increasingly meager, as crucial sectors of the economy—from agriculture to industry to resource extraction—faltered. To take one indicator, although in most economies energy efficiency increases over time, in the Soviet Union the opposite was true, and energy usage grew faster than industrial production over the entire period from 1940 to 1985 (Iasin 2002: 64). The planned economy's inherent propensity to eschew innovation was reinforced by the alleviation of central pressure to increase productivity and became an obstacle to development even in such strategically crucial sectors of the economy as oil and gas extraction (Goldman 1980; Rosser and Rosser 1997). The government's refusal to address these issues—indeed, its implicit promise to the elite that it would not address these issues in any fundamental way—simultaneously freed and forced the elite (and pretty much everyone else) to pursue the alternative, semiclandestine strategies of *blat* and pseudo-market exchange that would quickly become the only means to keep the system functioning (Ledeneva 2000; Goldman 2003a). More on these strategies will be said later. Suffice it for now to quote Bunce: "Instead of generating stability and growth, the corporatist deal generated neither, and political bankruptcy went hand in hand with economic bankruptcy" (Bunce 1983: 136).

Rather than erupt into crisis, however, the logic described by Kornai—combined with the failure of official reforms to rationalize that logic—forced the adaptation of the system's participants to existence in what Naishul and Kordonskii termed the "administrative market." This market, according to Kordonskii, can be defined as a "strictly but multifariously hierarchical syncretic[2] system (the economic and political components of which are inseparable even analytically), in which social status and consumer well-being are mutually convertible according to defined, in part unwritten rules, which change over time" (Kordonskii 2000: 11).[3] Unlike the mechanisms that traditionally govern capitalist goods and services markets, in which buyers and sellers are on an equal footing and relations between them are horizontal, relations between buyers and sellers on the administrative market are arranged according to a hierarchy defined by values that have more to do with politics than economics. As such, Kordonskii wrote:

> Costs, goods, values, goals, and the means for achieving them were fused into a single administrative whole, and the possession of means for achieving various aims divided people into strata, social groups within the socialist society. The economic situation of a member of these socialist social groups was singularly tied to his political status (with the specific meaning socialism gave to this concept). The system of political statuses (social background, education, position in society, place of residence, and so on) determined a Soviet citizen's economic position. . . . The hierarchical nature (and, thus, political significance) of all forms of activity was combined with an all-encompassing bargain between the owners of administrative rights and of consumer values. The latter were always in "deficit," and they could only be obtained by presenting ones administrative rights to them, having beforehand stood in line and negotiated with those who distribute the goods. (Kordonskii 2000: 14)

Even on an individual level, decisions that would otherwise be political take on economic significance, and vice versa. Positions are held not for money, prestige, or even power, but for access and a place in the hierarchy; at virtually all levels, in virtually all spheres, the perks (legal or otherwise) became more important than the job. In the context of a state sustained by the total expropriation of property, this "administrative market" was reinforced by the consumer deficit inherent to the socialist command economy. For the average citizen, subsistence on what the state allotted was impossible. For the elite—the *nomenklatura*, with its privileged access to goods and services—such subsistence was undesirable. Every action becomes imbued with hidden meaning and is driven by motives that are ulterior and, because they run counter to official ideology, clandestine in nature. In other words, everyone in the system becomes to some degree a thief, expropriating from the expropriator (see, in particular, Kordonskii 2000: 13). Ironically, by easing subsistence and providing opportunities for mobility, it was this thieving that sustained the system and staved off crisis.

Clearly, much more could be said on these and a number of other structural points. For our purposes, however, this analysis of the institutional political economy of "really existing socialism" is sufficient to suggest a model for analyzing late- and post-Soviet institutional and elite developments. For help, I turn to the concept of collective goods, specifically "club goods," to which I alluded earlier in describing the Soviet elite as a "club." Like public goods, club goods are (usually) noncompetitive in their consumption, but, unlike public goods, they are excludable in their distribution, with access limited only to members of an actively constituted group who agree to make more or less equal contributions to the production of the "club good." For the "club" to operate and for the good to be produced, two conditions must be met. First, the members of the club must perceive a need for the good on a sufficiently regular basis, such that they would prefer the good to be in constant supply. And, second, the good must be sufficiently expensive to produce, such that potential club members find it more beneficial to contribute to production even when they have no immediate demand for the good, rather than risk the necessity of having to produce the good alone at a later date. Should either of these conditions fail to be met, the club will dissolve and production will cease. Many clubs have enforcement mechanisms to prevent members from free-riding and/or deserting. If the bargain involved is substantially disadvantageous, however, no degree of coercion will be sufficient to hold the club together, especially as the coercers themselves will find it too costly to enforce their control.

The concept of club goods was promulgated by James Buchanan as occupying the middle ground between "private goods" and "public goods" (Buchanan 1965). As such, club goods are semirivalrous, in that consumption of the good (or a unit of the good) by an individual reduces the marginal utility that can be extracted from the good by others (unlike with public goods, whose marginal utility is not reduced), but not to zero (unlike with private goods). They are also semiexcludable, in that the good's inherent degree of "publicness" (because it is semirivalrous) makes total exclusion inefficient, but a degree of exclusion remains relatively efficient.

If the preceding describes club goods, the question remains of how to define the "club." Todd Sandler and John Tschirhart classically define the club as "a voluntary group deriving mutual benefits from sharing one or more of the following: production costs, the members' characteristics, or a good characterized by excludable benefits" (Sandler and Tschirhart 1997: 335). This definition subsumes six key characteristics (Sandler and Tschirhart 1997: 336–338):

1. "Privately owned and operated clubs must be voluntary; members choose to belong because they anticipate a net benefit";
2. "Club goods, unlike pure public goods, involve sharing that results in congestion or crowding," and, as a result, the net benefit enjoyed by club members must be sufficient to warrant forfeiting their ability to negotiate private (and thus potentially exclusive) access to the good;
3. "Club goods require an exclusive group whereby nonmembers are excluded";
4. "Partitioning is what permits competition among clubs";
5. "The presence of an exclusion mechanism that monitors utilization so that members can be charged tolls and nonmembers kept out";
6. "Club goods involve at least two allocative choices in contrast to the provision choice of pure public goods. Because exclusion is and should be practiced, membership size must be ascertained along with the provision level of the shared good. Insofar as the membership size affects the provision choice and vice versa, the decisions must be made simultaneously."

For analysis, it is useful to envisage the institutional structure of the Soviet regime—all of the apparatuses of ownership, control, and coordination that support the *nomenklatura*'s campaign for maintained power—as a club good. Thus, members of the ruling elite (the "club") perceive the need for a collective mechanism (the "good") that will maintain and/or increase their power as a group, while guaranteeing each member access to a secure supply of privileges. As a contribution to the good's production, members agree to forego a degree of freedom and the potential for greater individual reward that might otherwise arise from individual economic and/or political entrepreneurship. As long as this collective agreement is able to provide secure benefits to the elite at a price below what it would cost them to acquire similar benefits individually—or to provide benefits that no lone individual could ever obtain—the club will remain in place and the "club good" of Soviet control will be continually produced. This, essentially, is what Kornai and Kordonskii are (separately) referring to when they speak of the propensity of the system to reproduce itself. As soon as the bargain becomes disadvantageous, however, enforcement mechanisms will break down or be overcome, and the institutional structure of the regime will be dismantled in favor of a new arrangement.

I regard this conception of collective rule as a club good as more than simply a metaphor. Over the course of this book, names and appearances will change. The word *nomenklatura* will fall out of use, elections will feature independent political parties, economies will be privatized. The argument, however, is that none of those things matters if the fundamental nature of power does not change. And, in the last three decades or so of the Soviet Union, the crucial and particular aspect of Soviet power was its concentration in the hands of a club, which sought to maintain position and privilege by means of broad economic, social, and political control. But, just as Kornai wrote that socialist ownership of the economy was a symptom rather than a cause of Soviet power, so too should we remember that the mechanisms with which the club exercised control are of only secondary importance. The key is the existence of the club and the maintenance of its position. And the test of any "revolution"—whether in 1991 or 2004 or 2011—is thus whether the club is dismantled.

The club's rigid nature—the fact that, once entrenched, it had every incentive to hoard power and little incentive to share—eventually began to create socioeconomic and political tensions. By allowing individuals to remain in high-level posts for long periods, the "stability of cadres" arrangement severely limited younger functionaries' opportunities for career advancement. One result was to encourage officials and functionaries at all levels to maximize their extraction of privileges from the positions they occupied and were likely to occupy for the foreseeable future; this, in turn, supported the development of networks and horizontal relationships at middle and lower levels of the hierarchy. Another result of this increasingly Jurassic Party, however, was to create a generation of frustrated *nomenklatura* functionaries who had begun their careers under Khrushchev and were still young enough under Brezhnev to harbor ambitions for career advancement; notably, Gorbachev was among this generation (Bunce 1999: 59). In other words, differentiation began to appear within the "club," and its members were no longer wholly equal, even in principle. This potential conflict, as much as political stability and economic stagnation, was a key part of Brezhnev's legacy.

Macroeconomic troubles, meanwhile, only worsened the inbred inefficiencies associated with the "shortage economy" described by Kornai. In the extractive industries, as in the economy at large, the Brezhnev government attempted a number of minor restructuring programs, most of which were designed to consolidate enterprises and clarify lines of communication. The Soviet system, however, had no administrative solution. What it did have was a solution in the form of an informal institution, the under-the-table, off-the-books culture of transactions that allowed formal institutions to function and Soviet citizens to get by.[4] Often referred to by the Russian word *blat*, sometimes called the USSR's second economy, this was actually more than either term suggests. In some respects, this was the Soviet Union's primary economy, to which the structures of the "real" socialist economy were nothing more than an access point.

Alena Ledeneva defines *blat* as:

> . . . a distinctive form of non-monetary exchange, a kind of barter based on a personal relationship. In the planned economy, money did not function as an equivalent in economic transactions; things were sorted out by mutual help, by barter. Apart from official rations and privileges allocated by the state distribution system to different occupational strata, every employee had a particular kind of access (*dostup*) which could be traded in *blat* relations. The relative unimportance of money in the command economy brought into being this specific form of exchange, lying somewhere between commodity exchange and gift giving. (Ledeneva 2000: 184)

Thus, in a manner of speaking, *blat* was the currency of the administrative market Kordonskii describes. With it one could buy what could not be bought in any other way, anything from education to country houses and—as shortages intensified—just about everything else. Ideologically, *blat* was anathema. The political elite, however, came to rely on it not only to make life livable but more generally to make the economy as a whole function. Party officials, as Ledeneva writes, understood that "maintaining informal contacts in order to loosen the rigid constraints of the system was part of their function" (Ledeneva 2000: 196).

This was not, moreover, simply a secondary function of officials ordinarily tasked with pursuing official aims. In the context of Brezhnev's stagnant economy—the period that came to be known as *zastoi*[5]—numerous people made trading in *blat* their primary profession. On the consumer level, as Marshall Goldman describes, there were the *fartsovshchiki*[6] selling goods on the black market, *valiutchiki*[7] trading currencies, and the *deltsy*[8] providing private services; on the industrial level, *tolkachi*[9] moved goods and services, correcting the central planners' ubiquitous oversights (Goldman 2003a: 123–124). In theory, all of these people were marginal. In practice, however, they were crucial; no factory manager could make do without a reliable *tolkach*.

In an inherently inefficient system, *blat* was an ideal currency. It sustained the socioeconomic status quo and allowed business to be conducted at all levels. Most importantly, however, it was not threatening to the elite "club." Unlike money in a capitalist economy—where income can be turned into wealth—*blat* in the administrative market is difficult to accumulate and store. Its allocation is a factor of one's position in the hierarchy; thus, unlike money, it cannot be turned into an independent source of power. Once its owner places him- or herself in opposition to the system, his or her supply of *blat* loses value.

Officially, of course, there was "real" money in the Soviet Union, and after *blat* had been employed to negotiate access to a good or service, this money was used to consummate the transaction. *Blat*, rather than money, determined whether a good could be acquired. There was, moreover, no direct connection between *blat* and money. Money, as a general rule, could not buy *blat*, and because money on the internal market was only symbolic, there was no particular reason to use *blat* to acquire money. The exception to this rule was the black market, both in goods and currencies. Whenever a transaction involved a party outside the USSR, the most important use of *blat* was to acquire money, whether rubles or dollars, which would in turn buy access directly. This phenomenon could eventually become a threat to the system, especially were the government ever to lose control of the money supply, and indeed it did.

It is beyond the scope of this book to explain the demise of the Soviet Union. It is worth noting, however, what did not cause the system to collapse: There was no direct nonelite threat to the ruling elite's ability to maintain control, nothing akin to Solidarity in Poland or the mass exodus of East Germans to the West. Many of the elements that formed a potent counterelite in Hungary and Czechoslovakia were either absent or successfully accommodated by Gorbachev's glasnost. Thus, there was no need for a negotiated exit from power, for a handover of control to the opposition. What was in demand, rather, was a liberation of members of the ruling elite to pursue individual strategies. This liberation would include, first and foremost, the end of the Communist Party's "leading role" in elite recruitment, promotion, and hierarchical organization. Second, it would include the legalization of financial profit and personal enrichment. And, finally, it would give elites license to "cash in" the state resources available to them.[10]

The ruling "club" thus found itself in a qualitatively new situation. For a growing portion of the elite, the collective bargain that kept the club together was becoming increasingly unfavorable. If we recall the supporting components of the socialist system as laid out by Kornai, two things become clear. First, as the potency of ideology to promote cohesiveness dissolved, more emphasis would theoretically need to be placed on coercion, the legitimacy of which was, in turn, diminished by the decline of ideology. Second, the degree of control and privilege allotted to the elite was becoming increasingly expensive, even as individuals within the elite began to see greater opportunities for enrichment outside the confines of the club.

With the parting of ways by elites and the evisceration of the Party came the flattening of the hierarchy, the opening up of vertical and horizontal mobility within the elite, and the looting of state property. Regardless of the extent to which these effects were intended, elites adapted to changing domestic and international circumstances, seeking to maintain as much control and—more important—privilege as possible. The potential of a specific set of institutions to produce a specific "club good" had been exhausted, and the members of the club accordingly sought new institutional arrangements. As further developments demonstrate, however, many of them in no way intended to give up their ruling positions.

The Resource Curse in Russia

If power in the Soviet Union was generated at the nexus of the state and the economy (which, incidentally, separates the Soviet Union from no other country in particular), it is reasonable to assume that economic factors would help shape post-Soviet Russian political life, as well. And so an examination of contemporary Russia's political economy is in order.

Two things are notable about the post-Soviet Russian economy. For one, dependence on natural resources is considerable and growing. Hydrocarbons account for about 65 percent of total Russian export income, with other natural resources accounting for a further 18.8 percent (World Bank 2013). By relatively conservative estimates, the direct contribution to gross domestic product (GDP) in 2010 (not including multiplier effects) of oil and gas was 19.2 percent, while metals (ferrous and nonferrous) contributed 6.2 percent (World Bank 2004). Moreover, oil (again, alone) accounted for approximately one-third of federal government revenues in the mid-1990s and some 80 percent of the growth in budget revenues since the 1998 financial crisis (Ivanova, Keen, et al. 2005: 17). From 2001 to 2011, the share of oil in gas in budget revenues had grown from 20 percent to 49 percent: As Thane Gustafson wrote, "Dependence had become addiction" (Gustafson 2012: 5).

Secondly, ownership in the Russian economy is highly concentrated. At last count, twenty-three so-called financial-industrial groups (or FIGs), many until recently controlled by "oligarchs," controlled 35 percent of total sales and are most active in oil, raw materials, and machine building, including automobiles (World Bank 2004: 99, 105). By the end of the 1990s, the oil sector was dominated by thirteen companies (two state owned), producing 87 percent of total crude output and 88 percent of total refining output; another 113 small companies account for 10 percent of total value; the state-controlled natural gas monopoly Gazprom also controls some 3.2 percent of crude oil (Curkowski 2004: 288). What's more, the entirety of Russia's pipeline infrastructure is controlled by two sets of (state-owned) hands. Notably, these FIGs compete among themselves considerably more on political rather than economic battlefields (Barnes 2003; Yakovlev and Zhuravskaya 2004).

Recent research has shed considerable light on the web of causal mechanisms that underpin the negative impact that abundant exportable natural resources seem to have on democracy—the so-called resource curse. Most simply put, the presence of significant resource wealth—particularly oil, gas, and minerals—is argued to have a gravitational pull on a country's political elite, increasing the price they place on power (to the detriment of democratic practice) and decreasing the price they place on everything else (to the detriment of everything else). Clearly, though, the resource curse does not affect every country the same way; oil wealth does not skew politics in Norway the way it does, say, in Venezuela. In a static model, this seems easy enough to explain; as James Robinson and colleagues write, countries with "good institutions" get by just fine, while countries with "bad institutions . . . may suffer from a resource curse" (Robinson, Torvik, et al. 2003: 5–6).

In an environment such as Russia, in which institutions are weak and fluid, things are more complicated. Some of the effects that might be predicted in theory—such as a positive effect on regime durability—have not stood up to empirical analysis (Smith 2004). Michael Ross (2001), however, identifies three primary "effects" within the causal relationship between resources (in this case, oil wealth) and democracy that do prove robust: the "rentier effect" (in which states are pulled into the orbit of rents and rent seekers); the "repression effect" (in which elites use repression to maintain power); and the "modernization effect" (in which income leads to socioeconomic development and the effects predicted by modernization theory). I will focus here on the rentier effect.

Ross further breaks down the rentier effect into three submechanisms (Ross 2001: 332–334):

1. The taxation effect, which implies "that when governments derive sufficient revenues from the sale of oil, they are likely to tax their populations less heavily or not at all, and the public in turn will be less likely to demand accountability from—and representation in—their government";
2. The spending effect, which suggests that "oil wealth may lead to greater spending on patronage, which in turn dampens latent pressures for democratization"; and
3. The group-formation effect, which "implies that when oil revenues provide a government with enough money, the government will use its largesse to prevent the formation of social groups that are independent from the state and hence that may be inclined to demand political rights."

Taken as a whole, the rentier effect implies that "a state's fiscal policies influence its regime type: governments that fund themselves through oil revenues and have large budgets are more likely to be authoritarian; governments that fund themselves through taxes and are relatively small are more likely to become democratic" (Ross 2001: 335). In particular, Ross finds that the taxation effect alone accounts for some 17 percent of the total negative correlation between oil revenues and democracy (Ross 2001: 348).

Testing these and other hypotheses on Russia and the resource-rich Central Asian Soviet successor states—which, because of near identical initial conditions, provide a particularly effective laboratory for evaluating divergent outcomes—Pauline Jones Luong and Erika Weinthal draw attention to the ways in which the distribution of benefits from resource wealth either reinforces or undermines entrenched patronage networks and patterns of political competition (Luong and Weinthal 2001; Weinthal and Luong 2001). In their research, they adopt an approach that does not "view the state as captured by dominant economic interest groups but rather as captured by the interests of its own elites who are primarily concerned with staying in power"; the analysis is thus based on two assumptions: that rulers are interested in maximizing sovereignty, and that

. . . all state leaders are concerned primarily with staying in power and that to do so they must satisfy those interests that support their rule and appease or defeat those that do not. More specifically, they must continue to satisfy the status quo set of political and economic expectations that the state is expected to fulfill. This will vary according to the particular system of patronage and the particular cleavage structure on which patronage is dispensed in a given state. State leaders in energy-rich states will therefore choose development strategies that enable them to achieve a maximum level of sovereignty over their natural resources without threatening their continued rule. (Luong and Weinthal 2001: 373–374)

In this context, the resource curse is seen to be worse when the related benefits flow directly to state actors, whereas "private ownership results in the dispersion of proceeds from resource wealth, and hence, the generation of new interests outside the state apparatus" (Weinthal and Luong 2001: 216–217). It should be noted, however, that the link between the diversity of beneficiaries and the private ownership of resource-extracting companies is contingent, both on the relationship between ruling elites and private owners and on the nature and security of private property in a given state. Indeed, it is not difficult to imagine a situation in which state actors, with assistance from or in the guise of private actors, benefit directly from privately owned resource wealth. Thus, the lesson to be taken from this research is that, from a democratic point of view, the optimal distribution of resource wealth is one that supports the development of a diverse and competitive group of stakeholders.

The standard approach to the relationship between states and state-linked firms is as "a game between the public, the politicians, and the enterprise managers," which assumes "that, because the public is disorganized, politicians cater to interest groups, such as labor unions, rather than the median voter" as well as "that the relationship between politicians and managers is governed by incomplete contracts, so that residual rights of control rather than incentive contracts become the critical determinant of resource allocation" (Shleifer and Vishny 1994: 997). In this model, politicians use firms to win political points among their constituencies. Because the model is designed for electoral democracies, it assumes that this constituency comprises a broad electorate; the implications change, however, if the constituency is narrow.

In a number of postcommunist countries—including Russia—reforms initially (or, at least, nominally) intended to create a broad democratic and proreform constituency instead created a narrow constituency that was certainly in favor of the freedoms implied by the market but not necessarily the restrictions implied by democracy. As Joel Hellman wrote, "Instead of forming a constituency in support of advancing reforms, the short-term winners have often sought to stall the economy in a *partial reform equilibrium* that generates concentrated rents for themselves, while imposing high costs on the rest of society" (Hellman 1998: 204–205; italics in the original). Following Hellman, Venelin Ganev describes the "Dorian Gray effect," in which "private groups strong enough to resist the government may also be strong enough to undermine the organizational basis of effective democratic governance" (Ganev 2001: 2). This is reflected in what David Woodruff calls Russia's economic backwardness, in which Russia has "created market institutions that function like their international models on the transactional level, but not on the juridical level" (Woodruff 2000: 439).

The presence in transition economies of what Hellman and colleagues call "influential firms"—companies with either current or historical ties to the state and thus the ability to influence state policies and actions—encourages other firms to engage in the capture of state institutions in order to compete (Hellman, Jones, et al. 2003). Politicians and bureaucrats, in turn, may have their own rent-seeking interests, leading many to argue that Russia and others have replaced the "invisible hand" with the "grabbing hand" (Frye and Shleifer 1997). This "grabbing" might seem an unwanted cost, but recent research suggests that it may be more of a tax—a price major economic interests are willing to pay for their extremely privileged positions (Hellman and Schankerman 2000). Indeed, these actors may even prefer to maintain insecure property rights, as it is precisely that insecurity that allows them to maintain their domination of politics, jurisprudence, and the most lucrative sectors of the economy (Glaeser, Scheinkman, et al. 2003; Sonin 2003).

Taking all of these phenomena together, the result goes well beyond traditional conceptions of capture and intervention. Rather, what we are left with is a picture of almost total mutual permeation, in which the lines between the political elite and its very specific and narrow constituency are often blurred. Put in this perspective, the distinction between state and private ownership used as an explanatory variable for the resource curse becomes problematic. Therefore, before conclusions can be drawn about the impact of resource wealth in a country such as Russia, it is imperative to conduct a careful investigation of the relationship between political and economic interests.

The Potemkin Revolution:
Disengaged Authoritarianism in Russia

During the early reform period, economic interests—including oil companies—and political interests were often at odds with each other. Taxation in particular was a sore point, as the government continually raised rates and firms found new ways to avoid payment (Luong and Weinthal 2004: 140). Shortly into Vladimir Putin's first presidency, however, something of a truce was called, and the two sides appeared to come together around an agreement, at the center of which was a new tax code. To understand how and why this happened, and its broader significance, it is necessary to look a little further back into history.

Much has already been written about the degree and character of elite continuity in post-Soviet Russia. Early studies—most prominently that by David Lane and Cameron Ross (1998)—suggested that the transition had severely dislocated the *nomenklatura* and created significant opportunities for the advancement of new elites. Some recent and in-depth studies, however, have shown quite a different picture. Thus, Ol'ga Kryshtanovskaia claims that as much as 77 percent of Russia's political elite and 41 percent of the business elite in 2001 had their roots in the *nomenklatura* (Kryshtanovskaia 2002: 34). A number of other analyses, meanwhile, have demonstrated the considerable overlap of and blurred distinctions between Russian political and economic elites, both the national level (see, for example, Hough 2001; Simonia 2001; Goldman 2003a) and on local and regional levels (see, for example, McAuley 1997; Hughes, John, et al. 2002). Still others have echoed Kordonskii's "administrative market" thesis and questioned whether the Soviet system left any institutional room for the conception of embryonic autonomous elites (see, for example, Etzioni-Halevy 1993).

The key, however, is not which elites are in power, but how they got there. Many of Russia's most important political figures—the likes of Yeltsin, Putin, Luzhkov, Primakov, Chernomyrdin, Yakovlev, most of the regional governors, ad nauseam—are old *nomenklatura* cadres. This is all the more true of Putin's more recent appointments from the ranks of the old KGB. But even those figures who tend to be seen by Western academics as members of an old counter-elite—Yavlinsky, Gaidar, Nemtsov, Chubais, and so on—rose to power through traditional nomenklatura mechanisms (Davydov 2000; Hoffman 2002). The same is true for much of the economic elite, not coincidentally. Berezovsky and Khodorkovsky are only two of the best examples (Goldman 2003a). This is not to say that they rose through the Komsomol and Party apparatus, although Yavlinsky and Gaidar did. Many of those in the elite whom Lane and Ross would see as newcomers relied on the old networks of patronage and cronyism to build their careers. Nemtsov, now an opposition leader, is an excellent example, for much of his career pushing his reformist agenda by currying favor with those, such as Yeltsin, who could give him power (Davydov 2000: 142–155). Some of his "liberal" colleagues—Kirienko and Stepashin, most prominently—continue to employ that strategy.

Throughout the government and the civil service, this had perpetuated an atmosphere not dissimilar to a "royal court," in which service to superiors rather than service to the public or even the state was the surest way to advance (Afanasiev 1996). Indeed, a study by the Russian Academy of State Service found that fully 45 percent of those government officials surveyed believed personal relationships to be the key to career advancement; only 19 percent gave the same weight to performance (Afanasiev 1996: 153). This approach appeared to extend to the highest levels of power, as Yeltsin tended to select prime ministers and other key politicians based more on personal preferences and gut feelings than real policy concerns (Davydov 2000).

Reddaway and Glinsky suggest that the Yeltsin team made a conscious decision to preserve the old, closed channels of recruitment rather than open up the political system. "Such a scenario [of an open system]," they write, "would threaten Yeltsin and his entourage by turning them into transitional figures for whom competition with rising politicians from outside the *nomenklatura* could end in their own weakening or even in their retreat from the political stage" (2001: 33). The result was that the old *nomenklatura* became the "center of crystallization of the new Russian political elite," while outsiders, rather than coalescing into a counterelite, "'grew into' the body of the elite" as a kind of "'service sector' for the elite. . . . More precisely, this second group was incorporated into the first in the course of structuring the new Russian political elite" (Kodin 1998: 76–79).[11] This both facilitated and was facilitated by the concentration of power in a strong presidency.

A relatively smooth transition for the old *nomenklatura* from status-based wealth (by virtue of membership in the *nomenklatura*) to property-based wealth (by virtue of ownership of capital) could conceivably have been endangered by market-oriented reforms and privatization. That portion of the old elite who had elected to go into business, as it were, mobilized effectively to ensure that such threats were never brought to bear. Using their leverage through the Congress of People's Deputies (the holdover Soviet parliament until the new constitution in 1993), they demanded and won a privatization plan that favored insiders through a variety of means, including barring substantial foreign participation and leaving significant room for corruption and back-room maneuvering (McFaul 1995; Glinski and Reddaway 1999; Luong and Weinthal 2001). This arrangement also suited those who chose to remain in politics, as it allowed a wide range of valuable goods that could be traded on the "administrative market" (Luong and Weinthal 2001). Finally, it suited bureaucrats as well, who were only too happy to see a flourishing market economy, so long as there was sufficient (and sufficiently Byzantine) regulation to ensure a steady stream of rents (Al'bats 2004). Thus, as Hellman (1998) and Ganev (2001) both described, a coalition of initial winners essentially conspired to prevent further reforms from depriving them of their gains.

Clearly, some felt there were even further gains to be achieved through continued intraelite competition, which explains why oligarchs and politicians spent much of the 1990s at odds. As Luong and Weinthal note, though, "The August 1998 financial crisis, which resulted in enormous losses in profits and tax revenue . . . revealed the extent to which these equally powerful actors were both vulnerable to global markets and, thus, the costliness of their previous failure to cooperate" (Luong and Weinthal 2004: 145). Both the state and the firms had an interest in clarifying what Berkowitz and Li call "tax rights," that is, "the property rights that a government appropriates over its own tax base" (Berkowitz and Li 2000: 370–371). The result was something of a corporatist agreement, in which the FIGs agreed to a substantial real increase in their tax burden in return for relative but—as the dismemberment of Yukos Oil Company has shown—not entirely concrete guarantees of property rights.

This has led some analysts to reevaluate traditional notions of Russia as a weak and captured state. In a recent article, Philip Hanson and Elizabeth Teague argue that in Russia—unlike many middle-income states, where the state has frequently been "captured" by big business interests—"the state is in a position of strength vis-à-vis big business that is unusual for a middle-income country—or, indeed, for any country" (Hanson and Teague 2005: 657). In this context, they argue that Russia is closer to what Schmitter defined as "state" (as opposed to liberal) corporatism, in which "the state unilaterally designates particular organizations as interlocutors and excludes others; it may still derive information useful for policy from these exchanges, but it sets the terms of the dialogue" (Hanson and Teague 2005: 658).

TABLE 3.2. Percentage of GDP spent on public health and education in postcommunist states.

Country	Item	2002	2004	2006	2008	2010
Bulgaria	Health	4.6	4.4	3.9	4.1	4.2
	Education	3.5	2.4	4.0	4.4	4.1
Czech Republic	Health	6.1	6.2	5.8	5.6	6.3
	Education	4.1	4.2	4.4	3.9	4.2
Estonia	Health	3.7	3.9	3.7	4.7	5.0
	Education	5.5	4.9	Na	5.6	5.7
Hungary	Health	5.5	5.7	5.8	5.0	5.0
	Education	5.3	5.4	5.4	5.1	4.9
Kyrgyz Republic	Health	2.1	2.3	3.3	3.1	3.7
	Education	4.4	4.6	5.5	5.9	5.8
Latvia	Health	3.3	3.7	4.4	4.1	4.1
	Education	5.7	5.1	5.1	5.7	5.0
Lithuania	Health	4.8	3.8	4.3	4.8	5.1
	Education	5.8	5.2	4.8	4.9	5.4
Romania	Health	3.8	4.1	4.1	4.5	4.8
	Education	3.5	3.3	Na	Na	Na
Russia	Health	3.5	3.1	5.4	3.4	3.8
	Education	3.8	3.5	3.9	4.1	Na
Slovakia	Health	5.8	5.3	5.0	5.4	5.8
	Education	4.3	4.2	3.8	3.6	4.2
Slovenia	Health	6.3	6.1	6.0	6.1	6.5
	Education	5.8	5.7	5.7	5.2	5.7
Ukraine	Health	3.5	3.9	3.9	3.8	4.4
	Education	5.4	5.3	6.2	Na	Na

Source: World Bank, World Development Indicators (September 2013).

One notable peculiarity of this supposedly "corporatist" arrangement, meanwhile, is the fact that it essentially excludes labor. Indeed, despite their considerable contribution to the economy and pride of place among the governing elite, the mining and extraction industries account for only 1.9 percent of Russian employment (World Bank 2004: 80). This dislocation of economic production from the bulk of the population also corresponds to a growing distance between the state and the population. For one, Russia provides a notably lower level of public services even than other postcommunist states (see Table 3.2). The government's recent unpopular decision to switch from indirect

TABLE 3.3. Percentage of consolidated tax revenue
from individuals in postcommunist states.

Country	2000	2010
Bulgaria	20.66	14.00
Czech Republic	22.66	19.00
Estonia	34.10	26.19
Hungary	27.70	25.49
Kyrgyz Republic	9.82	15.17
Latvia	na	29.40
Lithuania	39.56	22.14
Romania	na	19.31
Russia	na	17.06
Slovakia	na	16.77
Slovenia	25.14	27.20
Ukraine	na	21.65

Source: International Monetary Fund Current Government
Finance Statistics, 2013.

to direct monetary subsidies to pensioners, veterans, people with disabilities, students, and others is another example of this dislocation.

Partly as a result of these dislocations, Russia's tax system revolves to an unusually high degree around corporations (see Table 3.3). In comparing tax strategies in transition, Gerald Easter noted, "While Poland worked out a social pact with labor over household incomes, Russia developed a system of elite bargaining over corporate profits" (Easter 2002: 599).

It was in this context that a new term came into being: *administrative resources*, shorthand for the ability to turn "state goods" into "economic goods" and vice versa. A new term, however, does not denote a new phenomenon; *administrative resources* simply refers to the liberated incarnation of what was once monopolized and selectively distributed by the Communist Party of the Soviet Union. Thus, over the course of the 1990s, the old administrative resources were traded, consolidated, divided, and multiplied. In some cases, they were used to control privatization; in others to maintain control of enterprises that had been privatized. Regional elites used them to consolidate power locally and then as bargaining chips versus the state (see, for example, Ross 2000). (Indeed, much of the tension that developed between the federal center and the regions in the early and mid-1990s was both instigated and resolved by issues of administrative resources (see, for example, Hughes 2002).) The state, in turn, used administrative resources to create political parties and other movements that could counteract local leaders (see, for example, Hale 1999). The balance of resources was always uncertain. One telling (although possibly apocryphal) story occurred in the aftermath of the August 1998 financial meltdown, when then-Prime Minister Sergei Kirienko paid a visit to Gazprom's then-CEO Rem Viakhirev to demand that the state-controlled natural gas monopoly begin paying taxes. Viakhirev's reply was reportedly abrupt: "And just who do you think you are?"

Also during this period, new, nonadministrative resources began to develop, giving rise to new "currencies" that could be exchanged for political or financial capital. One group is fairly straightforward: economic resources. The opportunity for businesses to operate openly on international markets and at world prices meant that, unlike in the Soviet Union, money now had a meaning beyond that defined by the state. This was a resource that could be mobilized either to trump administrative resources or to purchase them. The second group of resources, for lack of a better term, might be called "civil." In a regime that does not practice outright repression, public opinion can, at least theoretically, be mobilized and used either against and/or within the administrative system. The best example of this sort of resource in Russia is the extra-administrative political power once wielded by such media magnates as Boris Berezovsky and Vladimir Gusinsky (see, for example, Mickiewicz 1999; Belin 2002). Another example is the clout wielded by Gusinsky and fellow oligarch Leonid Nevzlin as successive presidents of the Russian Jewish Congress. The result was a tremendous degree of uncertainty, as this expanded "administrative market" searched for the proper values of all of these various goods.

Here, even as we observe the Soviet "club" disintegrating, it is useful to return to the theory on club goods. The dynamics of how and why clubs form and thrive has made the concept rich for use in political economy, and thus in our case as well. In laying out the initial theory of clubs and club goods, Buchanan noted that the optimal club size naturally changes depending on the size and nature of the resource base, with equilibrium reached "at the point where the derivatives of the total cost [to members] and total benefit functions are equal" (Buchanan 1965: 8). Other writers, particularly Eitan Berglas (1976), showed that economic actors would prefer club arrangements to private markets only when they stood to "gain other advantages for which they pay in the form of a loss of efficiency" (Berglas 1976: 119). In the most common instance, this "advantage" is to be found in segregation: Although private, competitive markets most efficiently serve heterogeneous groups, clubs are the most effective arrangement for serving actors who derive utility from consumption in an artificially homogeneous environment (Berglas 1976: 119–120; Berglas and Pines 1981: 148–152).

Considerations of efficiency in private versus club provision of a good also stem from the optimal size of the firm(s) providing the good. Thus, Berglas writes, "Whenever the optimal firm providing a service is small relative to the market and exclusion is possible, the competitive market solution is possible. . . . where the optimal firm is large relative to the market, then increasing returns are dominant and the competitive markets fail" (Berglas 1976: 121). In the case of Russian power, the question thus arises of why the political "market" favors a large "firm" size. Although this question cannot be adequately answered here, the suggestion is that the answer will have to do with a combination of the "rentier effect" and the weak diversification of political demand (due either to unanimity of demand or to unanimity of nondemand).

To Berglas's conditions, Robin Broadway added the cost structure of the good, arguing that club goods will become efficient if "the club good [cannot] be expanded at constant cost" (Broadway 1980: 132). Berglas and Pines (1981: 145) dispute this, to the extent that private provision of goods can survive such conditions, but the general argument should still hold, particularly in our Russian case, where the members of the club are essentially passive "takers" of the quantity of the "good" to be provided, due to the reliance on income from commodity exports.

The concept of club goods, since the inception of the concept in 1965, has worked its way deeply into the analysis of authoritarianism and such democratic political "market failures" as clientelism. Thus, Jonathan Hopkin writes, "Club goods, such as fiscal or regulatory advantages for particular industrial sectors, or public investments for specific territories, are collective goods, but of more narrow scope than the purer public goods. . . . Such goods can be conducive to clientelistic exchange, but at a group, rather than an individual level" (Hopkin 2006: 6). In his study of authoritarian Portugal, Nuno Luis Madureira writes of industrial fishing concerns that forfeited commercial liberty to a consortium, which became the key source of finance for the members in return for limits on production and effective price controls. Thus, "In effect, the price controls established through the regulation of minimum prices for exports created a 'club good,' which yielded the individual cost of a decrease in production" (Madureira 2007: 84). In the Portuguese case, then, actors agreed to the forfeiture of economic liberty in return for price controls, economic stability, and political stability. Similarly, in the Russian case, economic and political actors agreed to the forfeiture of economic and political liberty (in particular, the right of permanent accumulation) in return for guaranteed access to large-scale consumption of private goods. In the classical conception, members of the club contribute money (or flows of money) to obtain utility. In the Russian case, members contribute utility (in the form of competitive liberty) to obtain money.

Clearly, what is often described as the "chaos" of the Yeltsin era reflects the uncertainty involved in the apparent disintegration of the Soviet "club." This also, however, explains what has often been described as the "democracy" of the Yeltsin era. The collapse of old mechanisms of coordination, combined with the collapse of global commodity prices, made the maintenance of the old, Soviet "club" impossible. Without the club, competitors for resources and power will naturally seek a minimum of restrictions on the ways in which they can compete. Thus, the liberalization of political and economic institutions, following the explosion of the Party and its apparatuses, opened up myriad opportunities for political entrepreneurs. But that was not the end of the story. As in the case of Portugal alluded to earlier, liberalization also imposes costs, not least of which was uncertainty. It should have been at least conceivable, then, that the demand for a new club could arise, particularly if the elite should desire "segregation" from the masses as insurance against possible disenfranchisement. With the demand in place, all that was needed was supply, in the form of high and rising commodity prices.

The old administrative market, meanwhile, remained intact, and almost all of the "new" elites continued to act accordingly. Very little attention was paid to the development of de novo enterprises or even reinvestment into old ones, as resources continued to be hoarded. Insider privatization ensured that political standing was still more important than managerial prowess, although enterprises were routinely mismanaged for the sake of political expediency.

What we might call the Putin era has seen some changes to this landscape, although not as sweeping as has sometimes been suggested. One change has been the remonopolization of administrative resources under the presidential administration and its electoral wing, the United Russia party. This has been a gradual process, beginning by co-opting a number of other parties (most notably the Fatherland bloc and associated groups loyal to then-Moscow Mayor

Yury Luzhkov, ex-Prime Minister Evgeny Primakov, and a number of other regional and central politicians and business leaders), supported by domination of the federal and regional parliaments, and culminating (until 2014) in the elimination of directly elected governors and parliamentarians (see, for example, Alekseev, Chernov, et al. 2004; Drankina 2004; Konitzer-Smirnov 2005; Lipman and Petrov 2007). This has been accompanied, meanwhile, by the renewed influence of the police, secret service, and other coercive institutions (see, for example, Shevtsova 2004).

The second change has been an attempt to eliminate or at least marginalize nonadministrative resources, evidently to ensure that no threats to the position of the elite can be generated from outside the "club" of those granted access to administrative resources. The clearest example of this has been the effective nationalization of the two main independent television stations, NTV and Channel 1 (formerly ORT), early on in Putin's first term. Another example is the infamous Yukos affair, in which the various political, coercive, and economic forces collaborated to dismantle a business that had gained significant leverage vis-à-vis the state. These developments must be carefully interpreted. The seizure of television stations should not be confused with state censorship, though this exists, and some independent voices do remain on other media. The state, meanwhile, continues to encourage the development of large, powerful, and private corporations, many of which remain owned and run by oligarchs (Hanson 2001b: 333; Goldman 2003b: 326; Grivach, Gorelov, et al. 2004).

The policies aimed at monopolizing administrative resources and marginalizing other sources of power are most clearly seen in aggregate. Thus, the Kremlin pushed through a variety of new election-related laws between 2002 and 2006: raising the barrier to entry in the Duma to 7 percent of the popular vote (and to as much as 10 percent in some regional parliaments, such as the Moscow City Duma); increasing state financing for parties that do overcome the barrier; eliminating district voting in favor of pure proportional representation; eliminating the "none of the above" option on the ballot; dropping the requirement that turnout top 25 percent and 50 percent for parliamentary and presidential elections, respectively, for those elections to be valid; increasing the number of signatures required to initiate a referendum by 450 percent; and increasing the regulatory "opportunities" for election officials to remove parties and candidates from the ballot (Aptekar' 2004, 2005; Guseva 2006; "Kak pravilis'" 2007b). The outcome has been a dramatic reduction in parliamentary competition, with the liberal Yabloko and Union of Rightwing Forces parties unable to garner 7 percent of the vote, and the remaining parties—including the opposition Communists—in one way or another owing their success to administrative support.

Similar tactics have been employed against civil society. Evidently spooked by the mass demonstrations that precipitated "revolutions" in Georgia and Ukraine, beginning in the spring of 2004 (after the Georgian revolution but before the events in Ukraine), the Kremlin and its friends in the Duma began devising rules that would allow them to more closely control the country's streets and squares (Guseva 2004; Rudneva 2004; Sadchikov 2004; Riskin and Pipiia 2005; Stepovoi 2007). Indeed, the first reaction, in April 2004, was so draconian in its restrictions—which would have banned protest in all "strategic" locations, including in front of government buildings—that Putin himself revised it.[12] The new law still gave the authorities broad powers to decline permission for rallies, marches, and other protest activities, without clearly stating the reasons that could be used to justify such a refusal. Protests could be held near the Kremlin or on Red Square only with the permission of the president. Meanwhile, in early 2007, as the country geared up for parliamentary and then presidential elections, the Moscow City Duma passed an ordinance banning protests near major thoroughfares, courts and other pipelines, factories, and other "potentially dangerous" sites, a rule that has repeatedly been used to ban opposition marches along Moscow's main streets. Likewise, in an evident reaction to the "revolutions" in Georgia and Ukraine, which the Russian leadership saw as fomented by Western NGOs, in late 2005 the government increased regulation of Western nonprofit groups operating in Russia, as well as Russian organizations that receive Western grant funding; again, a draconian law was eventually softened, and few NGOs have been closed down as a result, but the administrative pressure on NGOs has increased across the board (Redichkina 2005; Moskovkin 2006; Pavlikova, Mukhamed'iarova, et al. 2006).

The Russian state's newfound wealth allowed it to be proactive in these endeavors as well. Thus, in addition to building the walls around itself described in the previous paragraphs, lavish resources have been spent on building what Andrew Wilson calls "virtual politics," in which "politics is 'virtual' or 'theatrical' in the sense that so many aspects of public performance are purely epiphenomenal or instrumental, existing only for effect or to disguise the real substance of 'inner politics'" (Wilson 2005; see also Sestanovich 2007). Thus, parties are invented, purportedly complete with platforms and constituencies; staffed by Kremlin loyalists; funded through the presidential administration;

and then dismantled when no longer needed. Three state-run television channels offer ostensibly "alternative" views of the current events, all carefully choreographed and sanctioned from above (Lipman 2006). The Public Chamber, created in 2005 nominally to serve as a forum and platform for civil society, was filled through a rigged selection process, as a result of which only those approved by the presidential administration could gain access (Lipman and Petrov 2007). Rather than work with the institutions of Russian civil society, such as they were, the elite chose to build simulacra and, in effect, carry on the political conversation exclusively with itself.

Conclusions: The Apex of Putin's Russia

It has been argued, at times, that Putin's Russia is a regime of personalized power (see, for example, Shevtsova 2007 or Kryshtanovskaia 2008). Certainly, Putin is more powerful than his predecessor. Yeltsin, similarly endowed with a strongly presidential constitution (of his own creation), wielded his tremendous formal and informal powers sporadically, frequently delegating them to (or allowing them to be usurped by) others. Putin was more consistent in his presidency, never leaving any doubt that he, personally, was at the center of the ruling apparatus.

I would argue, however, that by 2008, at the end of Putin's second term as president, Russia's power structure had become *personified*, not personalized. Personalized power implies that power accrues to the ruler by virtue of some attribute of the individual. In Russia, however, the ruler rules on behalf of an elite—a competing, often chaotic group that I nonetheless refer to as a "club"—rather than in place of that elite. Putin serves functions, both internal and external, vital to the survival of the club. Internally, he appears to be the arbiter of competing "clans" (Kryshtanovskaia and White 2005). Externally (and more important to this argument), he is legitimator. In the modern world, with its democratic sensibilities, a Russian regime that came to power without a modicum of free and fair elections would be unpalatable, with attending risks to the elite's European lifestyles. An elite "club" cannot win an election, but a popular leader can.

All of the foregoing discussion in this chapter—save for brief references to Kornai's analysis of the Soviet period—is devoid of any mention of ideology. Ideology was, in the end, a burden on the Soviet regime, constraining elites and forcing them to maintain an expensive and problematic coercive apparatus.

The post-Soviet Russian elites have carefully avoided this pitfall. Certainly, Russia has no transformative, totalitarian ideology, and Russian citizens are free to travel, read, worship (generally speaking), and speak (at least individually). Putin's ruling party, United Russia, has only the most modest rudiments of an ideology, proclaiming that Russia is following some evolving double-epithetic system (managed-democratic initially, then sovereign-democratic later). While sometimes coddling true nationalists, the state itself pursues only an idea of "national unity," creating what Ken Jowitt refers to as a "castle identity" (Jowitt 2008). It is, in essence, a hodgepodge, ideally suited to the sort of "virtual politics" described by Andrew Wilson, in which ideology is stage decoration for a play with no plot.

The plot, of course, occurs behind the scenes and has no direct relationship to the ideology. A fierce competition for resources unfolds backstage, with only one clear rule: Whatever the circumstances, no one is allowed to step through the curtain and appeal to the audience for sympathy. Those with backstage access agree to forego popular politics (and, thus, a degree of independence) and are rewarded with the opportunity to compete. It is the job of the legitimator—in our case, Putin—to take to the stage and entertain the audience. This job is, of course, empowering, because he can at any minute bring the whole thing (or any particular part of his choosing) crashing down merely by raising the curtain. But he himself is not the power structure; he simply represents it on stage.

If we agree that the system of relationships that make up the power structure is at least as important as the person who personifies that structure, then we arrive at a picture that is much more complex and rigid than the idea of personalized autocracy might initially imply. This may be, to some extent, why Putin had to stay on as prime minister and head of the United Russia party, even as democratic legitimacy demanded that he cede the presidency to Dmitrii Medvedev: The informal mechanisms that Putin used to mediate and perform are his own and do not transfer easily to a successor. Medvedev would have to develop such mechanisms for himself, if he is to wield them. But that may also be why Putin is unable (assuming he is willing) to deal with systemic inefficiencies: He is beholden to his constituency and cannot risk disrupting the backstage machinations for fear of undermining his own enviable position.

Looking more broadly, the terms in which I have described the Russian regime in this chapter may seem to suggest the symptoms of clientelism: the privatization of law, rent-seeking behavior, predatory relationships between bureaucrats and citizens, and, crucially for our study of civil society, civic atomization and impediments to democratic political accountability (for a discussion of the definition and parameters of clientelism, see Roniger 1994: 3–5). Indeed, some authors have sought to attach the clientelism label to Russia, arguing that "access to public and private goods [is] still largely the object of clientelistic exchange. These goods included government jobs, housing, medical services, and economic resources" (Vorozheikina 1994: 114).

The difficulty with this argument, however, is that clientelism in Russia, if it is the dominant game, looks very different than it does in more classically clientelistic environments, such as Latin America. For one, classic clientelism generally involves the exchange of votes or political support for private goods (jobs, homes, and so forth) or public goods (social services or infrastructure projects) and often involves well-developed political party structures on one side and well-entrenched social structures (such as religious, ethnic, or regional groups) on the other. Neither is the case in Russia. Moreover, clientelism leads to the development of deep and durable relationships between patrons and clients, based on a degree of trust and on expectations of continuity (Auyero 2001: 175–179); relations between citizens and bureaucrats in Russia, by contrast, are more often furtive and characterized by a lack of trust. Thus, although it might be tempting to blame the atomization or, perhaps more accurately, the individualization of Russian state–society relations on clientelism, the evidence does not support such an argument.

Rather, Russia may be a case of what Anna Grzymala-Busse (2008) describes as a "predatory" rather than a clientelistic regime, in which the lack of competition and the ability to avoid the social distribution of rents makes it possible for the elite to eschew the costly exchanges involved in maintaining patron–client relations. The deal making between officials and citizens is corruption, devoid of the social meaning of patron–client relations (though not devoid of social meaning altogether; see Ashwin 1996). Claus Offe (2004) writes that corruption facilitates microlevel trust but undermines the development of macrolevel trust of the kind that could be useful to collective action. In this view, then, corruption and predatory governance could, in theory, be enough to generate the individualized state–society relationships that seem to stymie Russian civil society.

This occurs, again, behind a stage set of democratic legitimacy. Russia has held and continues to hold elections that are outwardly competitive even if closely controlled. Official rhetoric proclaims Russia's adherence to European democratic values. The leadership enjoys high levels of popular support, for the maintenance of which it touts increased stability and economic welfare. The Russian public, on the other hand, very well understands the meaninglessness of formal political participation but has no access to the informal political relationships, which are deeply unsystematic.

What we are left with, then, is a political system that actively seeks to divorce the public from politics and policy, limiting competition to those within the elite who can be "trusted" not to bring down the system of unaccountable privilege and power, but without placing undue strain or burdens of consent on ordinary Russians. The balance struck is uneasy, and elites will find it easier to maintain stability by strengthening authoritarian institutions rather than by building democratic ones.

In this view, Putin's "reforms" can be seen as a "response" rather than a "solution" to the developments of the Yeltsin era (Mohsin Hashim 2005). He has not truly resurrected the Soviet administrative market nor dismantled Yeltsin's. He has instead presided over a long-awaited codification of rules, a convening of a new, somewhat modified club of elite interests. Indeed, if we return to our club–good analysis, a conclusion suggests itself: The selective incentive of increased certainty for the controllers of administrative resources (and of those assets capable of generating such resources) proved sufficiently strong to encourage the reorganization of a club. This club leaves its members with substantially more leeway and room for personal advancement than did the Soviet system and even leaves open the opportunity for exit. What it does not permit, however, is the mobilization of extra-administrative resources for advancement, as this would endanger the integrity of the entire arrangement and, thus, the welfare of all of the club's members. This, essentially, was the sin committed by Gusinsky, Berezovsky, and Khodorkovsky; the reason why television had to come under central control; and the motive behind the increased pressure on NGOs.

It would be wrong, however, to ignore the fact that Russia, while authoritarian, was not in 2014 a police state. Until the first nervous election season of 2007, arrests of political activists, journalists, and other potential troublemakers were few and far between. Opposition newspapers and radio stations continued to get their message out, and the Internet was already rife with alternative opinions and news coverage. Holding protests had become more difficult, but it could be done. Opposition parties were harrassed, but they continued to exist. Owners of major businesses knew that they must be servile to the state, but they were still allowed to get rich.

This is not meant to be an apology for authoritarianism or to minimize the significance of the changes. It is noteworthy, though, that none of this appears to have had a real impact on civic activism in Russia. Indeed, none of the contemporary cases reviewed in the chapters to come are significantly affected by repression, even when they fail. Likewise, none of this prevented the extraordinary mobilization of 2011 and 2012. This, and the fact of the consistent failure of Russian civil society to mobilize from 1991 to 2011, suggests that the root cause is not to be found in the repressive policies of Putin's Russia. Such repression is little more than a restraining order, an attempt on paper to draw boundaries between two parties who no longer enjoy each other's company. The root cause, I argue, is deeper, the product of the long processes described in this chapter, through which Russian elites, enticed by power and privilege and inured to accountability by abundant natural resources, have divorced themselves from the Russian people.

By emphasizing simultaneously the continuity of elites and patterns of elite behavior and the discontinuity of the political regime, I am not suggesting that we have witnessed an authoritarian restoration or a backlash against the "democratization" of the 1990s. Rather, what I am arguing is that the mode of politics shifted—first, in the early 1990s, toward greater "democracy," and then, at the end of that decade, toward greater "authoritarianism"—in response to changing political-economic opportunities available to elites. Simply put, what looked like democracy in the 1990s was indeed a form of pluralistic competition, but its emergence was driven by political economic necessity rather than ideological adherence to democratic principles. At the end of the twentieth century, however, something happened that allowed the Russian elite to reconstitute a club similar in some respects (but not all) to what they had enjoyed in the Soviet period, and that "something," I argue, was the reappearance of natural resource wealth as a significant source of rents.

This, then, is the backdrop against which this study of Russian civil society will unfold: a withdrawn, disengaged state; a regime built for the purpose of autonomy, fueled by revenues from natural resource exports; and an environment in which state–society relations are individualized by a system that empowers elites rather than citizens. We will see this from various angles in the following chapters, as civic initiative is stymied by citizens' inability to arrive at a stable "working" relationship with the state but eventually flowers in the rare instances when the state, for various reasons, decides to act institutionally.

4

Civil Society in Russia
What We Do and Do Not Know

To the extent that there was consensus in the literature regarding Russian civil society prior to December 2011, it was as follows: Russians exhibit low levels of participation and mobilization, and they face a significant degree of repression on the part of the state. It is not, however, a simple and straightforward story. Russia has a large (though shrinking) number of nongovernmental organizations, including at least some high-profile social movements, and protest does from time to time occur. Moreover, the state, while far from democratic, is equally far from totalitarian, and there is a significant public space in which civil society can operate. There are three broad sets of hypotheses most commonly promulgated to make sense of this situation: The first concentrates on issues of culture and history, the second is built on arguments about trust and social capital, and the third focuses primarily on the regime. Each of these will be reviewed in this chapter, but prior to doing so it is worth delving a little deeper into the puzzle.

If the story of Russian civil society were a simple and cohesive one, it would probably read something like this: Russians, not socially and historically predisposed to collective action, are beset by an authoritarian state that only deepens those atomizing tendencies, thus effectively stymieing the development of civil society. While I do not want to prejudge my case studies here, it is worth noting even at this early stage that observation of Russian protest movements reveals neither deeply engrained social or cultural obstacles to mobilization nor overbearing repression from the state. And there are facts that point to this disconnect between theory and observation even in the existing literature.

The first of these facts is the movement of Soldiers' Mothers. Begun in the late 1980s, the movement, first in the Soviet Union and then in Russia, has evolved into perhaps Russia's greatest civil society success story. Loosely united under the Union of Committees of Soldiers' Mothers of Russia, the movement consists of regional and local committees of activists, almost all of them volunteers, throughout the country, who pursue a twofold strategy of providing services to individual draftees and their families and lobbying the government and the military for reform to end brutality and the abuse of soldiers' rights. They have been successful on both fronts, becoming an important resource for soldiers and an accepted participant in the policy discussion on military reform (such as it is) (Sundstrom 2006b). Were the simple, blanket explanation I described earlier to hold, no such movement would persist in Russia, while any exceptions would be seen as unsystematic aberrations. Yet there are movements that persist in Russia, and the purpose of this project is to determine whether they are truly as aberrant as the blanket explanations would suggest.

The second of these facts is the short-lived but remarkably powerful *l'gotniki* protest wave. In January and February 2005, Russia saw a series of protests in cities across the country, in opposition to proposed reforms that would have replaced subsidized transport, pharmaceuticals, and other goods for pensioners, students, and others with monetary handouts. The timing and content of these protests is explored in more detail in a later chapter, but they are worth noting here as the largest protests held in Russia under the rule of Vladimir Putin. The extent to which they were spontaneous, grassroots phenomena is a matter of some debate; while many of the local protests, including the initial protest in St. Petersburg, were apparently led by nonorganized citizens, the Communist Party, Yabloko, the National Bolsheviks, and others seem to have played a role in helping spread the protests around the country (Robertson 2009). Although the protests never posed an existential threat to the regime, the Kremlin was clearly nervous (perhaps because they followed so closely on the protests of the Orange Revolution in Ukraine) and, while working to keep protestors off the streets, gave into their demands almost completely (Robertson 2009). Thus, if Russian civil society is weak, the Russian state would appear to be even weaker; either that, or civil society is not as weak as we have been led to believe.

A review of the dominant stories in the literature, and a recapitulation in that context of my own hypothesis, will suggest a way out of this dilemma.

Culture and History

One set of hypotheses regarding the weakness of Russian civil society—indeed, the weakness of the Russian democratic project more generally—focuses on Russia's culture and history as an obstacle to the adoption of new, democratic modes of behavior and interaction. Although many Western writers have avoided such arguments, seeing them as deterministic and path-dependent, they remain popular among Russian writers and continue to influence analysis in the West, as well.

Among the first to put forward a systematically cultural argument was Oleg Kharkhordin, a St. Petersburg–based political scientist. He rejects what he calls "Catholic conceptions of civil society," with their "concentration of attention on the creation of free citizens' associations that (potentially) oppose the state and educate the citizenry," because they assume institutional structures found in Western contexts, but not in Russia; to create such a civil society in Russia, he writes, "One has first to re-create the absent monopoly of legitimate violence" (Kharkhordin 1998: 963–964). Given what he perceives as the weakness of the Russian state, Kharkhordin suggests that "instead of trying to re-concentrate violence—that is now diffused among many actors—in the single hands of the state once again, one may counteract this diffusion of violence by the diffusion of a civil way of life"—what he refers to as the Orthodox or Dostoyevskian project of civil society (1998: 963–964). Moreover, Kharkhordin suggests that the tendency toward such "Orthodox" conceptions is reinforced by historically engrained habits of particular forms of collective action, which persevered even through Soviet times, according to which collectives seek not to gain sovereignty over the state in an Enlightenment sense but rather to protect members from the state's more pernicious encroachments. Here, he echoes the leading Western proponent of path-dependent theories of Russian history, Richard Pipes, who argues that Russia continues to be beset by a self-reinforcing tendency toward "patrimonialism," "rooted in the failure of Russian statehood to evolve from a private into a public institution" (Pipes 2005: 181).

Iurii Afanas'ev similarly—but considerably more forcefully than Kharkhordin and with a more exclusive focus on the past rather than the present—posits deep historical roots of Russia's current dilemma, which rest on a fully "unique" relationship between Russian Power (*Vlast'*) and the people. But whereas Kharkhordin and Pipes see the tradition of state and society as symbiotic in their relative dysfunction, in Afanas'ev's view the traditions of the state are clearly primary and the traditions of society secondary. Thus, he writes:

> Our *vlast'* is not only peculiar, as every power is in one way or another. There is every reason to state that Russian *Vlast'* is unique and worthy of being designated with a capital V. This type of power was formed through the many centuries of Russian history and entirely determined the general picture of Russia's history itself. This power contains both the riddle and the answer. It combines the autocratic with the socialist,

the personal with the communitarian, the creative initiative with destructive reactionism. It is lord and murderer. Great and useless. . . . Our power has always been somehow outside of society, self sufficient, not dependent on society and yet always provoking and repressing it. The population has been forced to develop concomitant strategies for dealing with *that kind of power* and, in the end, developed such a strategy in the constant movement into the "shadows," in a way of life that is "distributed" *between the normative and the real, between lies and the truth.* (Afanas'ev 2001: 20–21; emphasis in original)

The depth of the roots of such "archaic" tendencies, however, is a matter of some debate. Kharkhordin's argument itself differs crucially from Afanas'ev's, positing that the salience of historical modes of behavior is contingent on contemporary dysfunction (which it in turn reinforces), while Afanas'ev sees contemporary dysfunction as itself rooted in history. The bulk of the analysis in the literature seems to come down on the side of Kharkhordin, however. Andrey Ryabov, for example, argues that Russia's current political structure is "feudal" and in that respect mirrors some historical phenomena from Russia's past, suggesting that "the emergence of archaic [structures] is to a significant degree a reflection of the unpreparedness of the transition society for further change and the accompanying new risks; society instead seeks to steady itself not only on familiar forms of social existence, but also on those forms that are hidden in the deepest archetypes of mass consciousness" (Ryabov 2008: 7). The phenomenon, then, may have historical roots, but it is caused by contemporary realities.

Turning a clearer focus on culture, some writers have argued that the failure of some civil society organizations to mobilize the public successfully stems from a misalignment of cultural frames, caused in part by the influence of foreign donors, who pull activists in directions that may be too dissonant with discourses in Russia. Thus, Lisa McIntosh Sundstrom delivers a powerful indictment of the impact of foreign funding for Russian NGOs, based primarily on two observations. First, she writes, "Foreign donors on the whole have focused heavily on internal development and professionalization of the Russian NGO sector, but have largely ignored external mobilization" (2006a: 17). Second, taking the example of organizations for the advancement of gender equality, she finds that:

Foreign assistance efforts have failed to produce significant NGO mobilization when emphasizing norms that are not universal in nature but instead are specific to Western contexts. Women's issues that are difficult to frame without using feminist principles—such as workplace discrimination and sexual harassment—are examples of areas in which foreign donor efforts have largely failed from the standpoint of developing democratic civil society. (2006a: 170)

The result, Sundstrom argues, is that those relatively few Russian activists interested in such issues more easily align their "frames" with Western conceptualizations, which are, in turn, poorly received by the broader public in Russia. (Valerie Sperling reaches similar conclusions, also about women's movements, writing that "movement globalization may run the risk of leaving broad segments of the Russian population out of the equation" (Sperling 1999: 265). While this seems true enough, it is worth asking whether similar issues of frame alignment and misalignment might not have arisen just as problematically without foreign donor support.)

In sum, then, while the historical and cultural arguments enjoy the benefit of a deep understanding of how action and reaction may be perceived in Russia and thus have important and powerful things to say about processes of framing, when it comes to the broader questions of the development of Russian civil society they are causally ambiguous: Beyond being deterministic (which is, after all, more of a normative failure than an analytical one), they cannot clearly distinguish between those effects that are truly historical and/or cultural in nature and those that are contemporary factors masquerading in historical guise. Moreover, because they rely on broad, all-encompassing categories from which no member of a society or polity is assumed to escape, historicist or culturist arguments inevitably deal poorly with diversity. Additionally, there is division within the literature between those who trace contemporary challenges back to problems of societal development and those who "blame" the character of the state. And although they may be convincing in the aggregate, such arguments do not provide useful analytical tools for explaining exceptions to the rule of low levels of civic mobilization. Some of these themes—including the division between state-centric and society-centric viewpoints—resurface in the following pages, in the discussion of social capital and of the Russian regime, while other, more "contemporary" approaches may provide more ready tools of analysis; they all, one way or another, return back to Russia's history and culture.

Social Capital and Trust

Those writers who have sought broad, if not to say blanket, explanations for the weakness of Russian society but who have been for whatever reasons dissatisfied with the historical and cultural arguments have turned to conceptions of social capital and trust. Such arguments also point to causes and effects that are pervasive and deeply engrained, but, unlike in the previous section, they are rooted in a clearer theoretical and empirical basis and thus may do a better job of dealing with diversity.

Unfortunately, the evidence on trust and social capital has proved vexingly hard for analysts to interpret. In his highly influential work on civil society in Russia and the former East Germany, Marc Morje Howard writes, "A great number of citizens . . . feel a strong and lingering sense of distrust of any kind of public organization, a general satisfaction with their own personal networks (accompanied by a sense of deteriorating relations within society overall), and disappointment in the developments of post-communism" (Howard 2003: 145). It is this, rather than "an immutable set of cultural values and predispositions," he argues, that leads Russians to reject collective solutions to shared problems. However, an analysis by Nina Belyaeva and Liliana Proskuryakova (2008: 83) of data from the 1999 World Values Survey found relatively scant differences in levels of generalized trust between members of civil society organizations and nonmembers; thus, 28.3 percent of members of civil society organizations agreed that "most people can be trusted," compared to 22.0 percent of nonmembers. Although these numbers cannot be fully parsed without knowing the sorts of organizations to which respondents belong—state-backed versus independent unions, for example, or opposition groups versus government simulacra—it hardly appears a ringing endorsement of an argument that trust is a deciding factor in whether people participate in civil society, nor does it lend strong support to the conclusion that participation in civil society helps build significant degrees of generalized trust.

Polling data on generalized trust do not lend themselves to easy interpretation, neither in isolation nor in the context of civic mobilization and participation. Levels of generalized trust (as measured by responses to the question, "Can people be trusted, or do you need to be careful when dealing with people?") have indeed evidently declined in recent years. Thus, according to surveys conducted by the Public Opinion Foundation, 36 percent of respondents in 2005 said that people could be trusted, while 58 percent said that caution was required; in 2008, those numbers shifted to 33 percent and 60 percent, respectively (Zvonovskii 2008: 112). The propensity to trust is higher among those with higher incomes and more education but still does not overcome the propensity to mistrust, with the exception of the highest income earners in 2005,

TABLE 4.1. Sources of influence on the local situation (percentage of respondents).

Who has the greatest influence on the situation in your city (town, village), in deciding issues of local life?	Population at large	Groups				
		Social base				Outsiders
		Core	Satellite	Buffer	Periphery	
Local government (mayor, administration, legislators)	72	75	76	71	72	59
Regional government (governor, administration, legislators)	40	43	45	35	41	29
Federal government (cabinet, ministries, State Duma)	19	24	20	17	20	16
President	14	15	14	13	15	13
Population	12	20	15	11	10	7
Local business, entrepreneurs	12	17	14	10	12	8
Enterprise managers	12	16	13	11	11	8
Criminal structures, Mafia	9	14	11	7	9	5
Media (print, radio, TV)	7	14	9	5	5	2
Political parties, movements	4	7	4	3	3	1
Local self-government	3	6	3	3	2	2
Civic organizations and NGOs	2	5	3	2	2	1
No one	3	2	1	3	3	9
Difficult to say	6	3	3	8	6	16

Source: Mersiianova 2008: 144.

and that trend has since been reversed (Zvonovskii 2008: 117). There is nothing in the data to indicate, however, whether these are the results of more deeply historic trends or the outcomes of processes "native" to the post-Soviet era.

Looking at the question of trust from a political culture perspective that can be linked to civic participation, polling data reveal relatively low levels of confidence in citizens and civic organizations—including NGOs, the media, and political parties—to deliver solutions to citizens' problems (Table 4.1). Moreover, attempts at cluster analysis, dividing respondents into groups by their degree of involvement in organized civil society, including core civic activists, "satellites" of civil society, "buffers" between the active community and the inactive, the inactive "periphery," and social "outsiders," reveal very little in the way of meaningful differentiation. Core activists, unsurprisingly, are somewhat more likely to trust citizens and civic groups, but they also see a larger role for the federal (as opposed to local or regional) government, as well as for organized crime (though the implications of that are left unexplored). On the whole, however, there is general consensus across the various groups (Mersiianova 2008). Taken together with the findings from Belyaeva and Proskuryakova (2008), then, this suggests that trust per se—neither person-to-person nor in collective and political institutions—is not a strong determinant of civic participation and mobilization.

Writers in the trust/social-capital school of thought have looked also at trust as actuated through social networks, but here, too, the evidence is contradictory, with writers falling broadly into two camps: those who are optimistic about networks and the associated social capital and those who are pessimistic, believing that informal "network solutions" undermine formal institution building. Among the optimists, James Gibson writes, "It appears from [the] data that social networks bear few scars from the era of communist domination in Russia" (2003: 69), contradicting Howard's conclusion that the Soviet past has undermined confidence in the motivations of fellow citizens who become involved in organized civic activity and, consequently, in collective action. Gibson goes on to write:

> Russians have extensive social networks that are highly politicized and that often transcend family units. . . . Unable to organize publicly, Russians may have substituted private social networks for formal organizations. But Russians are not atomized, and, as a consequence, Russian social networks have a variety of characteristics that may allow them to serve as important building blocks for the development of a vibrant civil society. In addition to carrying considerable political content, these networks are characterized by a relatively high degree of trust. Because the networks are not closed (strong), they link Russians together to an extent not often recognized by most analysts. (Gibson 2003: 69–70)

Gibson's conclusion that Russians may use informal networks to replace formal organizations—though the question of why these organizations are undermined, and whether it matters, is left to other researchers—echoes the arguments of Burawoy, Ashwin, and others cited earlier in this book. And it is echoed again by Richard Rose, who writes that networks of social capital are critical to welfare in Russia: for example, "Social capital networks are the predominant source of income security in Russia today" (1999b, 19).

Writing on migrants, who tend to prefer informal networks to formal NGOs, Moya Flynn observes:

> The existence of strong informal networks cannot be assumed to prevent interaction with more formal NGOs, although it does lessen the need for such interaction. Some migrants justifiably see the concerns of their individual everyday lives as best managed through informal networks, not by an organization that represents them as migrants. Furthermore, in some cases, informal networks of family and friends may choose to adopt a more formal, although temporary, participatory public role when the need arises. (Flynn 2006: 260)

In interpreting this evidence of the strength of some types of networks rather than others, writers on social capital have found a degree of common ground with the culturists and historicists. Thus, Rose writes that, in Russia, "pervasive anti-modern networks are . . . an obstacle to democratization," (1999a: 30) insofar as antimodern behavior "actively rejects modern organizations and procedures" in favor of nonmodern ones (Rose 1999a: 6), a rejection motivated in part by historical affinities. But, as in the historicist arguments that could not clearly distinguish between historical and contemporary causes, Rose and other "social-capitalists" find more recent roots. Thus, Rose writes that antimodern social capital in Russia is produced at least in part by the nature of the state:

> In effect, the Russian Federation has begun democratization "backwards," for it has introduced free elections before establishing institutions of the modern state, whereas in first-wave democracies the rule of law, civil society institutions and the accountability of governors was established before the introduction of free elections with universal suffrage. (Rose 1999a: 30)

Complicating matters further, it is increasingly frequently argued that the strong social capital sometimes observed in Russia does not have to be seen as a benefit to civil society. Rose first suggests this with his emphasis on antimodern networks, and this is picked up on by Nicolas Hayoz and Victor Sergeyev, who:

> . . . stress the two-faced character of networks, particularly in underinstitutionalized Russia, where nothing works without networks of trust and power but where networks of trust are also useless if they are not connected or combined with the "right" networks of power. In Russia, the problem of unbalanced informal connections with

power is particularly virulent. The chances of achieving a positive collective output are diminished because these networks risk adopting strategies of exclusion in order to maintain the existing power configuration. These strategies of exclusion, enforced by a "weak" state, promote personal trust instead of institutional trust. (Hayoz and Sergeyev 2003: 56)

As a result, although empiricists working in the trust/social capital vein have more evidence and a more analytically robust theoretical basis with which to work, there is neither consensus about the facts on the ground nor, moreover, about causality. Trust is indicated as the decisive independent variable, but insights from interviews and focus groups (of the types conducted extensively by Howard) are not borne out by statistics. Social networks are observed to be strong, but this is shown to favor in Russia noninstitutionalized mobilization rather than institutionalized (or institutionalizing) organization, and that is argued to support society (that is, through helping migrants and bolstering income security), while damaging civil society. (The latter conclusion, of course, rests on an equation of civil society with formal organizations, an equation I have questioned earlier.) And this bent toward informal rather than formal organization is argued at turns to stem from historical or contemporary factors. Indeed, approaches to social capital dating back to Robert Putnam's work in Italy, and even further, have seen the phenomenon as historically conditioned, stemming from long-established institutions and traditions. Thus, it is unclear exactly what the difference is between positing history and culture as the direct cause of contemporary effects, on the one hand, and positing social capital as the mechanism through which history and culture operate. The difference may be that social capital can be engineered, thus providing a way out of historical path dependency, but that is a quandary for another project.

Leaving aside questions of theoretical taste, there are quite concrete elements in this body of work that bear further exploration in the case studies presented later, including two key questions. First, where does the preference for informal versus formal mobilization come from, and what is its relationship to engrained patterns of (mis)trust? And second, how much does that perceived preference really affect outcomes in civil society?

The Regime

A third set of writers has focused primarily on political factors—and the structure and agency of Russia's political regime—as the independent variable in the equation of Russian civil society development. Under this political heading, there are at least two broad (though overlapping) sets of arguments. One group looks primarily at structural arguments. Of these, emblematic is M. Stephen Fish (2005; see especially ch. 6), who argues that "enduring economic statism," supported by the "rentier effect" of the "resource curse," "retarded the development of independent societal organizations and the socioeconomic bases for the development of such groups, and it circumscribed the autonomy of the organizations that did emerge" (2005: 192). Kelly McMann (2006) develops a similar argument, according to which the structure of the state and the economy deprive citizens of economic autonomy and thus stymie activism.

Any focus on regime structure, though, must inevitably recognize the very real differences between the Soviet Union and post-Soviet Russia, and numerous researchers have noted the proliferation of NGOs reflected in the statistics presented earlier and the increasingly diverse strategies that those NGOs pursue. Thus, Diana Schmidt-Pfister opens her own recent chapter with the sentence, "Throughout the 1990s, new possibilities of participation have triggered the emergence and development of a civil society or third sector in post-Soviet Russia" (2008: 37), going on to note, "Recent empirical evidence indicates the emergence of new strategies, reflection and adaptation on part of all parties involved and reaction to each others' changing courses" (Schmidt-Pfister 2008: 41).

A second group of arguments has focused more on agency. Thus, Michael McFaul and Elina Treyger (2004) note the depredations of the "Putin regime" on civil society, including pressure on domestic and international sources of funding; legal changes to allow the state to rein in labor unions, political parties, and NGOs; attempts to co-opt civil society groups financially or otherwise: and the curtailing of independent broadcasting. This is not, however, an entirely one-way street. Writing on civil society organizations in Karelia, Ilkka Liikanen observed that civil society has been able to adapt and reorient itself to this shifting political landscape: "It is possible that the ongoing change of political frame towards the federal level does not necessarily signal a mere shift in the balance of power between civil society and the state—from the regions to the centre. It can be perceived even from below in terms of the formation of new alliances and hegemonic blocs operating within a federal frame" (2008: 34).

Vladimir Putin began his rule in 2000 with a passively ambivalent approach to civil society, suspicious of its independence and particularly of its often foreign sources of funding and thus its goals but content to let the NGOs assumed to represent civil society function more or less freely while the state established tighter controls over political parties, media, and business. Nonetheless, toward the end of his second year in power Putin began applying to civil society the same approach he had taken to other sectors, that is, co-optation. Thus, he brought together a so-called Civic Forum, including some 4,000 NGO representatives from around the country, outwardly intended to establish new channels of communication between civil society and the state (Knox, Lentini, et al. 2006: 9). That initiative, repeated the next year, was formalized with the creation in 2005 of the so-called Public Chamber, a permanent body of 126 representatives of NGOs, one-third of whom are selected by the presidential administration, one-third of whom are nominated by regional bodies, and the remaining third of whom are nominated by the first two groups together (Lemaitre 2006: 397–398). As discussed in further chapters, members of the Public Chamber have at times taken up the causes of protestors, and they do issue reports on issues of social importance that are often critical of government agencies and the parliament, but the Chamber depends for its funding and, indeed, its membership and existence on the presidential administration, and members are careful not to criticize the top leadership (Evans 2008: 349–350).

After the Orange Revolution in Ukraine in 2004, in which NGOs organized street protests against a falsified election and forced a transfer of power, however, the state took a more active stance vis-à-vis NGOs. In addition to cooptation, the Russian state added three other cannons in its arsenal:

1. *Impede:* Relying on the various laws governing the registration and oversight of NGOs, particularly as revised in 2006, the state places an onerous bureaucratic burden on the operation of noncommercial and nongovernmental organizations, particularly those that have foreign funding (Lemaitre 2006: 395). It should be noted, however, that this has not led to a large-scale closure of NGOs, nor has it had any noticeable effect on the overall number of NGOs operating in Russia, as discussed earlier;

2. *Attack:* The state and state-run media periodically engage in smear campaigns against individual NGOs and the sector in general, accusing them of being covers for espionage or otherwise serving foreign interests, and a handful of organizations have closed down as a result (Lemaitre 2006: 396);

3. *Replace:* To displace and prevent autonomous mobilization, the state has generously funded so-called government-organized nongovernmental

organizations, or GONGOs, such as the Nashi youth group, a progovernment organization charged with occupying all of central Moscow's main squares during the most recent presidential elections (Lemaitre 2006: 396; Robertson 2009).

Over time, the regime has apparently mastered an increasingly sophisticated repertoire of managing civil society, in which all of the above methods have been combined with the creation of GONGOs and "virtual" organizations designed to crowd out genuine mobilization; thus, Graeme Robertson writes, "Within a political system that is a hybrid of open competition and authoritarian control, the Russian authorities are constructing a hybrid system of state–society relations in which independent organizations are allowed to exist, but where they compete with state-supported groups on a highly unequal basis" (Robertson 2009: 531–532). Similar strategies are seen to be applied to political parties (Wilson 2005; March 2009).

While these effects are doubtless real, it should be noted that it is difficult to measure their overall impact or differentiate among the effects of the various "cannons" in the regime's arsenal. Statistics from *Goskomstat* do show a decrease in the number of NGOs in Russia, but this decrease began before the Putin era's ramping up of pressure on civil society and has not noticeably increased in speed since then; nor has there been a drop-off in the number of new organizations created each year, which we might expect to have seen if there was growing pressure on the sector.

If these regime-related factors are not direct, mathematical inputs into the equation of civil society—and, in any case, we are not overly convinced of the value of numbers of NGOs as an indicator of activism—it may still be the case that the nature of the regime and the way elites behave have some impact through the more "sociological" factors that emerged in the prior two hypotheses. As mentioned earlier, several of the writers focusing on social capital and networks pointed specifically to the nature of politics and the economy as determinants of the types of trust and networks that are valued by Russian citizens. And, if credence is placed in the historicist hypothesis, it may still be argued that the perseverance of archaic or historically engrained modes of interaction is predicated on the political elite's refusal or inability to institute qualitatively new relationships. Because various aspects of the regime are dealt with at length elsewhere in this book, I will not dwell on them here, other than to note that the regime is inevitably a part of any explanation.

What We Still Don't Know

What we "know" about Russian civil society is at once a great deal and not much. There is a relative wealth of statistical data, a portion of which is presented at the beginning of this chapter, but which bears little direct relevance to questions of mobilization, participation, or the sort of ground-up aggregation and mediation of grievance that this project understands to be at the heart of civil society. There is a rich literature on cultural and historical aspects that, while they cannot be asserted to be determining and are unable to shed light on the exceptions to the rule of civic inactivity at the core of this project's puzzle, must also not be discounted entirely without further investigation. A lively debate rages over the levels and meaning of trust and social capital observed in Russia, giving rise to important, unresolved questions about why Russians mobilize in some ways and not in others. And the study of the Russian state and the regime that governs it—a discipline unto itself—yields a panoply of potential causal mechanisms but very little systematic understanding of how they interrelate to produce the overall result of Russian civil society as we know it today.

As discussed in Chapter 1, I have elected to pursue a series of case studies to help untangle this web of contradictory theory and evidence. Earlier, I have explained why I believe the cases presented in the following chapters—a human rights organization failing to achieve systemic change, an array of housing rights protest groups that succeed in generating conflictual "heat" but fail to coalesce into a social movement, and a spur-of-the-moment motorists' protest that evolves into a sustained and institutionalizing social movement—are adequate to the task of resolving my research question as to whether an examination of exceptions to the rule of civic inactivity can yield better understanding of the rule itself. Inevitably, that also means sifting through the implications of this literature.

But they are not the only cases, and they must be situated in context, the broad strokes of which have been presented earlier. But three other "exceptions to the rule" have also been discussed in the literature, and they help frame the empirical and analytical tasks I will pursue in the following chapters. The first two of these "exceptions" were described briefly at the beginning of this chapter.

The first of these is the Soldiers' Mothers' movement, arguably the most sustained social movement in post-Soviet Russia. A handful of studies have been made of the movement, the most prominent and thorough of which, by Lisa McIntosh Sundstrom, notes that the movement's experiences "diverge from Western theory on democratization, practices in foreign democracy promotion, and the experiences of American social movements specifically concerning successful mobilizational strategies in civil society" (2006a: 179). The key difference, she argues, is that the movement has "not succeeded best through rights-based argumentation"; rather, the movement's success owes to its ability to mobilize universally held conceptions of justice and injustice, thus marshaling public support for the righting of wrongs, rather than the exercise of rights. Thus, Sundstrom attributes the Soldiers' Mothers' success to their ability—in large part coincidental—to frame their advocacy in terms that were already well aligned with existing (if immobilized) injustice frames in Russia, regarding such issues as the injustice of bodily harm, the role and responsibility of mothers, and antimilitarism (Sundstrom 2006a: 185–188).

Although Sundstrom does not use the social movement theory "tool kit" or engage with the sociological processes of framing injustice, the Soldiers' Mothers' case as she presents it provides an initial illustration of the hypothesis that emerges from my own interpretation of the social movement literature, specifically the importance of sustained interaction with a state that presents coherent and cohesive policy interventions into private life in ways that allows citizens to identify themselves as groups. The Soldiers' Mothers act in reaction first and foremost to the draft and interact primarily with the military, which is a coherent and cohesive institution par excellence. Although the movement has not been universally successful in achieving its stated aims—far from it—due to the institutional nature of its interlocutor it has been uniquely successful in consolidating and continuing its mobilization.

The second case also demonstrates the durability of injustice frames in Russia to a degree not predicted by those writers who focus on alleged apathy. In the aftermath of the *l'gotniki* protests described at the beginning of this chapter, the Public Opinion Foundation conducted an almost yearlong series of surveys, yielding an interesting combination of observations. First, generally fewer than a quarter of Russians at large said at any point during 2005 that they would be prepared to participate in benefits-related protests in their town, should they be held, whereas consistently more than half of those who would be affected by benefit reform—the so-called *l'gotniki*—indicated that they would participate. This suggests that, although more than half of the population approved of the protests themselves (Klimov 2008: 156), there was no immediate connection between conceptions of injustice and readiness to protest. Second, readiness to protest among *l'gotniki* themselves actually grew throughout 2005, from 54 percent of respondents in January to 68 percent in October, suggesting that the *l'gotniki* injustice frame was sufficiently stable to maintain opinion for a considerable period of time and, indeed, strengthened even without the fact of ongoing protest. (See Figure 4.1.) This supports two key hypotheses: First, the experience of successful mobilization appears to be sufficient to overcome any preexisting antipathies toward mobilization that Russians may harbor; and, second, the resulting mobilizational and injustice frames are potentially durable.

The third "exception" was not described previously, but it serves to reinforce the prior observations. Through interviews and participant observation of housing movements in Astrakhan', Carine Clement eschews the statistical clustering that large-N studies sometimes pursue and developed instead a conception of three groups: ordinary citizens (*obyvateli*), "situational activists," and "dedicated activists" (Clement 2008). Rather than attribute membership in these three groups to sociodemographic factors, Clement sees group membership as a factor of experience, as a result of which the dominant "*obyvatel'skii*" frame shifts. According to Clement's research, "ordinary citizens" tend to reject collective action either because they are egotistical and selfish, because they are generally apathetic, or because they harbor grudges against their fellow citizens (where these subframes come from is another question, which Clement does not address directly, but which is generally seen as stemming from combinations of all of the factors hypothesized earlier in this chapter). When faced with a crisis, and when there are no immediate social barriers disuniting the potential victims of that crisis, the frame may shift to one of situational activism. This shift is further predicated on a process through which citizens lose their faith in the ability of government to resolve the crisis and in which some knowledge of the power of activism gained, either through first- or secondhand experience. A further process of action and interaction with the authorities—very much in the mold of social movement theory, though Clement does not refer to that particular literature—is seen to support the consolidation of the situational frame into a frame of committed activism.

For various reasons, I have not selected these cases for my own study. In the instance of Soldiers' Mothers, the group's history stretches back into the Soviet past, and to gain purchase on the initial genesis of mobilization, my own observation needs to be present as close to the beginning of the story as possible.

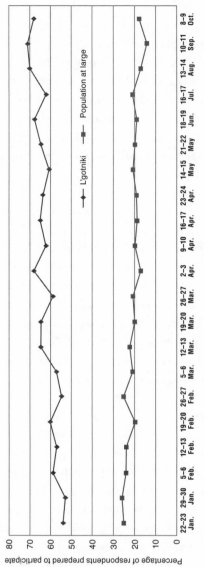

FIGURE 4.1. Readiness of Russian citizens and *l'gotniki* to protest.

Source: Klimov 2008: 158–159.

In the instance of the *l'gotniki*, while the protests were high profile, they were not long lasting, and there are as a result simply not enough data to work with. And in the third instance, the Astrakhan' case is colored somewhat by Clement's dual role as both a researcher and an activist, and many of the strategies pursued by the local activists were introduced by her.

These three "exceptions," nonetheless, lend initial support to my core hypotheses and suggest some of the dynamics that I will be looking for in my cases, particularly regarding the nature of the state's intervention and subsequent response, and the generation and consolidation of injustice frames. My cases must do more, however, than simply describe three more "exceptions" to the rule: They must help shed new light on the broader theoretical and causal arguments described in this chapter.

5   Private Brutality and Public Verdicts
Defending Human Rights in Russia

If states are held to wield a monopoly on legitimate violence, and if the legitimacy of a regime stems from its defense of citizens' lives and livelihoods, then it must be among the most important goals of civil society to defend citizens against abuse by those who act in the name of the state. Even under the most despotic regimes, when civic initiative withers in the face of repression, there invariably remain small groups who seek to bring the state to task for the violent injustices it commits against its subjects. Russia, though not such an extreme case in the period covered by this work, is no exception: Numerous human rights organizations track the excesses of Russia's coercive agencies, demanding justice and providing help to those afflicted.

This chapter explores the work of one such organization, "Obshchestvennyi Verdikt," or Public Verdict. Launched in February 2004, Public Verdict and its network of partners provide legal and public relations support to the victims of physical abuse, unlawful arrest, and other injustices committed by Russia's law-enforcement agencies. With its staff of half a dozen employees—including lawyers and administrators—and a network of human rights lawyers around the country, the organization has been able to achieve significant results: In the period from July 2005 through June 2006, Public Verdict dealt with some 136 cases, of which ninety-five (or 70 percent) involved the unlawful use of force by law enforcement officers. In the ten cases in which verdicts were reached, ten officers were jailed, three were given suspended sentences, and law enforcement agencies were required to pay 310,000 rubles (approximately $10,000) in compensation (Public Verdict 2006). In all, in 2006 Public Verdict took on sixty new cases; results of the organization's management of those cases and others continued from previous years included the opening of four criminal investigations that had been unlawfully stymied by prosecutors, the revocation of ten unlawful decisions by prosecutors to close criminal cases, and charges filed in court against thirty law enforcement officers. Of those, eleven received guilty verdicts: Five were jailed, four were given suspended sentences, and two were ordered to pay fines (of 5,000 and 6,000 rubles respectively, or about $161 and $193). The other nineteen cases are still in court. None of the accused has been acquitted. In addition, Public Verdict assisted in sixteen civil lawsuits, seeking total compensation of 4.66 million rubles (approximately $150,000), of which only 768,200 rubles ($24,780) were awarded (Public Verdict 2007).

It should be made clear from the outset that this chapter does not deal with a social movement. Public Verdict is a professional nonprofit organization of paid "activists"—some working full time, some on a case-by-case basis—who are brought together by a shared belief in a common cause. (The term *activist* is, I believe, appropriate, despite the fact that the organization's members receive a salary or honorarium for their participation; invariably, the staff, most of whom are lawyers, could be earning considerably more if they were in commercial practice, and thus they are making a significant sacrifice for their cause.) As a result, Public Verdict could come in for much of the same criticism that a number of analysts level at Russia's other human rights organizations—that they are "too professional," lack grassroots support networks, and thus may not be true mediators between the state and society (see, for example, Carothers 1999; Ottaway and Carothers 2000; Henderson 2003).

It is true that Public Verdict is not a grassroots organization, but that should not disqualify it from a study of civic activism. For one, the work that the organization does, regardless of whether its participants are reimbursed for their time, certainly qualifies as activism. And its twin stated goals—to provide pro bono legal aid to victims of police and prosecutorial abuse and to "create an atmosphere of intolerance toward violations of human rights by law enforcement"—are certainly civic. In interviews, as well as in the organization's promotional materials, the leadership and activists recognize the public component of their work. "It is practically impossible to root out abuse in Russia by legal and judicial means alone," the group states on its website.[1] As a result, significant emphasis is placed on public outreach: The organization manages a legal advice hotline that receives, on average, more than 1,000 calls a month; it conducts opinion surveys together with a leading sociological research center; and it works actively with the news media, leading to mention of the organization's activities in more than 2,000 articles since its founding.[2]

What Public Verdict does not do is seek significant public support for its activities. It was initially supported by grants from the Open Russia Foundation, until that foundation was closed in the aftermath of the jailing of its primary benefactor, the oil magnate Mikhail Khodorkovskii; it has been funded since then primarily by Western donors, including the European Commission and the Open Society Institute. It has made meager efforts to raise money publicly, but these have been entirely unsuccessful. Indeed, in the view of one foreign donor, these efforts were "halfhearted" because the organization "never really expected to succeed."[3] In any case, Public Verdict never set out to become a mass movement. (In that respect, it is no different from its predecessors in the Soviet human rights "movement.")

I argue that Public Verdict's failure (or refusal) to become a grassroots social movement is not a failure in its own right. The literature on both the defense of human rights and the social construction of (in)justice is remarkably focused on collective constructions—that is, on acts of perceived injustice or violations of human rights that afflict and mobilize individuals by virtue of their (generally accidental) membership in predetermined groups (see, for example, Moore 1978; Folger 1984; Shaver 1985; May and Milton 2005). Movements for human rights and social justice become tied up with issues of identity and are thus more easily absorbed into the identity-specific social movements and other networks that grow out of socially ingrained institutions of ethnicity, religion, employment, gender, culture, and so on. What is so problematic in the Russian case, however, is that the injustice is inflicted on individuals entirely arbitrarily, without reference to any categories they may happen to fall into. Although it is true that non-Slavic individuals—particularly from the Caucasus and Central Asia—are disproportionately targeted for document checks (Adjani 2006), Public Verdict's case archive does not seem to indicate that non-Russians are significantly more likely to be the victims of abuse than ethnic Russians. Indeed, the risk group for police brutality in Russia, if there is one, is best defined as adult Slavic men with blue-collar jobs and a drinking habit. That is hardly fertile ground for identity politics.

Rather, it would be more appropriate to judge Public Verdict on the success with which it achieves the two goals, described earlier, that it sets out for itself and with which it appeals for support from donors and the media: (a) to help individuals in need; and (b) to "teach," by means of carrot and stick, the state to behave better. I will argue in the following pages that the organization is considerably more successful at the first task than at the second. In numerous cases, Public Verdict is able to achieve some measure of justice for those it represents, overturning decisions, jailing police officers, and winning compensation. It is unable, however, to move the system in the direction of reform, and the punishments it is able to afflict on the state—in some cases severe—are demonstrably insufficient to induce systemic change.

Public Verdict's success in achieving justice for individuals suggests that the state apparatus, or at least the individuals who populate that apparatus, can be made to feel pressure. The evidence, though, suggests that pressure is effective only when it comes from within—or at least is channeled through—the system itself. Bureaucrats respond, I suggest, not because they feel pressure from the public but because of the realities of internal subordination and competition within the bureaucracy. This is important, because it will help to explain Public Verdict's failure to achieve systemic change. Elsewhere in this book, we will see civil society organizations challenge the state and force the political elite to change the way it devises and implements policy in an area in which the state intrudes into people's lives. Here, too, there is a clear intrusion into the private lives of Russian citizens; indeed, what could be more intrusive than brutality? And yet, a professionally strong and outwardly successful organization is unable to budge "the system." The reason, I will argue, is that when it comes to the abuse of the law by law enforcement agencies, there is no "system" at all: The relationship between individuals and the representatives of the state is essentially unstructured.

The chapter will continue with four brief studies of cases taken on by Public Verdict since its inception, falling into four distinct categories: a "difficult" and an "easy" case involving a single victim and a "difficult" and an "easy" case involving large numbers of victims. From there, I will attempt to gauge potential public reception of these cases through an analysis of media coverage. In the absence of open public protest, coverage in the media is the next best indicator of public interest in a case; moreover, media coverage is among the most common potential mechanisms of pressure on the apparatus. And, finally, based in part on what we know about the Russian legal and criminal justice system from other literature, I will attempt to sketch out a logic of interaction that will explain why the efforts of Public Verdict, while of immense value to the victims of the state, are, at the end of the day, unsuccessful in achieving lasting change.

The Beatings of Sergei Oleinik and Nikita Gladyshev

On November 16, 2000, Sergei Oleinik and a friend, Viacheslav Pigalev, walked into a mini-market in the city of Nizhnii Novgorod, where they bought cigarettes and vodka and joined two other friends at a small table in a corner of the store. Several minutes later, two local beat cops, Nikolai Khor'iakov and Mikhail Frolov, walked into the same store, likewise to buy cigarettes. While the officers were in the store, the janitor noticed that Oleinik and Pigalev were smoking and asked them to move outside. When Oleinik and Pigalev did not immediately leave, the police officers approached them and repeated the janitor's request, at which point all four men left the store.

Outside, Oleinik asked to see the officers' badges and identification. The officers initially obliged. But when Oleinik decided to inspect Khor'iakov's identification more closely, the officer became enraged, saying, "What, you don't respect a major?" and punched Oleinik in the face. While Pigalev ran for help, Khor'iakov and Frolov continued to beat Oleinik, leaving him with a concussion, severe bruising to the face, abdomen, and genitalia, and spinal trauma that will leave him disabled for life. Oleinik was then taken to a local police station, where he was not booked but where Khor'iakov and another officer, Mikhail Nelidov, continued the beatings. As a result of his injuries, Oleinik was unable to maintain his commercial driver's license, depriving him of his livelihood and means of support for his two teenaged daughters.

Oleinik's case was one of the first taken up by Public Verdict, after a referral from the Committee Against Torture, a local human rights organization in Nizhnii Novgorod, to which Oleinik had appealed for help four days after his beating. Working together, the two organizations provided legal support and launched a media campaign to help Oleinik bring his attackers to justice and receive commensurate compensation.

The time line of what happened next (see Table 5.1) is indicative of the difficulties that victims of police abuse—even with significant help from qualified human rights lawyers—generally face as they pursue their complaints.

After the August 2003 ruling, Oleinik abandoned further criminal proceedings and concentrated on a civil lawsuit against local and regional authorities, claiming 73,000 rubles (approximately $2,354 at the time) in lost income and 100,000 rubles (approximately $3,225) in moral damages. The police offered a settlement of 2,000 rubles (approximately $65), which Oleinik refused. On February 28, 2006—more than five years after the incident—a court finally found in Oleinik's favor (Anisimov 2006). At the time this was written, however, Oleinik had not yet received the money.

Two things are notable about the development of the Oleinik case that are not immediately evident from the time line in Table 5.1. The first is the lengths to which the local authorities were willing to go to protect their own. Although

TABLE 5.1. Oleinik time line.[1]

Date	Event
November 16, 2000	Oleinik is beaten by officers Khor'iakov and Frolov
November 20, 2000	Oleinik appeals for help from the Committee Against Torture
December 15, 2000	Local police complete an internal review of the case, concluding that there was not enough evidence to convict Khor'iakov and Frolov of the beating but that they should be censured for failing to cite Oleinik for disorderly conduct
December 27, 2000	District prosecutor opens a criminal investigation
January 30, 2001	Local police censure Khor'iakov and Frolov for failing to cite Oleinik for disorderly conduct
May 27, 2001	District prosecutor closes criminal investigation
July 31, 2001	Oleinik complains to federal prosecutors
August 6, 2001	Federal prosecutors refer case back to district prosecutor, who reopens criminal investigation
August 28, 2001	District prosecutor again closes criminal investigation
September 12, 2001	After complaint from Oleinik, district prosecutor reopens criminal investigation
October 12, 2001	Request by Oleinik to have the investigation assigned to a new prosecutor is denied
October 24, 2001	District prosecutor again closes criminal investigation
November 19, 2001	Oleinik complains to regional and city prosecutors, requesting reopening of investigation and assignment to a new prosecutor
December 12, 2001	District prosecutor reopens criminal investigation; investigating prosecutor remains unchanged
February 21, 2002	Investigation assigned to a new prosecutor
April 22, 2002	District prosecutor closes criminal investigation
August 21, 2002	After repeated complaints, district prosecutor reopens investigation and qualifies Oleinik as victim
December 18, 2002	Court finds police officers guilty, gives them suspended sentences, and awards no compensation
December 15, 2002	Oleinik appeals
May 28, 2003	Court upholds initial ruling
June 5, 2003	Oleinik appeals
August 12, 2003	Court upholds initial ruling

Source: Public Verdict, Case File No. 6
[1]This time line and the related narrative are reconstructed from the aggregated contents of Public Verdict Case File No. 6. A summary of the case is also available at: www.publicverdict.org/topics/cases/olejnik.html.

the police and prosecutors are formally independent of each other, in this case they clearly worked together to avoid an investigation that would incriminate the officers. In their own initial internal review, the police did not make it clear whether they were willing to see their own punished, writing only, "The testimony of S. P. Oleinik, V. V. Pigalev, M. F. Frolov, and N. A. Khor'iakov as to the cause of bodily harm to S. P. Oleinik contains significant contradictions, which cannot be overcome within the confines of an internal review, as further investigation is required."[4] However, for reasons that are impossible to determine, the district prosecutor clearly decided that he would not bring charges against the officers. Thus, the police produced testimony from Gennadii Khavroshechkin, who said that he had seen Oleinik start the fight with Khor'iakov and Frolov. That testimony was cited as decisive by District Prosecutor O. V. Kiriukhov on May 27, 2001, when he closed the criminal investigation for the first time; he wrote that only Khavroshechkin's testimony could be trusted because the other witnesses were all friends of Oleinik. (He also wrote that it was impossible to determine whether Oleinik's injuries were inflicted by the officers.)[5] However, on May 29, 2001, Khavroshechkin delivered a sworn affidavit to the Committee Against Torture, recanting his testimony, which he said had been made to officer Nelidov under duress. In reality, he said, he had been nowhere near the site of the incident at the time it occurred.[6]

The second is the inertia of the system. Oleinik's case was opened and closed four times before a fifth relaunch finally led to a court hearing in December 2002. (That is by no means a record, incidentally.) District prosecutor Kiriukhov repeatedly closed his investigation, making legal and procedural errors along the way; generally, he failed to provide new justifications for closing an investigation he had been ordered to reopen. Consequently, his superiors repeatedly forced him to reopen the investigation. Thus, two questions arise. First, if the prosecutors wanted to protect the police, why didn't they just close the case and keep it shut? And second, if the prosecutors wanted to pursue the case, why didn't they take it away from Kiriukhov and assign it to someone else? When the district prosecutor's office did reassign the case in February 2002, the new investigator again closed it. Only after the case was taken over by the city prosecutors did it finally make progress. And, even then, the officers never received any real punishment.

Moreover, the Oleinik case is far from unique. Such dragging out of cases—*volokita*, to use the more concise Russian term—is common practice when citizens go up against the state, according to Public Verdict's activists. Nadezhda Smol'ianinova went through a very similar process when she pressed to have charges brought against police officers who, while interrogating her son, injected him with narcotics, as a result of which he died of an overdose. Smol'ianinova's case was opened and closed seven times before finally going to court two years after the incident, resulting, with help from Public Verdict, in a conviction but no compensation.[7]

Volokita does not permeate all cases, however. When the authorities themselves are keen to get a conviction, they can move fairly quickly. When those convictions turn out to be false, however, they are slow to back down. The police and prosecutors, for example, wasted no time in charging and trying Evgenii Maininger of the murder of a newspaper editor in the city of Tol'iatti: After he confessed under duress on October 16, 2003, he was in court by March 15, 2004. After he was acquitted on October 11, 2004, it took the prosecutors only seven days to file an appeal, which Maininger won in November of that year. Clearly, then, when the law enforcement agencies are interested in the swift resolution of a case, they are capable of abandoning *volokita* and acting quite quickly. In December 2004, Maininger filed suit against the police and prosecutors, claiming 10.37 million rubles (approximately $334,516) in damages. Four months later, on April 4, 2005, Maininger won, with legal assistance from Public Verdict, though he was awarded only 150,000 rubles (approximately $4,838). However, he was paid only on March 3, 2007.[8]

Similarly to the Maininger case, Airat Khalilov was brought to trial in 1998 on charges of murdering a taxi driver, based on the testimony of only one witness and despite exculpatory evidence. Over the course of six years, Khalilov was convicted three times, only to have the verdicts overturned by a higher court and sent back for retrial, until he was finally acquitted in August 2005. Similarly to the way in which Oleinik's case was repeatedly returned to the same investigator, Kiriukhov, Khalilov was repeatedly tried by the same judge, who wrote and rewrote virtually the same guilty verdict, with no evident reflection on the reversals handed down from the higher court.[9]

In this context, one case taken on by Public Verdict stands out. On April 6, 2006, three Moscow police officers responded to an alarm call from an apartment that was apparently being burglarized. When they arrived on the scene—before even entering the apartment building—they happened upon thirteen-year-old Nikita Gladyshev, who was walking out of the building, where he lived. The officers stopped the boy, asked him where he lived, whether anyone was home, whether he had keys to the apartment, and other questions. Gladyshev became suspicious that he was being questioned not by police, but by would-be thieves, and ran away. When the police caught up to him, they handcuffed him (in violation of the law, which forbids handcuffing a minor who does not pose a threat) and roughed him up, leaving him bruised and with torn cartilage in his larynx.[10] Unlike in the cases of Oleinik and others, however, in Gladyshev's case the authorities acted quickly. Eleven days later, on April 17, 2006, the prosecutors had finished their investigation, confirming that Gladyshev was the victim of a crime, and the case was sent to court.[11] On October 31, 2006, the Basmannyi District Court in Moscow—the same court that convicted Mikhail Khodorkovskii and whose name is synonymous with perversions of justice—sentenced the three police officers to three years in prison and awarded Gladyshev 100,000 rubles in moral damages (Rogacheva 2006).

What distinguishes the Gladyshev case from Oleinik, Smol'ianinov, Maininger, Khalilov, and others? On the face of it, there are two main differences. First, Gladyshev is a minor, and the injustice inherent in abusing a young boy seems more glaring than in the abuse of a grown man. Indeed, recent research has shown that Russians (as, probably, most other people) tend to perceive a much stronger injustice frame when children are involved (see, for example, Sundstrom 2006b). The second factor is that the Gladyshev case happened in Moscow, whereas all of the others occurred in provincial cities. Given the concentration of media and political attention in Moscow, that fact alone may be enough to guarantee a larger degree of media coverage. However, while these two facts are undoubtedly important, it does not seem that they were sufficient to ensure the quick achievement of a positive outcome. Indeed, in early May 2006, Nikita Gladyshev's mother Kira came to Public Verdict for help. She knew she would need it: Kira Gladyshev is a court bailiff in Moscow and, based on her own professional experience, felt that, without legal help and a PR campaign, her son's case would go nowhere.[12]

Pogroms in Sochi and Bezhetsk

On the evening of July 16, 2006, two off-duty officers of the OMON—Russia's riot police—were enjoying drinks at the Oasis bar near the beach in the small town of Nizhnii Makopse, near the Black Sea resort of Sochi, when they decided to pick a fight with a group of patrons of Armenian descent. Outnumbered, the officers found themselves on the losing end of the brawl, but they vowed revenge as they fled.

Two days later, late in the evening, some thirty OMON officers, uniformed, masked, and armed, raided the bar. Some twenty-one patrons—many of them teenagers, many of them Armenian—were kicked, beaten with truncheons, and shocked with stun guns, before being forced to lie face down in the sand, bound, and then piled face down on the floor of an empty bus. The OMON officers likewise rounded up potential witnesses, including the security guard of the nearby summer camp Druzhba,[13] who approached the bus to find out why it was parked outside the gates of the camp. Some of the victims and witnesses managed to call the parents and relatives of those who had been rounded up, and by the time the raid was winding down, a number of distraught parents had shown up. They were not allowed to see their teenaged children, however, nor were they able to prevent the bus from leaving. Instead, they followed it to the police station, where they were prevented from speaking to their children for some four hours, until they were finally released at around 5 am, without being charged with any wrongdoing and having been forced to sign statements saying they had not been mistreated by the OMON.[14] Two teenagers were hospitalized, one with a concussion and the other with trauma to his internal organs (Glanin 2006a).

What became known as the Sochi OMON case came to the attention of Public Verdict from a local organization in Sochi, Mothers in Defense of the Rights of Arrestees and Inmates. That NGO, in turn, had learned of the incident after getting a telephone call from an E. I. Titov, a journalist at *Vechernii Krasnodar*, a newspaper in the local regional capital. That referral set in motion a mechanism that had been developed after a notorious pogrom in the Bashkir Republic city of Blagoveshchensk, in which local police rounded up and beat allegedly hundreds of local young men. To better coordinate response to such incidents, a network of human rights NGOs from across the country—including the Committee Against Torture in Nizhnii Novgorod and Man and Law in Ioshkar-Ola and coordinated by Public Verdict in Moscow—resolved to create joint mobile task forces (JMTs). Consisting of half a dozen or so delegates from participating NGOs, these JMTs would travel immediately to the scene of a pogrom, support local rights defenders, collect and systematize information and testimony, and, where possible, support local prosecutors in their investigations.

In the Sochi OMON case, the JMT was run by O. I. Khabibrakhmanov, from the Man and Law organization in Ioshkar-Ola, and was on site in force by July 23, 2006. Public Verdict provided financial support, including for an attorney,

Nikolai Shakhovalov, to represent the victims. As early as July 25, 2006, Khabibrakhmanov reported that, "There is currently no reason to believe that the official investigation is being pursued ineffectively."[15] In an e-mail to Public Verdict director Natalia Taubina, Khabibrakhmanov reported on progress as of August 2, 2006: The JMT, he wrote, had established a close working relationship with the local prosecutor, who by August 1 had arrested four OMON officers, including two who would not have been identified without the work of the JMT.[16] By August 17, four more OMON officers had been arrested. On January 31, 2007, the local prosecutors wrapped up their investigation and submitted the case to court, and hearings began in February (Glanin 2007; Titov 2007).

The work done by the JMT was evidently critical to both the speed and scope of the prosecutorial response to the Sochi OMON case.[17] As is the case with most local prosecutors' offices, the local investigators suffered from a lack of people and resources and would not have been able to conduct interviews of all victims and witnesses as quickly and as thoroughly as the JMT did. In addition, the fact that the JMT was made up of legal professionals meant that the materials they handed over to the prosecutors were drafted in accordance with proper legal practice, couched in legal terminology, and generally suitable for direct incorporation into the prosecutors' own reports. And, while the JMT mission to Sochi was eventually closed, advisers from the coalition of NGOs continue to support the prosecutors. Indeed, early in 2007, on the advice of members of the JMT, the prosecutors requested the case back from the presiding judge so that they could improve various elements that might have otherwise been exploited by the defendants in court.[18]

This sort of cooperation should not be taken to mean, however, that everything went the NGOs' way or that the local authorities put up no resistance. In late July 2006, men who presented themselves as police officers started making visits to the victims, trying to convince them to drop their charges, in some cases in exchange for promises of compensation.[19] (None of the victims agreed.) In addition, the prosecutors refused to pursue charges of human rights violations that were sought by the victims and the JMT, limiting the case instead to charges of excessive use of force, which carries lesser punishment and has less potential to implicate higher-level officials.[20] In October 2007, three OMON officers were convicted and jailed in the incident. Various other aspects of the case, including the prosecution of some of the OMON officers and compensation for some of the victims, are still in court. Nevertheless, Public

Verdict has never had a more successful experience of cooperation with local prosecutors.[21]

This stands in sharp contrast to the case of the Bezhetsk pogrom. In November 2004 and March 2005, in the town of Bezhetsk, Tverskaia Oblast', local antinarcotics police rounded up, publicly humiliated, and then tortured eighteen local citizens, in an apparent attempt to get them to confess to false charges of trading in drugs and guns. The first group of victims was rounded up in a raid on the local market on November 24, 2004, where they were beaten, held face down in the snow, and then taken to a police station, where the beatings continued. On March 3, 2005, a second group was arrested in a local café, where the officers evidently forced one of them to call a third group and invite them for a drink. When that group arrived, they were dragged from their car, beaten, forced to lie face down in the snow, and bound before being dragged inside the café, where the first group was already lying, bound, on the floor. Inside the café—in front of employees and patrons, whom the police would not allow to leave—the victims were stripped naked and searched before being taken to a local police station. There, they were beaten and subjected to electric shocks. Unable to obtain satisfactory confessions, the police forced one of the victims to sign a statement saying he and others had resisted arrest, thus bringing their injuries upon themselves. Several of the victims were later hospitalized with severe injuries.[22]

Within days of the incident, a JMT was dispatched to Bezhetsk, where it began a long, slow process of trying to prod the local prosecutors into taking up the case. Eventually, in August 2005, the prosecutors recognized that the victims had indeed suffered from criminal activity. However, in September, JMT leader Aleksandr Kokorin wrote to Public Verdict director Natalia Taubina, saying, "The prosecutor's general approach to me is negative. He cannot understand why, in whose interests, I keep coming to Tver' from Izhevsk to work for [the victims] for free."[23] The Bezhetsk and Tverskaya Oblast' police accused the human rights organizations of "bald-faced lies" and threatened reprisal; General Aleksandr Mikhailov, head of the regional narcotics inspectorate, told a newspaper: "If someone is using them 'behind the scenes,' if someone led them astray, then we'll force them to reveal their source of information. If they acted purposefully, then we will force them to answer for their slander" (Mandrik 2005). In November 2005, the prosecutor closed the case, citing "the impossibility of identifying the individuals to be charged."[24] The case was eventually reopened, but it has gone virtually nowhere since then.

Public Pressure: Injustice in the Media

What might account for the discrepancies in the ways these cases were handled and the reception met by the NGOs? As we have seen in the case histories, the initial response by police and prosecutors in all cases was to ignore complaints and shield officials from prosecution. For reasons that are difficult to discern, however, prosecutors in the Gladyshev and Sochi cases eventually felt the need to "break with tradition" and push the cases forward. One partial explanation may have to do with timing: Media coverage of the Gladyshev and Sochi cases began considerably sooner after the incidents than in the Oleinik and Bezhetsk cases, allowing the authorities to become more deeply invested in their strategies prior to the appearance of public pressure. But this does not appear to be a complete explanation. Without the ability to interview the prosecutors, I am left to hypothesize and then to see whether the available evidence supports any of the hypotheses as to why this occurred more than the others.

There are two potential sources of pressure on prosecutors: sources emanating from within the system and sources that come from outside, that is, from the public. Inevitably, of course, these two sources coexist and influence one another. Thus, it seems likely that if public sources of pressure are sufficient to force a prosecutor to action, it will be because that pressure is somehow transmitted through internal channels, for example because the prosecutor answers to a superior, who answers to an elected official, who is afraid of the consequences of a public outcry. Indeed, I have already noted one potential hypothesis, stemming from existing literature and common perceptions, according to which the Gladyshev and Sochi cases were able to be more effectively pursued because they involved minors and because the victims were more blatantly innocent than the victims in the Bezhetsk and Oleinik cases, who were grown men, some with histories of run-ins with the law. To find support for the hypothesis that public pressure is capable of influencing prosecutorial decisions, we would need to find more public outrage over the Gladyshev and Sochi cases than in the Bezhetsk and Oleinik cases.

The difficulty, of course, is in assessing the degree of public outrage. No local or national public opinion surveys specific to these cases were conducted at the time, and, even if there were sufficient resources to conduct surveys after the fact, subjective memories would not be sufficient to demonstrate a link between opinions at the time and the degree of public outrage discerned by the prosecutors. And, as mentioned earlier, I cannot ask the prosecutors themselves (and even if I could, it would be impossible to know if they were telling the truth). As a result, I am left to look for a proxy, something measurable and potentially analytically valid, the presence of which would either support or not support the hypothesis.

One option, and the route I have taken here, is to review media coverage of the incidents and ensuing investigations, looking for clues as to the public frame of reference. Media coverage is obviously not the same as public opinion. At best, it is filtered public opinion, while, at worst, it is propaganda. To avoid the latter, I have reviewed only coverage from the print media, which is generally uncensored and subject to much less government pressure than television. There is, however, a logical connection to the hypothesis that supports the use of media coverage as a proxy: Any public outcry must necessarily be mediated, and politicians and government officials perceive public sentiment as aggregated by the media. Moreover, media coverage has the analytical advantage of being contemporaneous with the events at hand and thus not blurred by the passage of time and the subjectivity of memory. That said, there are limits to what a crude content analysis—and there are not enough articles available on these cases for a complex, quantified content analysis to be valid—can achieve. As a result, I am asking only very basic questions: Is coverage emotional or dry? Is the incident portrayed as clear-cut or nuanced? How much credence is given to the police's justifications? If the hypothesis is to be considered supported, there should be discernible differences in the answers to these questions for the Gladyshev and Sochi cases, on the one hand, and the Bezhetsk and Oleinik cases, on the other.

In the Sochi[25] and Gladyshev[26] cases, the fact that the victims included minors is indeed accorded special significance. In all but one of the newspaper articles reviewed on the Sochi case, the presence of minors among the victims figured in the first or second paragraphs; in many, it was in the headline (Glanin 2006b; Perova 2007). The same is true of the articles on the Gladyshev case. Closer analysis, however, reveals some differences. None of the articles on Sochi uses the word *child* or *children*, though some do use the word *offspring* to refer to the people parents tried to rescue from the police; generally, they preferred the colder, legalistic term *minor*. In contrast, articles on the Gladyshev case preferred words such as *child* and *schoolboy* and highlighted the fact that he was only twelve years old, while generally ignoring the fact that he was, at the time, 173 cm (5'8") tall (Lokotetskaia 2006). Indeed, the articles on Gladyshev are generally more emotive than the articles on Sochi. They include judgmental terms such as *cruel beating* (Zorin 2006) and *shocking incident* (Lokotetskaia 2006), which are not found in the Sochi articles. And while the Sochi articles are generally dry but thorough recounts of facts, the articles on Gladyshev are heavily laden with quotations, mostly from the boy and his mother, telling the story through their own eyes. While the point of view of the police is frequently missing in articles on Gladyshev, it is often the first point of view presented in articles on Sochi, most of which contain no quotations from victims at all. Over time, though, this dynamic began to change, and by the time the respective cases went to court, articles on Sochi treated the case as clear-cut, while some articles on Gladyshev began suggesting that the police—although undoubtedly guilty—perhaps did not deserve jail time. It is impossible to determine definitively whether the fact that the Sochi victims were mainly Armenian, while Gladyshev is an ethnic Russian, played any role in this discrepancy. However, the articles reviewed for this analysis on the Sochi case bear no evidence of ethnic prejudice or stereotyping; indeed, the Sochi victims were more likely to be referred to simply as "minors" than as Armenian.

What of the other two, supposedly less "media-friendly" cases? With the exception of the focus on minors, it is sometimes hard to tell the difference between the two groups. Both the Bezhetsk[27] and the Oleinik[28] cases received significant amounts of coverage at the national level (at least in newspapers). The general tone of the articles on these two cases, however, is indeed different from those on the Sochi and Gladyshev cases. In the Bezhetsk case in particular, much more credence is given to the police's version of the story than in the articles on Sochi. Whereas the journalists writing about Sochi treated the case as fairly clear-cut, some of those writing about Bezhetsk were more ambivalent, at least in part because the victims were involved in running the local market, a business assumed to be tied up with organized crime (Mandrik 2005; Sapozhnikova 2005). On the whole, however, it is difficult to identify a systematic difference in form or content between the articles on Sochi and the articles on Bezhetsk. Indeed, most articles on the Bezhetsk case give significantly more space to the victims rather than the police and come to the conclusion that the police are guilty. Remarkably, even the tabloid *Komsomol'skaia Pravda*—a progovernment newspaper that generally supports strong-armed policing—wrote, with characteristic irony:

> So, what are we left with? It's like the series *Brigada*[29] without the makeup. . . . All of the victims have characteristically shaven heads and wear the same leather jackets. Of course, this could just be the provincial fashion—well, maybe the 300 kilometers

that separate Bezhetsk from Moscow correspond to ten years of history, and people here still live according to the old canons. But no: There's one perfectly hairy individual walking down the street, and there's another . . .

Incidentally, none of that changes the point: By law, you can't beat anyone— not with shaved heads, not with long hair. Even those who themselves beat others. (Sapozhnikova 2005)

Coverage of the Oleinik case is even less ambiguous than the Bezhetsk case. Despite the fact that Oleinik, a grown man, was drinking at the time of the incident, the articles gave little credence to the police's version of events and treated the incident as "a clear case of a beating" ("Novosti: Proisshestviia" 2003). And while the articles on Oleinik are drier and less emotive than the articles about Gladyshev, they are generally indignant about the *volokita* and considered the suspended sentences given to the police officers to be unjust (Goncharova 2004; Anisimov 2006). What's more, the police were never given the chance in any of the Oleinik articles to justify their actions, in contrast to all of the other cases.

Does the source of the coverage have any impact on content? Generally speaking, it does not. State-run publications, such as *Rossiiskaia Gazeta*, and progovernment publications, such as *Komsomol'skaia Pravda*, *Izvestiia*, and *Gazeta*, did not differ in their coverage of these incidents, did not give more credence to the authorities, and did not shy away from criticizing the actions of the police and prosecutors. There is, however, one notable exception to this finding: the opposition newspaper *Novaia Gazeta*. In almost all cases, *Novaia Gazeta* wrote longer articles, giving significantly more space to quotations from victims and attacking the authorities with somewhat more bite. In some cases, *Novaia Gazeta*'s articles were even written by the human rights defenders who were investigating the case (who were identified in their bylines as special correspondents, rather than human rights defenders) (Khairullin 2005). If we disregard *Novaia Gazeta*, however, the tone of coverage from one newspaper to another, regardless of orientation or ownership, is remarkably consistent.[30]

Thus, the hypothesis with which I began this discussion is only partially supported by the evidence. Although the presence of minors among the victims certainly does lend itself to more emotional coverage, and thus perhaps to clearer senses of injustice, in reality all of the cases reviewed received significant amounts of coverage, and all of the reports gave more credence to the victims than to the police. Moreover, almost all of the newspapers in all of the cases gave prominent place to the human rights organizations that became involved in the investigations, including Public Verdict, the Committee Against Torture, and Man and Law. This is broadly true, again, regardless of a newspaper's ownership or orientation. These findings suggest that the Russian media—or, at least, newspaper journalists, who are relatively more free than their television colleagues—do not discriminate in their construction of injustice: If they become aware of an event, they are likely to give it "standard" coverage, regardless of where it happens or who is involved. This, incidentally, is good news for Russia's human rights defenders.

If we move beyond the initial hypothesis, however, one important difference emerges. The coverage of the Sochi case began on July 21, 2006, three days after the incident itself; likewise coverage of Gladyshev began on April 13, 2006, less than a week after the incident. Coverage of Bezhetsk, on the other hand, began on March 16, 2005, only eleven days after the second round of beatings, but four months after the first round; even more egregiously, coverage of the Oleinik case began only on April 17, 2003, two and a half years after the incident. While it is impossible to know whether and how media coverage directly affected decisions made by police and prosecutors, it is noteworthy that the two cases where coverage began almost immediately were handled quickly, while the others suffered from *volokita*. Again, this is good news for Russia's human rights defenders: Getting the word into the media quickly seems to have an impact. This, then, does lend some support to the hypothesis, suggesting in particular that public opinion may be fruitfully mobilized early in a case's arc. The fact that I have not found more conclusive evidence for the hypothesis, however, suggests that the search continue.

Internal Pressure: Russia's Criminal Justice System

There is another potential hypothesis alluded to in the case studies, which again differentiates the Gladyshev and Sochi cases from the Oleinik and Bezhetsk cases: the significance of location. The Gladyshev case occurred in Moscow, the capital and the focus of political and public life. Sochi is Russia's most popular resort, site of Putin's summer residence, and, at the time, a bidder for the 2014 Winter Olympics. The Oleinik case, on the other hand, took place in Nizhnii Novgorod, an important industrial center but a relative political backwater, while Bezhetsk, in Tverskaya oblast', is a small town of which Russians know little. This may help explain why the media reacted more quickly to the Gladyshev and Sochi cases: There is simply much more media attention focused on those cities than on Nizhnii Novgorod and Bezhetsk. But it also may help explain why—given broadly uniform coverage of all four cases—prosecutors in Sochi and Moscow felt compelled to react: There was a greater chance that their superiors (and their superiors' superiors) would be paying attention.

This distinction alerts us to the importance of internal sources of pressure. We might imagine a chain of accountability modified slightly from that outlined at the beginning of the previous section: A prosecutor answers to a superior, who answers to a politician, who is afraid not of electoral accountability but of disfavor from above. This model of vertical accountability looks particularly attractive in the Russian context, where semiauthoritarian rule has been concentrated in the hands of the president and transmitted downwards through the so-called vertical of power.

This hypothesis is considerably harder to test than the previous one because there are no valid, measurable proxies. The proposition that scandals in Sochi and Moscow are more politically sensitive than scandals in Nizhnii Novgorod and Bezhetsk is a fairly safe assumption. However, if we are to assert that this sort of political sensitivity is a stronger explanatory factor than public pressure, we will need first to examine how Russia's legal and criminal justice systems function, not in terms of formal rules and procedures but as living social institutions. If we are to put any credence in this hypothesis, then we should see an environment that somehow shields individual officials from public or even professional accountability while simultaneously leaving them vulnerable to hierarchical pressure.

Recent research on the Russian bureaucratic elite has shown that behind the façade of corporate solidarity, increasing centralization has given rise to fierce battles at all levels of power for a place in the hierarchy (see, for example, Petrov and Riabov 2007). As a result, the instinct to avoid accountability at all costs is forced to coexist with the reality that any lapse in judgment can be used by superiors or competitors to deprive a person of access. This is why prosecutors "cover their rears" by continuously reopening cases that they would much rather close once and for all. And it is also why a prosecutor in Sochi is more likely to cooperate than a prosecutor in Bezhetsk; should a mishandled case overshadow the city's Olympic bid or a summit at Putin's summer residence, the career consequences could be catastrophic.

This may also explain the one major exception to Russian government agencies' general reluctance to pay court-ordered compensation. Notably, Russia is fairly conscientious about paying the compensation ordered by the European

Court of Human Rights (ECHR) to plaintiffs. No bureaucrat in Moscow wants to be responsible for causing Russia embarrassment in Strasbourg, lest a senior diplomat, parliamentarian, minister, or even the president be asked an uncomfortable question while traveling abroad.

However, Russia has failed to make any of the systemic changes demanded by the ECHR (Jackson 2004). This was also noted by Anatolii Kovler, Russia's delegated judge to the ECHR, who complained in an interview with *Novaia Gazeta* that the state has done virtually nothing to address the systemic nature of human rights violations (Nikitinskii 2007). Likewise, the experience of Public Verdict reveals virtually no learning process on the part of the authorities. Neither Public Verdict, nor indeed Russia's total helplessness at the hands of the ECHR in Strasbourg, has succeeded in instilling a sense of discipline among Russian police, prosecutors, or other public officials. Infractions remain just as ubiquitous; reactions and remediation remain just as ad hoc. Clearly, embarrassment is capable of forcing remediation but only on a case-by-case basis. Russia has attempted to remove the source of embarrassment by strengthening its representation in Strasbourg, or by punishing a police officer here or there, but not by rooting out the misbehavior that gets them there in the first place.

How does this interplay with the media effects discussed earlier? Given what we know about Russians' relationship with their justice system, as well as about how the law is used by those who inhabit the system, we might posit that the media effect becomes meaningful because of the pressures it places on individual bureaucrats within the system, in an argument similar to the hypothesis we tested originally but with one correction: The impact of the media effect is limited by the inertia created by the system. In other words, an immediate media response creates pressure on bureaucrats within the system to avoid a potentially costly scandal before investments have been made in avoiding the impact of the case itself. Once those investments have been made to shield oneself or one's colleagues from accountability, and presumably in the absence of media pressure, the media effect seems insufficient to overcome the internal incentives to stay the course. Thus, the initial lesson, at least, seems to be that internal and external pressures cannot be demarcated in any satisfying way. External pressure, such as from the media, is effected inevitably through the mechanisms of internal pressure. And internal mechanisms, which have evolved in large part to avoid external interference, nonetheless cannot fully avoid pressure from without.

The State–Society Relationship and the Meaning of Law in Russia

Beyond the issue of why some of Public Verdict's cases succeed and some do not, there is the broader question of why the organization and its allies have been unable to effect systemic change. The failure is double: On the one hand, the regime and its agents seem impervious to any impetus to reform, while, on the other hand, the Russian public has not assimilated Public Verdict's appeal to see the issue of police and judicial abuse as systemic. Here, the cases suggest a different logic, which has more to do with public perceptions of state–society relations than with the inner workings of the law enforcement apparatus. Unsurprisingly, what the law means to Russian citizens is as important as what it means to Russian officials.

Returning for a moment to the press coverage and the discussion of external sources of pressure suggests one important distinction between the cases. Almost all of the articles on Bezhetsk and most of the articles about Sochi mentioned those incidents in the context of other police pogroms that had occurred across the country since the "cleansing operation" in Blagoveshchensk. Only one of the articles on Oleinik, however, and none of the articles on Gladyshev made any mention of other, similar beatings. (In the one exception about Oleinik, the article mentioned another beating case only because it had also taken place in Nizhnii Novgorod.) This suggests that the journalists, their editors, and, perhaps, their readers see the relatively small number of beatings of large numbers of people to be systemic—and thus in need of a systemic response—while the relatively larger number of beatings of individuals is not seen as being a collective issue.

Taken alongside the media effects described earlier, this distinction between group and individual grievances may provide part of the explanation of why Public Verdict is more easily successful in some cases than in others. With these two effects taken together, we begin to get a more complete picture, in which our four cases can be divided into a simple matrix based on two criteria: on one axis, whether the media responded immediately or with a delay, and, on the other axis, whether the case involved an individual or a group grievance (see Table 5.2).

A quick media reaction, as in the Sochi and Gladyshev cases, does seem to help prevent *volokita*, while the fact of a pogrom seems to support identification of the incident as symptomatic of a systemic problem. If in the previous

TABLE 5.2. Matrix of cases.

	Immediate media reaction	Delayed media reaction
Group grievance (pogrom)	Sochi case: quick reaction, systemic identification, partial success	Bezhetsk case: *volokita*, systemic identification, no success
Individual grievance	Gladyshev case: quick reaction, no systemic identification, success	Oleinik case: *volokita*, almost no systemic identification, partial success

sections we dealt with the issue of case-by-case success, here the question is one of the degree to which the grievance in a particular case can be generalized—and assimilated as such—by the public.

As discussed in other chapters, one of the keys to the development of an injustice frame is the question of who is to blame. Accordingly, frames in which the guilty are a very small number of individuals—such as a handful of police officers, who can be relatively easily arrested and jailed—may spawn short-term protests, up until the guilty are punished, but they are unlikely to give rise to enduring social movements, which aim to alter the system. Thus, for the development of sustained movements in the defense of human rights in Russia, it is of critical importance whether the sorts of infringements described above are seen as systemic or individual and random. Clearly, the professional human rights defenders who work for Public Verdict and their partner organizations see all of these cases as symptomatic of a larger, systemic problem, and their goal is to change the system. The question remains, however, as to whether the public sees it the same way.

Meanwhile, the public's view of the problem—and of the sorts of collective solutions offered by Public Verdict and its partners—will to a significant degree depend on how people in Russia view the legal and criminal justice system with which Public Verdict interacts. For one, if we are to accept the argument that the legal and criminal justice system is divorced from public accountability, then this should be reflected in the way the public relates to that aspect of the state. And, second, a review of the state–society relationship in this area relates back to one of the core arguments of this entire project, namely, that an unstructured, individualized approach by the state to its subjects discourages collective responses to injustice.

To understand why this might be, we need to understand Russians' relationship to their legal and criminal justice systems. According to surveys conducted by the independent Levada Center in September 2005, only 12 percent of Russians fully trust their police, while 13 percent trust prosecutors and 16 percent trust the courts; meanwhile, 82 percent felt unprotected against abuse by law enforcement, and 73 percent believed that they could become the victims of such abuse (Dubin and Gudkov 2005: 11). In their analysis:

> Dissatisfaction with the police stems first and foremost from the fact that, without fulfilling the function of maintaining social order and defending citizens against crime, the police do not bear any accountability before "civil society." Indeed, this distinguished and continues to distinguish the Russian police from the police institutions of Western democratic countries, seemingly analogous in their functions. The Russian system, and much less its Soviet predecessor, has never known such forms as municipal police, elected police chiefs, parliamentary oversight of internal affairs, etc. . . . The coordinated efforts of authorities at various levels to stymie all attempts by society (civic organizations, parties and human rights defenders) to establish the accountability of coercive structures for violence and abuse is simply a continuation under new conditions of the old tendencies of corporative isolation of these agencies from independent external control, self-defence against "external" forces, and the desire by the leadership of the police and the coercive structures to create a zone of autonomous management. (Dubin and Gudkov 2005: 13–14)

Most Russians' opinion of the police is based either on their own personal experiences of dealing with law enforcement officers or on that of their relatives and close friends (Shepeleva 2005). People want the police to defend their lives, well-being, and property, although they do not actually expect the police to do so (Shepeleva 2005). Fully 41 percent of Russians and 56 percent of Muscovites are afraid that they themselves will become the victims of police brutality (Shepeleva 2005). People are aware of the fact that the police cut corners, refuse to open difficult cases, and generally do not share complainants' priorities, significantly undermining public trust in the police (Novikova 2005; Shepeleva 2005).

These opinions, meanwhile, are reflected in behavior. Despite relatively high levels of crime, Russians are remarkably reluctant to go to the police for help. (See Table 5.3.) And, as shown in Table 5.4, while Russians do fear violence from the police, they are primarily worried that the police will be rude and ineffective and may even refuse to investigate their cases.

Strikingly, the values gap between the police and the public is not as large as it might otherwise seem. In particular, Russians appear to be somewhat ambivalent about violence by the police, to a certain extent sharing the police's conviction that illegal force may be justifiable. The difference comes in the

TABLE 5.3. Victims of crime: Which of the following has happened to you? (percentage of respondents in large Russian cities; N = 1,200)

Was a victim of . . .	In the past three years	In the past year	Reported to the police	Satisfied with police work	Criminal caught
Pickpocketing	20	12	1	0.4	0.3
Attack by hooligans	15	10	2	0.3	0.6
Sexual assault	15	5	0.1	0	0.1
Fraud	11	7	1	0.1	0.1
Mugging	11	6	2	0.3	0.3
Theft from automobile	9	3	6	0.3	0
Blackmail, racketeering, extortion	5	3	0.3	0.3	0
Rape, attempted rape	3	0.9	0.1	0	0
Theft of automobile	5	3	2	0.5	0.7
Apartment burglary	2	1	2	0.1	0.5

Source: Public Verdict 2006.

definition of the target; the public does not share the police's evident view that suspects are guilty until proven innocent. Thus, Ol'ga Shepeleva writes:

> The average, law-abiding citizen is generally not opposed if a police officer beats up a criminal. . . . At the same time, citizens' preparedness to tolerate the excesses of "law enforcers" is not without its limits. Infringements by law enforcement agencies are permissible only if they are undertaken in order to fulfill the function of defending society. A law-abiding person, who might agree with the beating of a criminal, will be extremely upset if he learns that police officers beat an innocent man. (Shepeleva 2005: on-line source, no page numbers)

This goes partway to explaining why the press reports on the case studies presented above reflect a feeling of more "systemic" injustice in cases of pogroms than in cases of individual beatings: It is hard to imagine that a large group of people, minding their own business, could all be simultaneously guilty of whatever infraction provoked the police to raise their truncheons. But it is clearly insufficient as an explanation. To understand public perceptions, we need to take a closer look at how Russia's law enforcement and judicial institutions function in practice.

TABLE 5.4. What sorts of police infractions do citizens most often face?

	Rudeness	Inaction, *volokita*	Extortion	Unlawful arrest	Refusal to investigate	Physical violence	Cover-up	Blackmail, threat of violence	Racketeering	Repression
Entrepreneur	61	55	59	47	33	27	23	17	20	14
Company director	—	—	58	—	—	25	38	17	—	13
Middle management	—	57	52	45	31	—	—	—	—	10
Office worker	—	55	51	42	36	25	19	—	—	8
Skilled worker	61	53	53	46	—	25	18	18	—	—
Unskilled worker	58	53	—	48	31	31	—	—	—	—
Unemployed	57	—	—	57	—	35	21	18	17	13
Retiree	—	—	—	—	—	—	—	—	—	—
Homemaker	55	—	—	—	35	—	—	—	—	—
Student	63	54	54	53	33	42	23	30	14	11

Source: Public Verdict 2006.

It makes sense to start with the police, both as the "front door" of the criminal justice system and as the source of the injustice addressed by Public Verdict. The behavior of Russia's police is shaped by their institutional environment, a centralized bureaucracy managed by the Ministry of Internal Affairs in Moscow. This management, perhaps inevitably for such a large and unwieldy machine, depends heavily on statistics. Thus, the salaries of individual police officers and the budgets of their departments depend to a significant extent on the number of cases they solve, without regard for the importance of the case. As a result, officers will often refuse to accept reports of crimes they do not think they can solve (such as purse snatching or theft from an automobile) and will put off the investigation of major cases to pursue smaller, more easily solvable investigations. When the hierarchy becomes aware of a case that has drawn some degree of public or political attention, the police will pursue it but find themselves under tremendous pressure to cut corners to reach a swift conclusion. This modus operandi, incidentally, has not changed significantly since the Soviet era (Shelley 1996).

Underpaid, understaffed, undertrained, and under siege, police officers often take an adversarial view of society. One study found that:

> If citizens' mythology about the police is more or less accurate, the police's mythology [about citizens] abounds in negative stereotypes and is based, with rare exceptions, on an undifferentiated approach to society. Society is seen as a monolith. "Yes, I'm deeply convinced that our people, at least the average person, they still can't understand what can be done. You need to keep in mind the peculiarities of our country. We either have hunger or terror, half of the country was sent to the camps; it's been worked into people's genes that we have to run after them with truncheons." "The people go crazy at night," and "we work like we're on the front lines"—that is approximately how the situation is seen from within the police department. (Novikova 2005)

And so it may be unsurprising that the police seem to have few qualms about using excessive force, even when they know it violates the law. The Levada Center found that 63 percent of police officers felt it was acceptable to use illegal force against suspects in criminal cases in the interest of solving the case, while only slightly less—60 percent—felt it permissible to use illegal force against people who insult a police officer (Dubin and Gudkov 2005: 30–31). Again, these practices carry over from Soviet times (Shelley 1996).

If the police, at least in theory, exist to enforce the law, the courts and prosecutors exist to uphold it. There is, unfortunately, little literature available on

Russia's courts, and even less on its system of prosecutors. What literature is available, though, suggests that, as with the police, the dominant practices in the courts have their roots in the Soviet past. Tamara Morshchakova, a former constitutional court judge in Russia, wrote: "[In the Soviet Union], the courts played the rule of a supporting agency of punishment, a secondary addition to the state's other agencies of punishment. Courts were organs for the implementation of state policy. . . . Courts were part of the law enforcement system and were not seen as an independent power" (Morshchakova 2003).

Today, the court system remains—like the police—hierarchically organized, with the result that "the independence of judges is increasingly infringed upon within the court system itself. Judges depend on chief judges, on higher courts and on material benefits" (Morshchakova 2003: on-line source, no page numbers). This leads to two problems. The first, as noted by Frye (2002) and Hendley (1999), is a tremendous reluctance to rule against the state in cases that may involve overturning a bureaucratic decision or awarding compensation to the plaintiff. The second is what has become known as the "no-acquittals policy":

> Judges are afraid to render decisions consistent with their conscience and the pertinent legal rules, if such decisions would violate policies established the superior legal bureaucracy. For example, rendering a judgment fully exonerating the accused involves a serious risk to one's career, since it transgresses a no-acquittals policy imposed and consistently enforced by the regional court. The doctrine of no acquittals has never been articulated because it represents an obvious violation of law, both municipal and international. Nevertheless, it has been consistently applied sub silentio, with the message effectively conveyed. (Pomorski 2002: 112)

This, in turn, leads to bizarre situations. In his ethnography of criminal courts in the Siberian city of Krasnoiarsk, Stanislaw Pomorski found that:

> In the majority of the trials observed, the prosecution was not represented at all. When prosecutors did attend, their performance was, in most cases, weak or worse. Thus, the legally mandated adversariness of the trials, with the prosecution shouldering the burden of proving the defendants' guilt, remained an unqualified fiction. In reality, the judge, guided by the policy of no acquittals, sought to prove the defendant's guilt. (Pomorski 2002: 114)

As a result, judges remain too closely linked to prosecutors (Solomon and Foglesong 2000). Indeed, this has come back to haunt Russia in its cases at the European Court of Human Rights in Strasbourg, where, as William Jackson writes, "Among the most problematic aspects of Russia's legal system are the sweeping investigative powers assigned to prosecutors and police agencies and the inadequate rights possessed by defendants" (Jackson 2004: 26).

There is also a third problem: Courts in Russia are frequently unable to enforce their verdicts. As Nikita Gladyshev's mother knew well, bailiffs have insufficient resources and authority to force losing parties to pay their court-ordered compensation. Thus, as mentioned earlier, Sergei Oleinik is still awaiting the money he was awarded by the court. Vladimir Lukin, Russia's then human rights ombudsman, admitted in an interview with the state-run newspaper *Rossiiskaia Gazeta* that government agencies frequently go out of their way to avoid paying compensation, even when ordered to do so by a court (Kulikov 2007).

The resulting system of incentives for police officers, prosecutors, and judges in many ways resembles Janos Kornai's (1992) description of the state of Soviet industry: The production of the nominally intended good (whether automobiles or justice) inevitably takes a back seat to the twin production of indicators (for consumption by superiors and the bureaucracy) and rents (for consumption by the individual functionary). Given the degree to which contemporary practices replicate Soviet practices, this is not surprising. The law, in the traditional sense of a more or less universally enforced set of rules, is thus much less important to the functioning of the system than abuse and *volokita*. Indeed, as with so much else in Russia (see, for example, Ledeneva 2006), these seemingly informal practices are not by-products of a poorly functioning system; rather, they are the core practices that allow the system to function (however dysfunctionally from a normative standpoint).

The literature on Russians' relationship to the court system is, unfortunately, less rich than that on the police. Scholars studying Russia's arbitrage courts find a lack of trust in the courts on the part of would-be plaintiffs to rule against the state (Frye 2002). Likewise, Kathryn Hendley argues that Russia suffers from a deficit of demand for law, not because Russians are conceptually averse to the rule of law but because in reality they are faced by a system in which the law is not generally a tool they can use to their own advantage. Hendley writes: "Why should they place their faith in the law—and alter their behavior accordingly—when they have so little experience with law as a means of protecting and advancing their interests and so much experience with law as an instrument of the state?" (Hendley 1999: 91).

Given the potential cost of litigation, both financially in terms of fears of reprisal, as well as the likelihood of failure, there is a tremendous "first-mover" problem, exacerbated by the fact that Russian law does not allow for class-action lawsuits. As Kathryn Hendley writes, "The shift to a reliance on law makes sense only if it is made almost simultaneously by a substantial majority of potential litigants" (Hendley 1999: 92). This, then, may explain why Russians may be more likely to respond to pogroms than to individual beatings: The victims can challenge the state as a group.

Indeed, whenever a pogrom occurs, the case inevitably finds its way to Public Verdict and its partners. The same cannot be said, however, for the cases of individual beatings. It is difficult to determine an exact logic that would explain why some victims approach human rights defenders and others do not. A certain amount of the explanation is almost certainly accidental: A victim in a city with a strong and well-known human rights organization, such as in Nizhnii Novgorod or Ioshkar-Ola, is much more likely to seek and receive help than a victim in a city with no such organization. In the analysis of Public Verdict itself, however, there is more to it than that. According to the organization's deputy director, Oleg Novikov, there appear to be two main groups of people who seek help: those, like Sergei Oleinik, who have been left without a livelihood and who are forced to seek compensation as a means of survival; and those, like Nikita Gladyshev's mother, who know that justice is possible but that they will need help to get it.[31]

In the vast majority of cases—and we do not know how many people are brutalized by the Russian police each year—the victim is likely to fall somewhere in between those two groups. As Dubin and Gudkov explained, the police have become "privatized," insulated from the public and serving interests—whether their own or those of politicians, big business, or other "clients"—that the public do not perceive to be their own. Indeed, this privatization of the law by those endowed by the state with power can be extended to the courts, prosecutors, and entire system of justice. Vladimir Pastukhov writes:

> Russian laws exist, but they do not regulate the real relations of those subject to the law. And one of the main reasons for this situation is that the real relations among those subject to the law in Russia are established in a unique dimension that is parallel to the one at which formal legal regulation is only aimed. . . . Distinct from Western gray areas, Russian shadow spheres are formed not next to and contrary to the state but, instead, within the state's own functioning machinery and in collaboration with it. (Pastukhov 2002: 66–67)

What this means is that the law is a tool not in the hands of the citizen but in the hands of an individual employee of the state, whether a politician, a bureaucrat, a judge, a prosecutor, or a police officer. The access to the law that they enjoy allows them to solve problems—in particular, problems created by the public's own lack of access to the law. This is what allows a bureaucrat to demand a bribe in exchange for a building permit. It is also what allows riot police to beat teenagers as revenge for a lost bar fight, or a prosecutor to defend a police officer, or a judge to stymie the defense. As a result, whenever a citizen wants to negotiate access to the law—whether for a building permit or to punish his or her abusers—he or she must do so on an individual basis. The exception arises only when a number of citizens demand exactly the same access to achieve exactly the same result. Thus, the connection between Sochi and Bezhetsk is potentially more socially useful for the purposes of "using" the system than the connection between Oleinik and Gladyshev.[32]

This privatization and individualization of the law also helps explain why Public Verdict does not function as a grassroots movement. At various points in its short history, Public Verdict has attempted to garner public support. In a six-month public fund-raising drive, however, the organization was able to collect only about $140.[33] Some of Public Verdict's partners have been somewhat more successful, raising in-kind support from local printing presses, for example. But Russia's human rights community continues to subsist on grants from foreign donors. (Incidentally, Public Verdict was initially the only exception, funded by the Open Russia Foundation, which was shut down in the aftermath of the arrest and imprisonment of its founder, oil magnate Mikhail Khodorkovskii.)

The privatization of the law, however, has an important side effect: Because each agent of the state wields the law individually—in other words, because the law is not a public good, available for all without limit—access to the law becomes an object of competition. State agents may be expected constantly to seek to expand their access to the law (and the ensuing rents), to defend their access against competitors, and so on; access and rents may also be used within the hierarchy to encourage loyalty and punish disloyalty.

To illustrate, I will return to the Oleinik case, whose drawn-out history and long paper trail makes it relatively easy to interpret. As already mentioned, lower-level prosecutors repeatedly blocked the case's progress, in the evident hope that it would simply disappear. That it did not disappear is due primarily to the stubbornness of Public Verdict and its partners, who repeatedly appealed for help in letters to higher-level prosecutors. These letters—which require a formal response—become tools of control and subordination within the system, as higher-level prosecutors, not necessarily interested in the cases but averse to clear violations of protocol that could haunt them in political struggles, wield them over their underlings. And so, when the case finally did move forward, it was because the prosecutors' need to please their superiors eventually overcame their desire to protect their friends in the police. If there is a role for public opinion in this mechanism at all, it is in speeding up the process. Thus, a high-profile media case such as that of Gladyshev or Sochi with a strong human-interest hook may make the higher-ups antsier earlier, shifting the incentive structure for lower-level prosecutors. However, the failure to achieve any meaningful progress in the Bezhetsk case suggests that this shift need not ever occur.

Moreover, this instrumentalized use of law and procedure according to the logics of intra- and internecine politics rather than considerations of public policy seems inevitably to reinforce the privatization and individualization of the relationship between the citizen and the state. Without the law as a guide, an individual has no way of knowing what to expect from an interaction with a bureaucrat, while the bureaucrat manipulates procedure to his or her benefit in a manner and according to considerations that are not transparent to the citizen. That is why Gladyshev's mother, an insider to the law-enforcement system, went to Public Verdict for help: No amount of inside knowledge would have been sufficient to guarantee a satisfactory outcome, and thus another strategy was needed. That is also why Public Verdict has been unable to develop a consistently successful strategy of engagement with the state that would be comprehensible and attractive to a grassroots following; the state's own inconsistency, driven by the highly atomized use of power, stymies common, collective solutions.

Epilogue: Russia Behind Bars

Aleksei Kozlov was arrested on August 1, 2008, on charges of fraud involving an approximately $1 million stake in a leather factory, ZAO Iskozh, in which Kozlov was a partner with Leonid Slutsker, a member of Russia's Federation Council (upper house of parliament) from the Republic of Chuvashiia, and a handful of smaller investors. Put briefly, Slutsker and the prosecutors argued that Kozlov had stolen, rather than bought, his stake in the company; Kozlov argued the opposite and believed the case was an attempt by Slutsker to grab full control over the company. On March 6, 2009, Kozlov was convicted and sentenced to eight years in prison, leading to a series of appeals that finally ended with his release on June 3, 2013, at the end of his sentence ("Delo biznesmena Alekseia Kozlova" 2011).

On the face of it, Kozlov bears little resemblance to the victims of police, prosecutorial, and judicial abuse profiled earlier in this chapter and defended by Public Verdict and other human and civil rights groups. Well-heeled and well-connected, Kozlov and his wife—Ol'ga Romanova, an award-winning television journalist for the station Ren-TV—never saw themselves as vulnerable, much less as victims. Until the arrest.

Kozlov, however, was far from alone. Throughout the latter part of the 2000s, Russian investigators and prosecutors had begun making more active—and, according to some, legally problematic—use of criminal statutes relating to "economic crimes." From 2000 to 2009, criminal investigations were opened involving "economic crimes" at more than 44,000 enterprises per year, leading to the opening of more than 130,000 criminal cases annually and 75,000 arrests per year; by the middle of 2011, more than 100,000 Russian businessmen were serving prison sentences for "economic crimes" ("Amnistiia predprinimatelei" 2011). A large number of such investigations—by some counts, between 40 and 60 percent—never make it to court, leading some analysts and observers to believe that the motivation in opening an investigation has less to do with law enforcement than it does with attempts at extortion and the transfer of corporate control (Volkov, Paneiakh, et al. 2010). Nor was Kozlov the only prominent case. Svetlana Bakhmina, a lawyer who had been on the defense team for Yukos, the oil company taken over by the government from Mikhail Kodorkovskii in 2003, spent almost four years in jail, from December 2004 through September 2008, before being released for good behavior ("Delo Svetlany Petrovny Bakhminoi" 2008). Sergei Magnistkii, a lawyer for Hermitage Capital, an investment fund whose director, William Browder, ran afoul of the government, was less lucky; arrested on November 24, 2008, and charged with fraud, he died in prison on November 16, 2009, before his case ever went to court (Sokolov 2011).

Another such case was that of Sofeks, a midsized chemicals company, whose chief executive officer Aleksei Protskii and chief financial officer Iana Iakovleva were arrested on July 11, 2006, on charges involving narcotics, money laundering, and fraud. That happened only after Protskii and Iakovleva refused to "cooperate" with a two-year investigation, in which context "cooperation" was understood to mean redirecting a sizeable portion of cash flow to the benefit of the investigators (Fedorin 2008). The defendants' lawyer, Evgenii Chernousov, took the case public, enlisting the support of opposition-minded politicians Aleksandr Lebedev and Vladimir Ryzhkov, human rights defenders including Liudmila Alekseeva and a number of prominent journalists. The "chemists' plot"—a moniker reminiscent of the Stalin-era "doctors' plot"—became a common topic in opposition-minded media, including the newspapers *Vedomosti* and *Novaia Gazeta* and the radio station *Ekho Moskvy*. A rally was held on Pushkinskaia Square in central Moscow. Prosecutors never brought the case to court, and Protskii and Iakovleva were released seven months later.

Romanova followed a similar tack. While pushing the case in court and making frequent visits to prison to ensure that her husband was relatively well treated, she used her position as a journalist to ensure that Kozlov's case was never too far from the public view. In September 2010, she managed to get a year lopped off of Kozlov's sentence; in July 2011 another two years were removed, reducing the sentence to five in total. And on September 20, 2011, just four days before Putin announced his plan to return to the Kremlin, Russia's Supreme Court overturned the verdict altogether, returning it for retrial to the Moscow City Court. Kozlov was freed—pending retrial—the next day.

While Public Verdict continued to support the cause of those maligned by an imperfect legal system largely on the back of foreign grants, with some pro bono support from lawyers, the Sofeks and Kozlov cases gave rise to more genuine grassroots mobilization, even if the "grass" in question was particularly and unusually green. Iakovleva enlisted the support of some ninety-one business owners and a range of public figures—Alekseeva, academic and former finance minister Evgenii Iasin, then-Duma Deputy Mikhail Grishankov, journalist Maksim Trudoliubov—to create Biznes Solidarnost' (Business Solidarity), an association dedicated to defending entrepreneurs and enterprises against abusive police, investigators, prosecutors, and judges.[34] Romanova, meanwhile, had become something of a magnet for the wives of other imprisoned businessmen (and, eventually, of prisoners of all sorts), who sought advice on how to deal with investigators, courts, and, particularly, prison officials (Beshlei 2011). Romanova began bringing them together once a week, creating an informal club dubbed Rus' sidiashchaia (Imprisoned Rus'), a mutual aid society, self-help group, and advocacy team rolled into one.

Why Romanova and Iakovleva succeeded in generating grassroots support and more of a "movement" environment, where Public Verdict could not, is an open question. Certainly, Iakovleva and her supporters could bring significantly more of their own resources to the table, simply because they had more resources to begin with; most of the people represented by Public Verdict and its partners were poor. But, although attracting the support of long-time rights defenders and a few prominent journalists, Business-Solidarity never attracted the active solidarity of sympathizers outside its core. Romanova's Rus Sidiashchaia, whose members would attend each others' court hearings, collect care packages for prisoners, and generally provide moral and material support, more closely resembles a traditional social movement, but its base is similarly narrow.

Notably, despite the high public profile that their cases have taken on and their relative successes in court and in the media, neither Business-Solidarity nor Rus Sidiashchaia have been any more successful than Public Verdict in pushing the state into rule- and law-bound practices. Taken together, the three groups and others like them—all with a common grievance and a similar approach—look a lot like the germ of a significant social movement for the defense of human and civil rights in Russia, but for one thing: the stubborn refusal of the state to engage them. Official letters are sent, court cases are fought, but the state continues to react to the movement's challenges as though they were one-off, ad hoc issues, rather than part of a systemic problem. Public Verdict and its comrades may be able to enforce the rights of Russian individuals, but because of the state's incoherence they remain incapable of enforcing the rights of Russians as a whole.

Conclusions

This chapter has attempted to answer the question of why Russian human rights activists have been successful in defending the rights of individual Russians, although failing in their stated goal of encouraging systemic change to ensure that fewer Russians have their rights abused. The approach has been to compare cases in which the organization at hand, Public Verdict, has more successfully defended individuals with cases in which it has faced more difficulties. This comparison was designed to uncover the sources of pressure that may force law enforcement officials to break from their usual routine of nonresponsiveness and pursue a case of injustice.

It has been a complex and difficult investigation, beset by a lack of verifiable evidence and useable methodologies, but I have attempted to triangulate the available evidence to reach at least some sort of valid conclusion. And the conclusion is that the insulation of the system from the public as a whole, combined with the individualization of the relationship between the state and its subjects (the privatization of the law, so to speak), means that there is, in effect, no system to change. If civil society is meant to mediate between two parties, one of which is the state, then Public Verdict finds an interlocutor with which to engage on the defense of individuals but finds none when it raises questions of policy. The reason for this, I have argued, is that a fortuitous confluence of external and internal pressures can create the right incentives for officials to act in citizens' interests; there are, however, no evident circumstances in which the system will reform itself, or allow itself to be reformed, even in the defense of what would outwardly seem to be the regime's own interests. The system, in other words, does not work, but it can be worked. In the remaining paragraphs, I will reiterate and contextualize this conclusion.

In all states, Barrington Moore Jr. writes, "What takes place . . . is a continual probing on the part of rulers and subjects to find out what they can get away with, to test and *discover* the limits of obedience and disobedience" (Moore 1978: 18). This, of course, implies a learning process, like a rat in a lab experiment, faced with a choice between cheese and an electric shock. What is remarkable in the Russian case is that the experiment—rather than being iterative, so that the subject can learn and correct its behavior accordingly—is seemingly reset each time, as though there were no prior experience. Clearly, there are limits to what the state (or those representing it) can get away with, and prices are paid when those limits are overstepped. But while it is hard to believe that Russia's rulers prefer the shock to the cheese, these limits are not transmitted down the chain of command, to police officers, prosecutors, and judges who continue to abuse the law as if Public Verdict had never won a case or as if Russia had never lost in Strasbourg. An alternative explanation is that the price of reform—and, thus, giving up the insulation and autonomy that the elite enjoy—is significantly greater than the pain from the occasional shock. In either case, there do not appear to be any tools available to civil society to alter this equation, all of whose variables seem to lie within the system itself.

Without access to the minds of officials, it is difficult to know whether the problem is one of interests or perceptions. The activists at Public Verdict approach their work as though they were faced with a system in the proper sense, which can be subject to reform. The ruling elite, on the other hand, while recognizing the failures and infractions of individuals, cannot or will not affect mechanisms of control that could alter the unaccountability that pervades the "system." To do so would imply that law and procedure exist to bind the bureaucrat—whether public official, civil servant, or law enforcement officer—into coherent, predictable, and logically transparent courses of interaction with citizens, ultimately accountable to the latter. That, in turn, is antithetical to the system of internal power relations that underpins the functioning of the contemporary Russian state. Recalling the argument about Russian power as a club good made in a previous chapter, the regime and all of its agencies can be expected to act first and foremost to produce power and privilege for the clubs members while making sure that they are insulated in the enjoyment of that power and privilege. The effects of this arrangement are perhaps more starkly seen in this case study than in any other part of this investigation, in some instances costing Russian citizens their lives and health. But these effects pervade the remaining cases as well, as ad hoc policy making in the defense of elite autonomy at turns stymies and encourages civic reactions.

In the final calculation, interests and perceptions are part of one and the same process: Elites perceive and approach the state in ways that are shaped by their interests, and these perceptions inevitably reflect on how they perceive those interests. They may, indeed, misinterpret threats, just as surely as activists may misinterpret the vulnerability of the elites to pressure. In any case, for the elite, the justice system is not a system at all but rather a network of positions of power, each endowed with certain procedural and legal instruments, employed according to the judgment of whichever individual is fortunate enough to wield them.

This, then, suggests that the problem is systemic, but not systematic. And the public seem to incorporate this distinction into their own frame of reference, accepting (and thus socially reinforcing) the lack of a causal link between policy and outcome; they understand the way that bureaucrats use power, the way the state functions (or does not function). And if police maltreatment is not a matter of policy, there is accordingly no use in collective mobilization to alter policy. There remains only individual defense. Thus, Public Verdict, despite its name, remains a very private affair.

6

Our Home Is Russia

Russia's Housing-Rights Movements

The early years of Vladimir Putin's second term as president of Russia brought discontent even to many Russians who haven't been victims of direct abuses of their human and civil rights. In particular, two waves of protests began to sweep the country in late 2004, some of which are still reverberating today. The first was the protest of the so-called *l'gotniki*,[1] pensioners, invalids, students, and others who were affected by a reform that aimed to replace subsidies with cash benefits. And the second is the protest of the so-called *dol'shchiki*,[2] investors in real estate projects who lost their savings and, in most cases, their homes. This chapter will focus on the latter.

Our theory predicts that civil society in general and social movements in particular will thrive when they are able to engage with patterns of intrusion by the state into the private lives of its citizens that are both coherent (in that they affect citizens as a group rather than as individuals) and consistent (in that they affect citizens in ways that are broadly predictable by and understandable to those citizens). In the previous chapter, we saw how the privatization of power in the hands of bureaucrats, in that case law enforcement, inhibits the development of collective, systemic responses to the ubiquitous problem of abuse of human rights by law enforcement officials. This happens, I argue, because the state's intrusion has been haphazard, the product of a dysfunctional system that made power a tool in the hands of individual agents with little or no reference to law and little or no attempt at systemic control. Because the state and the political elite fundamentally refuse to acknowledge the problem as a matter of *policy*, a *political* response is useless. Thus, neither of the two criteria was met, and civic action failed in its stated goal of changing the system.

This chapter examines a case in which the first criterion seems to be met fairly clearly: The policies pursued by the state in general, and the city of Moscow in particular, in the realm of housing have created groups of disenfranchised citizens who stand to lose much—in many cases, their homes—and who are prepared, at least on occasion, to protest this injustice. What we will find, however, is a series of protests, some of them successful, that nevertheless fail to coalesce into a sustained movement. The reason, I will argue, is in the failure of the state to meet the second criterion: It is inconsistent in the way it deals with its citizens, even in matters that can be more or less clearly linked to policy. Citizens are unable to make reasonable predictions about what strategies might prove fruitful and thus are unable to develop the repertoires of civic action and the stable patterns of interaction with the state that social movements need to be successful.

The *L'gotniki*: Setting the Stage

Before examining the housing movements in clearer focus, it is worth taking a moment to review the case of the *l'gotniki*. Indeed, any study of protest in Putin's Russia would be incomplete without at least a mention of the *l'gotniki,* whose uprising first demonstrated the current Russian regime's vulnerability to public sentiment.

On August 2, 2004, between 600 and 1,000 protestors took part in a rally organized by the Communist Party to demand that the State Duma reject a law that would replace subsidies on transport, education, health care, and other needs for pensioners, students, invalids, veterans, and others with cash benefits. Later that day, thirty members of the radical National Bolshevik Party staged a sit in at the Ministry of Health Care and Social Development, while members of two other youth groups, the Red Youth Avant-Garde and the Union of Communist Youth, announced a hunger strike ("30 natsional-bol'shevikov" 2004). The law, which would have affected more than 40 million people, was widely derided, with conventional wisdom holding that the amount of money distributed would not be enough to make up for the benefits, such as free transportation and medicine, lost in the process (Liubarskaia 2004). The Duma, dominated since late 2003 elections by a propresidential supermajority, ignored the protests and passed the law by the end of that week. For the most part, the protestors went home (except for the thirty National Bolsheviks, who went to jail).

Russians came back out onto the streets in January 2005, just days after the law took effect. On January 10 and 11, tens of thousands took part in protests in large and small cities across the country, including Moscow, Nakhodka, Samara, Izhevsk, Penza, Podol'sk, Khimki, and elsewhere; in Khimki, pensioners blocked Leningradskoe Shosse, the main highway connecting Moscow to Sheremet'evo International Airport and St. Petersburg ("Po vsei Rossii proshli" 2005; Prokhorov, Irdullin, et al. 2005). The protests continued on into early February, spreading to Perm, St. Petersburg, Samara, Saratov, Kazan, Ufa, Ulan-Ude, and Vladivostok, while taking on an ever angrier and more overtly political tone (Bondarenko and Migalin 2005). In Perm, protestors went as far as to storm city hall and burn Putin in effigy (Migalin and Zhukova 2005).

Initially, the Kremlin and the leadership of Edinaia Rossiia (United Russia) in the Duma placed the blame on regional governors and bureaucrats, whom they accused of failing properly to explain and implement the reforms; meanwhile, in a number of regions—including in Moscow—local authorities unilaterally (and probably illegally) annulled the changes and reinstated subsidies out of their own budgets. But, by late January, the Duma was already backing away from the reforms, calling (vainly) for heads to roll in the cabinet (Visloguzov 2005). And, in February, Putin announced that the implementation of the reforms would be delayed and phased in over time, allowing many of the initial benefits to remain in place indefinitely, at a cost to the budget of some $10 million (Alekseeva 2005; Grozovskii and Ivanova 2005).

With the bulk of their benefits restored, the *l'gotniki* again went home. The protests, which had brought to the streets numbers of Russians unseen since the early 1990s, failed to yield any lasting organization; rather, protests appeared to be organized primarily by the local branches of the Communist Party, in some cases the Rodina party, which was gradually breaking its ties to the Kremlin (and would soon be disbanded as a result), and various affiliated groups (Bondarenko and Migalin 2005). As a result, what was a protest movement failed to evolve into a social movement.

Nevertheless, the government thought it unwise to tempt fate, and then-Minister of Health and Social Development Mikhail Zurabov in April 2005 announced that he planned to postpone reform of the so-called ZhKKh, the utilities complex, which would have raised rates for another 30 million or so Russians (Grozovskii and Ivanova 2005). Over the course of the rest of the year, however, Zurabov lost the battle with other ministers, and, in the end, regional administrations were given the choice whether to keep subsidies in their regions, starting from January 1, 2006. Thus, in a number of regions, pensioners, invalids, large families, veterans, and others who had been paying subsidized rates for water, heat, and electricity saw rates soar overnight by as much as 20 to 50 percent, while the bulk of the population saw a 10 percent increase (Selina and Riskin 2006). In response, during the second half of January 2006 protests flared up in cities around the country, including Izhevsk, Riazan', Tol'iatti, and Cherepovets, with at least 5,000 protestors braving temperatures of 25 to 30 degrees below zero Celsius (Selina and Riskin 2006). This time, however, the reforms remained in place—with the blame placed squarely on local authorities—and, eventually, the protests subsided. Nonetheless, according to polls taken two months later, 35 percent of Russians—and 46 percent of Russians living below the poverty line—said they were ready to participate in further protests (Chernega and Khamraev 2006).

The Butovo Uprising: Anatomy of a Protest

On June 8, 2006, city officials, accompanied by riot police and bulldozers, arrived at the one-story wooden home of Iuliia Prokof'eva in the neighborhood of South Butovo, on the outskirts of Moscow, to evict its owner and her adult son and tear it down. The Prokof'ev[3] home was to be the first to go, with city officials preparing to demolish two streets full of single-family homes to make way for new high-rises. The injustice was almost poetic: Most of the homes had been built in the 1930s by people evicted from prerevolutionary buildings in central Moscow to make way for Stalin's redevelopment of the city. Residents—most of whom owned their homes but had been prevented by local officials for the better part of a decade from privatizing the land on which they stood—were offered small flats in buildings elsewhere in South Butovo, usually according to the state-established norm of eighteen square meters per individual resident. Thus, Prokof'eva and her son were offered one room in exchange for their house and garden, an offer they refused to accept. When the bulldozers arrived on June 8, Prokof'eva and her neighbors barricaded themselves in her house, called the media, and refused to leave. Riot police succeeded in dragging most of the family's belongings out into the yard, destroying much of their furniture along the way, but, when the scenes made national television, city officials stayed the eviction order and agreed to negotiations.

In the days that followed, neighbors and other Muscovites organized a permanent vigil outside the Prokof'ev home, ranging from twenty to 200 protesters at any given time, complete with a tent camp and an almost permanent contingent of journalists. Within a few days, the protesters began receiving visits from members of the newly formed Public Chamber, a state-convened group of Kremlin-approved representatives of "civil society" charged with mediating between the public and the authorities. Two members in particular, the attorney Anatolii Kucherena and the television journalist Nikolai Svanidze, made a public show of excoriating city officials, including then-Mayor Yury Luzhkov and City Duma Chairman Vladimir Platonov, while promising to seek action on behalf of the Butovo residents. After a month of protests, the city scrapped the eviction order altogether and agreed to seek a negotiated solution. A year later, Prokof'eva and her son accepted two apartments in Stalin-era buildings in the prestigious Kutuzovskii Prospekt neighborhood, and Prokof'eva herself was made an adviser to the Moscow branch of the Kremlin-backed Spravedlivaia Rossiia political party. Less favorable outcomes were offered to other residents, and conflicts flared up from time to time, but the city eventually pulled down all the homes in the neighborhood.[4]

I first visited the Prokof'ev home on June 22, 2006, two weeks after the initial raid, when the protests had come off their peak but were still going strong. The house itself was covered in makeshift banners, with slogans including "Force is not an argument," "This is our land," and "One law for all." On one corner of the house, near the wall, hung a Russian flag, the state seal, the text of the national anthem, and a portrait of Putin. Another wall was covered in news clippings and letters and telegrams of support from around the country. When I arrived, there was a core of about twenty protesters, congregated around the house and six tents, watching World Cup football on television and conversing with visitors from other neighborhoods, activists from opposition parties, and journalists. By the time I left in the evening, the group had swollen to about sixty, several announcements had been read out, and a petition had been signed.

One protester, a woman in her late forties and a neighbor whose house was also slated for demolition, described the situation as follows:

> *Question:* How long have you been here?
>
> *Answer:* Well, we have been trying to do this the right way, the normal way, for six years, from the moment they started to put pressure on us seriously. But we've been standing right here in this place since the 8th, when they first stormed the house.
>
> *Q:* Do you have some sort of initiative group?
>
> *A:* Yes, we have an initiative group in the village. They are people who have been dealing with legal issues, trying to prove our rights in court. . . . They are residents of our village, who had just been studying the documents; someone had a legal education . . .
>
> *Q:* Is this a fairly typical scene right now?

A: No. The thing is, right now they're trying to solve the problem in the courts, and with the authorities, to get the decision reversed. So right now it's just a core group here, who get things organized, when we need to get people together for a message or when we need to make a decision and get it out to people. We gather everybody here. There are always at least five or six people on duty here, on shifts, plus the tent city, where people live full-time.

Q: And the people on duty are all local?

A: All residents of the village, whose flesh and blood depends on what happens.[5]

The protesters were joined by activists from other Moscow neighborhoods and suburbs, including Sokol'niki, Zhulebino, Kurkino, Kur'ianovo, Nizhnie Mnevniki, and Krasnogorsk, where residents face similar threats to their homes; they had come to Butovo mostly to provide moral support. A van full of police officers was permanently parked outside the gate, but the officers did not interact with the protesters, and law enforcement was otherwise nowhere to be seen. Just in case, however, the tent camp housed around ten muscular young men, in their twenties and thirties, whose function was to make it that much more difficult for the police to perform another raid. The protesters were periodically approached by representatives of opposition political parties, including the Communists and the Union of Right-Wing Forces. Journalists were broadly welcomed, particularly from the national television channels and from foreign news bureaus, but the protesters angrily evicted a camera crew from TV-Tsentr, a television channel loyal to Mayor Luzhkov. Periodically, conversation outside the Prokof'ev home was drowned out by the sound of demolition work on neighboring lots, where residents had already agreed to the city's terms and turned their homes over to the bulldozers.

Mobilization

The participants in the Butovo protest were a fairly motley bunch. At one end of the yard, nearest the Prokof'ev house, stood the organizers, the "professionals" and activists, and the visitors from other neighborhoods and Moscow suburbs, such as Larisa Solomatina, a municipal legislator from the Moscow neighborhood of Sokol'niki, who came to Butovo with her neighbors and fellow activists in their local campaign to stop unwanted construction. At the other end of the yard, seven men in their twenties and thirties sat, accompanied by three young ladies, drinking beer, eating baked potatoes, smoking, and watching World Cup soccer on a portable television. Although they came from all over Moscow, unlike the visitors from Sokol'niki they came not as part of a movement but because they are neighbors or friends or friends of friends of people living in the neighborhood. Although they asked that the tape recorder be turned off and that no notes be taken, one summed up the group's motivation as follows: "I will never let anyone beat my friend. I came to defend my friend." Although they were clearly an integral part of the protest, they had little or no interaction with the "professional activists," who tended to congregate closer to the house.

Between these two groups, what I will call "accidental" protesters were milling around. One of them, a man in his early fifties, wearing a tracksuit, explained his presence as follows:

> *Question:* What brought you here?
> *Answer:* I have the time. And nothing else to do. Also, I saw them on television. And it's all happening next door.
> *Q:* So, out of sympathy?
> *A:* Of course. I feel sorry for people who are being kicked out of their homes like dogs.[6]

Other, less "accidental," protesters included neighbors, owners of homes also slated for demolition, such as the forty-something woman quoted earlier. Their reasons for coming would seem to be clear: By defending the Prokof'ev home, they were defending their own. Indeed, this neighbor, who I'll call Irina, confirms that in her outlook:

> *Question:* Do you have the feeling that you can achieve some sort of result?
> *Answer:* You know, I hope so. I'm an optimist by nature. I hope. It's scary to think about how we'll go on living if we don't achieve anything. It's just lawlessness. We've run into the fact that we have no way of defending our rights whatsoever.[7]

But this is not a simple case of desperation leading to a need to act. One protester, who I'll call Vadim, a man in his late twenties or early thirties who, like Irina, owns a home slated for destruction, took a very different point of view:

> *Question:* Are you a local resident?
> *Answer:* Yes, I'm local, and a homeowner.
> *Q:* I understand that this battle has been going on for several years.
> *A:* Yes, yes.
> *Q:* Do you have any hope of success?
> *A:* Personally, no.

Q: So, you figure you'll end up living in one of those [big apartment] buildings?

A: For me, that's the worst possible scenario. In principle, I don't want anything. I want to be left alone to live in my own home. But I'm a realist, and I understand that in the end, nothing good will come of this. I'll have to [move] . . .

Q: So why are you spending your time here [at this protest]?

A: I'm an active sympathizer.[8]

This difference in outlook—and thus the different mobilizational logics driving the protesters—seems to stem primarily from personal experience. Irina and Vadim are a case in point. During our interview, I tried to challenge Vadim to explain his pessimism:

Question: But you don't think there will be any result . . .

Answer: I think that it's such an uneven battle . . .

Q: And what do you think these people are counting on, then?

A: These people? It's just desperation, a reaction to injustice. A human reaction. I understand that.

Q: And the fact that people came from other neighborhoods . . .

A: It's the same thing, because something's happening that's not right, and people just feel it.

Q: Does the solidarity make you feel better?

A: Personally, no. I think that if the authorities come to deal with me, I wouldn't call anybody to help me, I'd take it calmly.

Q: Why?

A: Well, how to put it. I don't want people to waste their time, when it's already clear how it's going to end.

Q: And if someone called you to help, would you go?

A: I'd go, yes. But I wouldn't call somebody for myself. Because, on the one hand, it's just financially difficult. Count the dough, lost profits, count up the losses. [Laughs] It's when they've got your back up against the wall, when you've got nothing to lose, then it's different . . . I had an episode, when my house here burned down. And I tried to get the right, although it sounds dumb, to rebuild it along the lines of the same foundation. Neither the district nor the prefecture would give me permission. And it was my only home. If my bathhouse hadn't burned down as well, I would have had to live in that, like in the olden days. After that, I gave up on it all, and I just built my house. On the lot my house used to be on, I built a house. I decided, in the end, I've got to live somewhere. And then I was able to go to court to get the rights to the house. Believe me, it wasn't easy. It took from 2001 to 2004. And to do that, you need to not work; you need to spend all of your time on it, and I wasn't the only one working on it. It's awful, really.[9]

Vadim's pessimism, then, is not normative, nor does it stem from a feeling of mistrust of other citizens; indeed, he has nothing but goodwill for his neighbors. Rather, his outlook is based in personal experience, an experience he believed showed the futility of fighting with the state, or even of trying to "use" the state in any normal sense. Instead, Vadim puts stock in solutions that are first and foremost pragmatic, avoiding the authorities whenever possible, not because he has an ideological aversion to authority but because, in his experience, dealing with the government makes life harder.

Irina's relative optimism, by contrast, is driven by exactly the sort of desperation that Vadim talks about, but it is also bolstered by experience with other protests that have brought at least incremental success and that are closely tied with her local interests:

> *Question:* Do you consider yourself a politicized person?
>
> *Answer:* I can't say I'm politicized. But in any case, I stay on top of events, and I'm not oblivious to what happens.
>
> *Q:* You vote . . .
>
> *A:* I go to the elections, yes.
>
> *Q:* And have you ever been to any protests or rallies?
>
> *A:* To the protests that affect me, yes; I go to all of the protests about this village, about the sale of the Butovo forest; I was at the protest for that, too. If the problem affects me . . .
>
> *Q:* In 1991 or 1993, did you go to the White House?
>
> *A:* No, in 1991 and 1993 I wasn't at the White House, not directly, but I was on top of all the events, I worried about them, sympathized. So, in that regard, political life doesn't pass me by.[10]

The most optimistic of all of the protesters I interviewed, meanwhile, was a woman I'll call Viktoria, who came in with Larisa Solomatina from Sokol'niki. In her interview, it became clear that her outlook derives directly from the experience of successful protests, described earlier in this chapter. To get a clearer picture, I asked her to describe how her movement got started:

> *Question:* How long has your group existed? When was it organized?
>
> *Answer:* In 2002. It was all started on Eger'skaia Street, when they wanted to build an illegal construction . . .
>
> *Q:* Pinpoint construction?
>
> *A:* Yes, yes. It was all over the television. We got it all on camera; there were camera crews, in the newspapers, everywhere. Against the pinpoint construction. The residents stopped it. We threw ourselves under the bulldozers. It was

everywhere. [Deputy Mayor Vladimir] Resin himself came. They banned that project, and the lot is still empty.

Q: And your initiative still exists?

A: Yes, yes.

Q: What keeps it going? Are you still battling against the same project?

A: Well, see, we have Larisa Ivanovna [Solomatina], our deputy in the local municipal assembly. We are residents. So, we elected two deputies from among the residents: Shevelev and Solomatina, here, who support us, and the residents support them, and they defend residents' rights in the municipal assembly. . . .

Q: I understand. So, how many people take part in your initiative?

A: There are a lot of us.

Q: For example, fifty, a hundred?

A: No. A lot. If there's this kind of situation, then very many. Because where we live, in Sokol'niki, the abuse by the authorities is horrendous.

Q: Where do you get the resources?

A: From the residents. . . .

Q: And has it been difficult to get people organized?

A: No.

Q: People have been eager to get involved?

A: We have a lot of educated, smart people among the residents. . . . Right now we're forming Residential Ownership Unions in our buildings so that we can at least somehow stand up to this abuse, as a legal entity, so we can talk to the authorities not just as simple residents. . . .

Q: Four years ago, when this got started, did someone come to you and say, "I can help you," someone like Solomatina?

A: No, we did it ourselves. We got ourselves organized, and then, when we understood that we are residents and simply as residents we can't get anything done, we understood that we need our own people, so we can at least know what's going on there [in government]. And there was an election campaign, and we nominated candidates, and we had a very tumultuous electoral campaign.[11]

Notably, Vadim, Irina, and Viktoria share the same basic view of the political system as corrupt, impenetrable, and stacked against the common citizen. The only place they differ is on the usefulness of protest: Vadim, having fought and lost, is pessimistic; Irina, having fought and survived to fight another day, is mildly optimistic; and Viktoria, having fought and won, firmly believes that solidarity brings results. Viktoria's view was by far the rarest, while Vadim's was easily the most common among the protestors present. This is perhaps unsurprising, except when taken in the context of much of the writing on Russian civil society, which generally argues that Russians are led by their Soviet past and their ostensibly low levels of social capital to be protest averse. The observation of this protest, at least, suggests the opposite: Russians are willing to protest when they believe it might work, and they lose faith in protest and grassroots politics more generally when their initial hopes are dashed.

The Broader Movement Environment

The Butovo protests were in no way unique. Although they are rarely written about in the press, and even many experts are unaware of them, the entire history of Putin's Russia has seen several small protests in Moscow every week, most of which involve housing: either demolition and/or eviction orders that are perceived as unfair; construction of new residential and commercial buildings in what used to be yards, parks, and playgrounds; failure of local officials to provide adequate maintenance; and so on. Most of these protests are small, with the involvement only of a dozen or two local residents. The available evidence, however, suggests that they are not necessarily short lived: From conversations with neighborhood activists, there is both a realization on the part of residents that mobilization is necessary and no shortage of issues around which to mobilize. Moreover, the leaders of these protests frequently seem to become movement professionals (though not professional activists): They are aware of precedents in other neighborhoods and are in contact with the organizers of other protests.

Perhaps the clearest example of this is the "delegation" from the northern Moscow neighborhood of Sokol'niki to the Butovo protests. In 2002, local officials tried to carry out plans for what is referred to as "pinpoint construction,"[12] placing new buildings in the yards of older buildings, only meters away from existing structures. One of the Sokol'niki protest leaders, Larisa Solomatina, later became a member of the local municipal council and now offers advice and moral support to protests across the city, including in Butovo. She recalls:

> We had a situation in 2003, when they wanted to build a building five meters away from an existing structure. And it's only thanks to the active position of residents [that we stopped it]. We fought for two months, brought in the media, CNN, BBC; we had radio, television, the same tents [you see here in Butovo]. They had already brought a truck with building materials, brought out the riot police, and people lay down under the bulldozers. Some of them ended up in hospital. And we understood that this is the only way we can defend our rights. Together, only together.[13]

Despite the activities of protest leaders such as Solomatina, however, most of these neighborhood protests remain disconnected from each other, and, while protesters may recognize common grievances, they do not perceive a common agenda.

Networked protest movements involving housing issues have arisen primarily in response to problems that affect more geographically dispersed groups of citizens in more or less the same way. The clearest case of this is the so-called movement of defrauded coinvestors or *dol'shchiki*, who bought the rights to apartments in buildings yet to be constructed—most often selling their previous apartments to raise the cash—only to have the developers either go bankrupt or simply abscond with the money. Unable to obtain their apartments or their money back from the developers—and unwilling to write off their losses in a city that saw property prices triple from 2004 to 2007—the *dol'shchiki* turned to city and federal authorities for help. This, however, has not been forthcoming, and protests have frequently been dispersed by riot police. To further their cause, the *dol'shchiki* have come together in two ways. First, they have created "coordinating councils" of victims of particular firms, a logical step given that each developer's case is unique in its detail. The biggest of these coordinating councils is made up of victims of the ironically named residential developer "Social Initiative." Several attempts were made to bring these councils together under a single umbrella. Although most of these failed to coalesce over strategy, the most recent attempt—an organization called *Pis'mo Vlasti*, or "Letter to the Authorities"—seems to have succeeded by seeking to concentrate not on strategic engagement with the state but on transmitting a basic list of common demands to the government. In addition to writing open letters and petitions, though, the group has been instrumental in organizing joint protests and a major hunger strike.

Unlike other recent Russian protestors, such as the *l'gotniki*, who rose up to demand that the government reinstate benefits and subsidies for retirees and the handicapped, the *dol'shchiki* took to the streets to protest not what the government did but what it didn't do: Namely, it failed to protect them from one of the most destructive and widespread scams in post-Soviet Russian history. Over the course of the building boom that accompanied Russia's rapid oil-fueled economic growth after the 1998 financial crisis, ordinary Russians across the country invested in something called *dolevoe stroitel'stvo*, or "share construction." Real estate developers would take payment up front from would-be apartment owners, prior to the construction of a building, and then use that money to finance construction, rather than taking debt or equity capital and building on speculation; in return for the wait—which was usually meant to be one to two years—buyers got deep discounts compared to the going rate for new apartments. For the majority of participants, it worked. However, in 2003 and 2004 news reports started appearing about unscrupulous developers who would sometimes sell the same unit two or three times prior to disappearing, leaving the buyers to sort out the mess in the courts, or, more frequently, the developers would abscond with the money without completing construction. By some estimates, some 10,000 people in the Moscow suburbs and 200,000 across the country—many of whom had sold their previous apartments to buy in—were taken in by such scams (Morochenko 2005; Grishin and Tsikulina 2006).

The defrauded investors, who came to be known as *dol'shchiki*, started holding small protests in which they called for local and federal authorities to bring the developers to justice and help them recover their investments. In early 2005, the Duma enacted a new housing law, which came into effect in April of that year, banning "share construction" altogether and retroactively mandating recompense for those who had lost their investments (Ignat'eva and Finaeva 2005). By the end of 2005, however, only some 6,500 people had seen their cases resolved (Granina 2005). As a result, the *dol'shchiki* began stepping up their protests, focusing increasing attention on federal authorities, who they demanded intervene directly in their plight; unlike the *l'gotniki*, however, the *dol'shchiki* did not criticize the government directly.

Events came to a head on May 19, 2006, when 1,500 *dol'shchiki* from Moscow, Voronezh, Smolensk, Belgorod, Tambov', Orenburg, and St. Petersburg gathered at the Gorbatyi Bridge, a symbolic place of protest outside the White House, the seat of the Russian cabinet of ministers (Petrenko and Stenin 2006). There, they set up a tent camp and vowed not to leave until someone from the government came out to meet them. Rather than ministers, however, they were met by riot police. The police set up a ring around the tent camp, with 600 *dol'shchiki* inside. As the day wore on, the numbers of protesters dwindled, such that at midnight, when the police charged, there were only 100 inside the tent camp. Of those, thirty-four were arrested, and the camp was smashed. On May 22, three days later, the leaders of the protest returned to the site, having been promised a meeting with ministers; instead, they were met by the head of the government's public relations department and asked to write a petition to Prime Minister Mikhail Fradkov and Regional Development Minister

Aleksandr Iakovlev (Kozenko 2006). The petition included three demands, none of which its signers thought would be met: a meeting with Putin, a demand that they be fully compensated or that the government complete their buildings, and confirmation that they remained loyal to the regime (Kozenko 2006). Two days later, on May 24, 2006, the Duma leadership of Edinaia Rossiia demanded that the government meet the demands of the *dol'shchiki* (Khmelev 2006). Whether that will actually happen remains to be seen; as of early 2014, no overarching resolution had been reached, and the cases of many *dol'shchiki* continued to languish.

The State and the Movement

In contrast to the *l'gotniki*, discussed briefly at the beginning of this chapter, the *dol'shchiki* did develop an organizational infrastructure. Largely, this happened out of necessity, as the investors in each particular development formed more or less formal coordinating committees to handle criminal and civil lawsuits against the developers (Grishin and Tsikulina 2006; Utkin 2006). These, in turn, formed the Union of Coordinating Committees, which, in its turn, created an Internet site with a forum for discussing problems and potential actions, akin to that of *Svoboda Vybora*, examined in more detail in the next chapter.[14] However, conflicts eventually arose within the movement, regarding how best to approach the problem, what demands to press on the government, and whom to criticize. As a result, some of the leaders suggested that the May 19, 2006, protest may have been the last joint protest that the movement holds (Kozenko 2006). Nonetheless, at least some progress toward consolidation has been made, making the *dol'shchiki* and the broader housing movement a useful case for study.

As a general tactic, the *dol'shchiki* movement developed a straightforward set of demands and vowed to hold regular protests until the demands were met. The *Pis'mo Vlasti* umbrella organization published the demands as an open letter to the government and the public: "We demand from the President of the Russian Federation, guarantor of the Constitution of the RF, the restoration of the abrogated rights and freedoms of the citizens of Russia suffering from abuse and fraud in construction."[15] The letter contained three points of action: (1) recognition that the situation of the *dol'shchiki* represented a national emergency; (2) the appointment of a person and the creation of an agency responsible for resolving the problems of the *dol'shchiki*, with representation from the *dol'shchiki* themselves; and (3) setting a deadline of September 30, 2007, to re-solve each individual case.

In the preamble to the letter, the movement notes that Putin, in one of his regular teleconferences with the nation, ostensibly recognized the state's guilt in the crisis, thus providing sufficient ground for the movement's demands.[16] The state, however, saw things differently. While Putin did from time to time decry the crisis, none of the demands was met. The closest the state came to compromise was creating a commission in the Public Chamber, led by Anatolii Kucherena, the same lawyer who had offered to help the Butovo protesters. The commission, however, is only an advisory body and has no executive or lawmaking authority.

The state's unwillingness or inability directly to address the problem led to an increasing number of protests, many of which were broken up by riot police. In April 2007, the *dol'shchiki* held a hunger strike, occupying the ground floor of one of the unfinished buildings at the heart of the conflict. Law enforce-ment officials encircled the building with riot police, boarded up the windows, cut off electricity, and forbade the passage of water and medicine to the hun-ger strikers, suggesting that to do so would amount to aiding extremists. The strike received no coverage on national television. The Unified Coordinating Committee of the Victims of Construction, which organized the strike, wrote that even the terrorists who took the audience of the Nord-Ost musical hos-tage in Moscow "were more humane" than the authorities who dealt with the *dol'shchiki* hunger strike.[17]

Reactions to protest by other parts of the broader housing movement have differed, however. As already mentioned, in the Butovo case the authorities called off the riot police, sat down with the Prokof'evs and others, and nego-tiated a solution. This, though, was only part of the difference. The conflict in Butovo was widely covered in the media, including on all of the Kremlin-controlled television channels, and most of the coverage was supportive of the protesters. Moscow Mayor Iurii Luzhkov himself came in for sharp criti-cism, while some of his cadres—principally Moscow City Council Chairman Vladimir Platonov—were forced to answer uncomfortable questions on televi-sion. While it is difficult to know exactly why this happened, it is clear that it was permissible to attack Luzhkov and the Moscow authorities for a local scan-dal, in a way that the media would not have been allowed to cover a national is-sue for which federal authorities might be held to account. Clearly, the political opportunity structure can make it possible for protesters to gain leverage, and this was certainly part of the story in Butovo.

That is not to say, however, that the state gave up. As mentioned earlier, the authorities identified the Prokof'evs as ringleaders of the protest, offered them a settlement that removed them from the neighborhood, and continued the demolition of homes. Meanwhile, in Sokol'niki, after local protesters were successful in stopping a construction project, city officials removed the district prefect and appointed a new one. In the words of local activist and council-woman Larisa Solomatina, "He is a military man, and he said, 'I'm a specialist in dislodging enemy troops.' And now that dislodging is going on in our neighborhood," through a combination of buyouts, harassment, and co-optation.[18]

This inconsistent approach on the part of the state—repressing in one case, undermining in another, and acquiescing (at least temporarily) in a third—impedes the development of the expectations that are needed for the movement to coalesce and institutionalize. As we have already seen, protesters' expectations regarding outcomes, and thus their willingness to invest time, resources, and effort in the movement, arise largely from past experiences. Wittingly or otherwise, by failing to be predictable the state deprives the movement of common experiences and expectations that cut across geography and time, with the result that protest is, at best, sustainable only on a very local level or on a narrow issue area.

There is an interesting, and perhaps unexpected, side effect of this mobilizational blockage, however. In theory, it would seem that there is common issue-oriented ground for the construction of an injustice frame that would unify the *dol'shchiki* with protesters in places like Butovo and Sokol'niki, namely the failure of the state to protect and enforce property rights (and, indeed, the state's frequent complicity in their infringement). I have just suggested, and social movement theory generally suggests, that, without reasonable expectations of success, such common grounds are insufficient. Interestingly, however, the issue of property rights is only rarely discussed as such by the protesters and activists. To be sure, they universally demand that the state defend their right to live in their homes. But the conversation very quickly moves on to what they perceive to be the crux of the issue: the disconnect between the Russian state and the Russian people.

In Butovo back in 2006, I asked "Vadim" whether he thought that the situation with housing and property rights would ever change. He replied, "Given the current regime, I don't think so." He laughed, before continuing: "For me, the situation is perfectly clear. As long as there is oil in the pipeline, none of these people is needed. There is a policy to destroy the population, naturally, or sort of naturally. They're counting on us to die off here on our own."[19] He laughed again. Not everyone has the same sense of humor, nor the same conspiracy theories, but the sentiment was almost universal. Thus, Larisa Solomatina said:

> There are little shoots growing here and there of self-awareness, of civic dignity. They are very small, but I'm afraid that, in Russian history, that's enough for an explosion. There's a feeling in the air that everybody's fed up—each in his own way, but everybody. Look, I'm a councilwoman, and people come to me crying, and I don't know how to help them, even though I know exactly how the executive authorities could do in two minutes what they haven't done in years, if they only had the will.[20]

After numerous failed strikes, the *dol'shchiki*, too, began to become convinced that no one "on high" really had the will to help. Starting from autumn 2006, most major threads on the largest *dol'shchiki* Internet forum—that of those defrauded by the Social Initiative company—became dominated by discussions of politics, with only tangential references to the housing issue. A typical example is an exchange that took place in October 2006.[21] The thread was begun by a suggestion that the government might offer interest-free loans to the *dol'shchiki*, which sparked an angry reaction from almost all activists, understandably indignant at the idea of paying again for apartments they had already purchased. Early into the discussion, one participant, using the nickname Shamov, wrote:

> Why should we pay more? How can you pay again for what you've already paid in full? That would be like going to a store, paying the cashier 30 rubles for a packet of milk, and then having the salesman come up and say, "Surprise! We've got a complicated situation here! So, we'll need another 100 rubles for that milk."

To which another participant, nicknamed Pero-ok, replied:

> Right, but that's in a normal store, where the laws to protect consumers function properly, and in our case the laws don't work!

Shamov replied:

> But is that really a reason to pay again? To my mind, it's a reason to do something to improve the functioning of the law.

Another activist, paz, interjected:

> And what, exactly, elect a new regime? The question is only, are we capable of doing that? Most residents of Russia are perfectly happy with the current situation. And with this regime, I personally doubt that we'll be able to achieve anything.

To which Shamov replied:

> Electing new people to power won't change anything at all. We simply have to constantly remind those in power that they serve the people, and not the other way around. Not directly, of course, but through those who sit higher up . . . through protests, expressing discontent. The majority of Russian residents—who are they? Even in Moscow far from everyone is happy. And the fact that they are silent certainly doesn't mean that they are satisfied with everything. What's more, they even talk about their dissatisfaction, but for some reason only among themselves, where nobody can hear them.

It is striking that, despite differing levels of success, different expectations and the resulting difficulty of forming a coherent movement, all the submovements and protomovements examined in this chapter share a common sense of injustice. This is of crucial importance, both practically and theoretically.

Epilogue: The Ballad of Khimki Forest

Mikhail Beketov, most likely, couldn't hear the songs, and even if he could, he couldn't sing along. It was August, 22, 2010, and Iurii Shevchuk—frontman of the rock band DDT, a mainstay of late-Soviet counterculture—was on the stage at Moscow's Pushkin Square, singing on behalf of some old oak trees 19 kilometers up the road. He was singing, too, on behalf of Beketov, once the editor of the local newspaper *Khimkinskaya Pravda*, which in the spring of 2007 began a long crusade against plans to run a new Moscow–St. Petersburg highway through the town's old-growth forest. About two years and nine months before the concert, on November 13, 2008, Beketov was attacked at his home, his knees and skull shattered. He died April 8, 2013, never having regained his ability to walk or speak.

After the attack on Beketov, the torch for the Khimki Forest was taken up by Evgeniia Chirikova, a young mother with an engineering degree, an MBA, and an electrical design business she ran with her husband. In 1998, the couple had moved to Khimki from their Moscow neighborhood, where the green, open spaces they had once valued were rapidly being bought up and given over to high-rise apartment developments. It was the very beginning of the "pinpoint construction" phenomenon, in which the city of Moscow began selling off the spaces between apartment blocks for new building. They found a place on the edge of the forest in Khimki, where they, and eventually their children, could enjoy walks and the fresh air (Svetova 2010). Many of those who could not or would not move joined the not-in-my-back-yard protest groups described earlier in this chapter.

But less than a decade after they moved, the suburban idyll came to an end. Soon after the announcement by Moscow Region Governor Boris Gromov in 2006 that the new high-speed toll road would cut through the forest, the bulldozers and tree-fellers rolled in. Like the local neighborhood protest groups described earlier, Chirikova and her Khimki neighbors quickly came to understand their struggle as simultaneously local and political: It was the local grievance, the not-in-my-back-yard anger, that mobilized them, but it was the frustration at a political system in which they had neither purchase nor franchise that kept them angry.

Chirikova began posting flyers around her neighborhood, telling neighbors about Gromov's announcement and Khimki Mayor Vladimir Strel'chenko's complicity. Along the way, she met Beketov. The attack on Beketov occurred three weeks before the start of the election campaign for the Khimki mayoralty, and Strel'chenko was up for reelection. Chirikova registered and campaigned with a single plank in her platform: Reroute the road. Strel'chenko won, while Chirikova came in third.

The bureaucracy and courts were no more effective than electoral politics. Official complaints and appeals, mostly centering on the legally protected status of the forest, and thus the illegality of the construction orders, fell on deaf ears. "Putin supports it, and that means it's law," she said she was told (Al'bats 2011). But more aggressive tactics, such as occupations and sit-ins in Iuzhnoe Butovo and other Moscow neighborhoods and suburbs, where people fought to save their homes, parks, and lifestyles, had shown the relative efficacy of active measures. Chirikova and others organized a permanent presence in the forest, a tent camp to monitor deforestation and construction activity. From time to time, activists would lie down in front of the bulldozers and tussle with security guards. Bruises and broken bones were not infrequent results.

But the carnage had little effect. Officials continued to press forward with the road, brushing the protesters out of the way. Chirikova took the fight to Paris, picketing the headquarters of Vinci, the French infrastructure company that had won the contract to build the road. The movement filed suit in the European Court of Human Rights in Strasbourg, alleging violation of Russia's own environmental protection legislation. But in February of 2010 the government issued a report claiming that the clearing of a 43-kilometer-long tract of the forest was the "most ecologically friendly" of all possible routes for the road, and in March the Russian Supreme Court confirmed transfer of the forest from the forestry department to the transport department of the Federal Property Agency ("Vse varianty dorogi do Petersburga" 2010).

If for the Khimki environmentalists the spring of 2010 was cold, the summer was hot. On July 23, private security forces cleared the monitoring camp out of the forest, roughing up the protesters in the process, as police and media looked on. A month later, Chirikova and her colleagues decided to take the fight out of the forest and into the center of Moscow. And so, on August 22, she found herself next to one of Russia's biggest rock stars. There were others there, too, including singer Mikhail Borzykin, pop music critic Artemii Troitskii, human rights leader Liudmila Alekseeva, and left-wing leader Sergei Udal'tsov. But it was Shevchuk who grabbed the headlines:

> It seems to me, the biggest problem in our country is that there's a whole lot of cynicism. For a little bit of profit we're ready to send nature to hell. I want to congratulate the police and the riot police, the most active participants of all the dissenters' marches. We are not enemies of the state. In fact, we're the patriots, but in the real sense. The enemies of the state are the corrupt bureaucrats who are right there next to the Kremlin. It's time to put an end to this bureaucratic abuse. We need a civil society. (Timofeev 2010)

While Shevchuk had long been close to the opposition—including serving on the board of *Novaia Gazeta*, a prominent antigovernment newspaper—this marked the first time a major celebrity had come to the forefront of a cause that was so blatantly political. It would not be the last.

Conclusions

In the previous chapter, I suggested that the haphazard way in which law enforcement agencies interact with citizens inhibits the development of a coherent sense of injustice regarding abuses of human rights. In this case, by contrast, the sense of injustice is both clear and clearly shared. It is worth recalling here social movement theory, which argues that "what is at issue is not

merely the presence or absence of grievances, but the manner in which grievances are interpreted and the generation and diffusion of those interpretations"
(Snow and Rochford 1986: 466; see also Jasper 1998; Kurzman 2004). The fact
of shared grievance—and the perception, at least among some protestors, that
their grievances are indeed shared—helps in the development of what Gamson
(1968) refers to as "solidary groups," "collections of individuals who think in
terms of the effect of political decision on the aggregate and feel that they are
in some way personally affected by what happens to the aggregate." This, again,
was demonstrably absent in the previous chapter.

Moreover, it is notable that the greatest injustice is perceived not in the core
movement issues of housing and property rights but in the state's failure to
engage with the movement in meaningful and constructive ways, in the state's
propensity to repress and disperse rather than to address and negotiate. This,
too, is predicted in social movement theory, and in particular by Gamson
(1968), who writes that citizens who are systematically unable to achieve redress will begin to lose trust not only in their officials but in the system of
power relations itself.

It is remarkable how quickly the protomovement and its participants rise
above the ground-level issues to much loftier considerations of rights and
their relationship with the state. Although the protests themselves are mostly
local, and although slogans seek primarily redress of particular grievances,
the protestors in conversation complain of much greater injustices. Rather
than citing the mundane interests that may be behind the decision to raze
any particular neighborhood, they rail against a state that refuses to take citizens seriously, that refuses to offer and play by consistent rules. Their despair
is driven by a feeling of powerlessness that goes well beyond their specific
grievances. And their hope is bolstered by the fact that they are joined in solidarity by protestors from other neighborhoods who, despite differing particular problems, share the same generalized grievance and speak the same
language of injustice.

And yet despite the movement's successes at aggregating the grievances of
its members, at framing those grievances politically, and at building a degree of
solidarity, the mobilization remains a failure. Although individuals are sometimes able to attain redress, and although some groups are able to obtain temporary victories, the state remains as unchastened as in the previous chapter.
It is the protestors who rise up to a higher level, ready to discuss their general

relationship with the state; the state, on the other hand, remains stubbornly mired in the mud of construction sites, unwilling or unable to talk about the bigger picture. Indeed, the protestors themselves—and even the most optimistic among them—do not believe that they can open up the system for their demands to be heard. Their only hope, they say, is to stand fast between the bulldozers and their homes.

7 Road Rage
Russia's Automotive Rebellion

Nikolai Gogol once wrote that Russia suffers primarily from two problems: fools and roads.[1] The misery is thus doubled when the two intersect. After all, as most Russians would undoubtedly argue, the roads are most often built, driven on, and policed by idiots. So, even to the casual observer, it comes as no surprise that Russians are perpetually perturbed by just about everything that has to do with automotive transport.

It was thus, perhaps, predictable that the government would meet some resistance when, in early 2005, it proposed banning all right-hand-drive cars. This would have posed a particular problem in Vladivostok, Khabarovsk, and most other cities east of Lake Baikal, where large numbers of drivers own used cars imported directly from Japan; indeed, in Vladivostok it is extremely difficult to find a car with the steering wheel on the left side. By some estimates, there are 1.5 million right-side-drive cars in the country (Buranov 2005). Few if any, however, expected a reaction with the scale and scope that was eventually witnessed. Within the space of a year, the resulting movement evolved into one of the country's largest grassroots organizations, tackling issues well beyond the right to drive on the wrong side of the car. In the ensuing years, it also proved to be perhaps Russia's most enduring movement, surviving the cooptation of its first leadership and regrouping in new configurations as circumstances demanded. In this case study, we will ask how and, more important, why.

Much of the analysis presented here is based on a thorough review of six topical "threads" from the movement's initial on-line forum, where issues are raised and debated and plans for action are developed and distributed. The threads analyzed run from January 13 to August 1, 2006, and comprise 816 individual messages or "posts." The first two of the threads document the development, planning, and execution of the group's largest protest in 2006. The third thread concerns interaction between group members and the authorities, particularly the traffic police. The fourth and fifth threads are dominated by discussion of potential new campaigns. And the sixth thread concerns the group's integration into the broader sphere of opposition groups in Russia. These are augmented by two in-depth interviews of the group's founder and first leader, Vyacheslav Lysakov, conducted in Moscow on February 20 and April 28, 2006. And all of this is supplemented by information drawn from dozens of publications in the Russian press, as well as by interviews with the second generation of leaders who began to emerge in 2008.

Before launching into the case, it is worth recalling one key aspect of social movement theory: Because social movements are *processes* rather than things, developed dynamically through action, reaction, and interaction, analysis requires not a static dissection of a movement at a given point in time but a study of development over time. This is all the more true if we aim to draw out evidence relating to the hypothesis of this work, namely that the successful crystallization of civil society requires sustained engagement by the state *over time*. Thus, the structure of the case study to follow echoes the theory as presented in earlier chapters and as drawn from social movement theory more broadly. I will begin with the movement's genesis, that is, the initial incursion into the private sphere by the state, the public response, and the state's reaction; once all of those have occurred, the conflict has been born. From there, I will review the development of interaction, as the movement and the state continue to challenge and push each other, trying to identify how and why strategies change and, more important, what remains constant. And finally, once that constant aspect has been identified, we can discuss consolidation.

May 19: Genesis

Initial Intrusion and the Injustice Frame

Cars manufactured by Russia's remaining domestic automakers have seen little improvement in their comfort and reliability since Soviet days, when they were virtually the only cars available in the country. To shield them from competition, the government has periodically enacted various protectionist measures aimed at driving up the cost of imports. The most onerous of these have placed customs duties on used cars brought in from overseas that often exceed the value of the cars themselves. Nonetheless, many Russian drivers still prefer to pay more for a used import than for a new Lada. Almost on an annual basis, the government has continued to raise import duties, while the increasingly affluent middle class has shown its discontent only by continuing to pay for imports. Never have there been any significant protests.

In early 2005, the government upped the ante by proposing a ban on all right-hand-drive cars. As mentioned at the beginning of this chapter, there are an estimated 1.5 to 2 million right-hand-drive cars in Russia, mostly imported used from Japan directly into the Far Eastern ports of Vladivostok and Nakhodka. Throughout much of the Far East, left-side-drive cars are a rare sight, while Japanese imports with the steering wheel "on the wrong side" are not uncommon in Moscow and other major cities in European Russia and Siberia.

Thus, it is not entirely surprising that the movement that grew up in response to the proposed ban had its genesis in Moscow. According to its initiator, Viacheslav Lysakov:

> On May 14 [2005], I was on-line, and I read that the government was going to have a meeting about banning right-side-drive cars. I've driven one since 1991, and I was upset. Within about ten minutes, I started posting to a Vladivostok website[2] where a lot of car owners of right-side-drive cars communicate.[3]

Lysakov's suggestion was that he and other owners of right-side-drive cars drive by government offices on May 19, the date the cabinet was scheduled to address the issue, honking their horns and blinking their emergency lights. He continued:

> The idea was to have one protest, not to create an organization. The initial reaction [to my suggestion] was indifferent. I had to shake them up a bit. . . . I expected about 200 cars.[4]

Lysakov himself, though, was shocked by the scale of the response. By the government's own estimates, more than 6,000 cars took to the streets of Russian cities in protest ("Avtoklub. Pravyi bunt" 2005). The largest protests were in Moscow, Vladivostok, Chita, and Novosibirsk, with smaller protests in as many as a dozen other cities, with hundreds of cars in each city, decorated with homemade signs and flags, forming columns, parading past government buildings, and paralyzing traffic on central streets. The slogans were largely apolitical and were aimed specifically at the ban. Although participants may have been angry at politicians, it was clear both from the events and from their coverage in the media that they had more to do with cars than with anything else. Typically, one participant said:

If [Prime Minister Mikhail] Fradkov wants to ride around in a Volga,[5] let him. I've been driving for eight years. Over that time, I've had three cars. And not one of them has been Russian. They're trying to force us to drive cars that don't stand up to any comparison with our Japanese cars. (Progonova, Gorbunova, et al. 2005)

Despite the fact that the largest number of potential "losers" from the new ban were in Vladivostok and the Far East, the focus of attention was Moscow, where the plan was to drive in circles around the White House, the seat of the cabinet of ministers. However, when some 500 cars showed up—as opposed to the 100 Lysakov had expected—he decided instead to move the protest to Kutuzovskii Prospekt and its continuation, Rublevskoe Shosse, the main thoroughfare high-ranking government officials use to get to their suburban cottages.[6]

The authorities' initial reaction was mixed. Most immediately, the concern was to stop the protests at any cost, particularly in Moscow. The traffic police, Federal Guard Service (FSO),[7] and Federal Security Service (FSB)[8] quickly got involved, detaining Lysakov and closing off the roads (Buranov 2005). Lysakov was brought up on charges of disturbing the peace and tried before a judge that same day; the judge, however, threw out the charges (Martovalieva 2005b).

Before the day was done, however, the government announced that it would delay the ban on right-side-drive cars indefinitely (Progonova, Gorbunova, et al. 2005). Thus, in essence, a mass protest that began with an e-mail message five days earlier had forced a change in government policy. Lysakov recalls:

I was euphoric. . . . That was a real lift, a feeling of freedom. We brought together an enormous number of people. People felt as if they had gotten up off their knees.[9]

Why should this intrusion have provoked such a response, although all of the previous protectionist measures failed to elicit protest? My hypothesis on the importance of interaction between the state and civil society argues that intrusion into private interests must be concerted to provoke a collective response; in other words, it must afflict people as a group, not as individuals, as the result of a blanket policy. Certainly, an increase in customs duties is a blanket policy that could be considered as a concerted intrusion. There are, however, two key points of difference. First, the pain inflicted by an increase in customs duties is marginal compared to that inflicted by an outright ban on the use of right-side-drive cars. The previous protectionist measures cost would-be car importers a few thousand dollars extra, and from an economic perspective this cost could be at least partially recouped should the car be sold on. The new law, on the other hand, would have destroyed investments already made, prohibiting the use of existing cars and dragging their resale value down to nearly zero. This is the sort of "potentially irreversible" threat of loss that Tarrow identified as key to the development of social movements. And, second, although the tariff hikes were no less concerted as a matter of policy than the Japanese import ban, as a matter of implementation the difference is important. The customs duties have an impact on individuals in an identical manner but at different times, that is, when each person crosses the border with a car to import. This thus disperses the timing of the impact. Individuals also have the opportunity to mitigate or even avoid the inconvenience of increased duties by deciding when and indeed whether to import a car. The right-side-drive ban, on the other hand, would have afflicted approximately 1.5 million Russian car owners all at once and with no opportunity for mitigation. This difference in the facts of implementation is no less important than the actual content of the policies.

Something from Nothing: The Germ of a Social Movement

On May 30, 2005, Lysakov and a handful of other activists opened a new website[10] dedicated to the movement, at the center of which was a forum for exchanging information and ideas for future actions.[11] They dubbed the movement Svoboda Vybora, referring to the freedom to choose what kind of car to drive, but the issues coming in on the forum began gradually to expand to include the various gripes common to Russian drivers. In particular, this meant the workings of the traffic police, notorious for demanding bribes for arcane infractions, and the privileges granted to the drivers of government officials, who are allowed to break just about every rule on the road.

In the movement's initial phase—up through May 2006—"membership" in the organization came to mean registration in the on-line forum, which reached 4,500 by March 2006; it is unclear exactly how many others also participate as unregistered "guests." The typical member is thirty to fifty years old, with a car (usually, but not always, imported), a mobile telephone, and access to the Internet; says Lysakov, "It is the middle class. . . . It is the most progressive and educated sector of society."[12] Lysakov describes himself as typical, although his personal background is somewhat out of the ordinary. Born in 1953, he has a degree in health care but has worked successively as a diamond cutter, a hair cutter, an ambulance technician, a doctor of traditional medicine, a masseur, and a mechanic of Japanese cars; it was as a freelance mechanic that he was making his living at the time the movement got started. And, notably, prior to May 19, 2005, he had never been involved in politics or organized civic activity.[13] What arose, then, was a network movement, existing entirely on the Internet, with no offices and no paid staff, although by the end of 2005 the movement had become a full-time (if unpaid) job for Lysakov. The initial idea was to stick to the original model, what Lysakov calls a "motorized flash mob," in which drivers arrange on the Internet to hold quick protests whenever and wherever they appear to be needed.[14]

Reliable statistics that would allow us to paint an accurate picture of the socioeconomic profile of Svoboda Vybora's potential support base do not exist. Those Russians who had imported cars, Internet access, and mobile telephones were predominantly either part of the middle class or higher on the income scale. Moreover, according to data from VTsIOM, one of Russia's largest polling groups, the total number of households owning at least one car increased from 25 percent in 2002 to 37 percent in 2006, while in Moscow and St. Petersburg that figure reached 42 percent. Moreover, car owners in Moscow and St. Petersburg are almost as likely to have a foreign car (52 percent of surveyed car owners) as a Russian-made car (54 percent).[15] Prior to the May 2005 protests, however, there was little or no sociopolitical infrastructure bringing drivers together. In some neighborhoods, car owners formed small groups to manage garages and parking lots cooperatively, and these could become politically active if there was a threat to their territory, such as from real estate developers. On a national level, State Duma Deputy Viktor Pokhmelkin heads the so-called Drivers' Movement of Russia (*Dvizhenie Avtomobilistov Rossii*), but the organization is essentially fictitious.

Russian car owners are, however, well served in terms of mass communication. There are numerous periodicals, many with nationwide circulation, offering a broad range of information for car owners, from reviews of cars and accessories to articles and advice on traffic rules, import regimes, and other legal issues, as well as copious amounts of display and classified advertising. This is reinforced by a strong Internet presence. Russia's leading Internet rating service lists 14,247 automotive sites, of which the top ten alone register approximately 170.6 million visits from 3.7 million visitors per month.[16] The bulk of this is taken up by sites offering a combination of advertisements for cars, parts and car-related services, and user forums, in which car owners share information on cars, road conditions, and various legal issues. That said, the subcategory of sites dedicated to "Auto & Law," in which Svoboda Vybora's site is the most popular, is relatively small, including 450 sites (3.2 percent of total automotive sites), registering 411,206 visits (0.2 percent of the total) by 59,102 visitors (1.6 percent of the total) monthly. A significant part of the content and user forums on other, broader-based automotive websites deals with similar issues, but the fact remains that legal and rights-defense issues do not appear to dominate car owners' attention and communication—far from it. Svoboda Vybora, then, did not tap into a preexisting current of activity or even discussion. Rather, it was able to succeed despite the fact that rights-related issues were outside the mainstream, even among car owners.

When Lysakov issued his call to arms, he was addressing a community that was networked but not organized and only weakly aware, if at all, of a group identity as political constituents. In choosing an Internet forum as his venue, he was tapping a resource he already knew would be effective, where he knew it would reach an audience. As mentioned earlier, the fact that the forum was on the Internet led to certain efficiencies in terms of the distribution of his idea and the ability of geographically dispersed participants to hold a coherent discussion. What Lysakov did not know—indeed could not have known—was whether his message would resonate. Car owners had not to date been a political force and had never mobilized in their own defense. The fact that the May 19, 2005, protest gave rise to an evidently sustainable social movement is evidence that something can be created from virtually nothing.

Choosing a Course of Action

Although Svoboda Vybora had struck an initial victory, they didn't have to wait long for another reason to protest. First, in the late summer of 2005 the customs authorities in Vladivostok revamped the procedures for importing cars, making them considerably more difficult. In October, local activists from Svoboda Vybora took to the streets of the city and delivered a petition to the customs office; on the day of the protest, local customs officials announced that they were scrapping the new rules (Klimov 2005).

Then, in the fall of 2005, the government announced a sweeping set of changes to the traffic laws, several of which caught drivers' ire. In particular, members of the movement were incensed by changes that would have required owners of many American- and Japanese-made cars to change the color of their headlights and taillights (Buranov, Iablonskii, et al. 2006; Sedel'nikov 2006). As a result, in late 2005 and early 2006, hundreds of drivers, again honking and blinking their lights and carrying placards, drove through Moscow,

St. Petersburg, Ekaterinburg, Tiumen', and other cities. Immediately after the largest protests in January 2006, the rules were repealed (Sedel'nikov 2006).

As the number of protests increased, a pattern of action began to crystallize. Svoboda Vybora's tactics remained largely the same at each protest: Cars would drive through highly visible parts of major cities, bearing placards and flags. In keeping with the philosophy set out early on by Lysakov, protests were kept apolitical:

> We are generally critical, but we try not to get into our political preferences. It could become a point of conflict. If we bring up politics directly, the movement will fall apart. That was my decision, despite the fact that I'm highly politicized myself.[17]

Thus, none of the protests called for the resignation of officials, and, although members of the cabinet might be criticized, President Putin was generally left alone. It was decided that there would be no alliance with any political party. To get the authorities' attention, however, two strategic decisions were made. First, protests would always be held as centrally as possible. And second, cars would carry orange flags and banners, the color of Ukraine's revolution. Lysakov explains: "Orange is a reflective color. It also annoys the hell out of the authorities."[18]

Notwithstanding their use of orange flags and banners, in conducting their protests the organizers actively sought to avoid confrontation or anything that could be seen as a provocation. To that end, instructions for protestors posted on the Svoboda Vybora website include the following:

> We will move 30 to 40 kilometers per hour in the far right lanes. We can and should move faster if doing otherwise would cause a hazard to other drivers. But only if that is the case. Cars passing by at meteoric speed are hard for camera lenses to catch, and your neighbors on the road will have an easier time reading our slogans. Keep the number of reasons for a traffic stop to a minimum. Your car should be in perfect working order, you should have all of the documents for the car and for yourself, and your seatbelt should be fastened. We will not break the rules, and we will behave properly and politely with other drivers. If someone wants to pass through the column, let them. We should not cause traffic jams! Obey the commands of the traffic police. If they stop one car, three will stop, the rest keep going. If they stop a column, everyone stops. If there is no clear place to park, stop somehow (just not in the middle of the road) and ask the officer where and how to park. Speak with the officer politely, though you are not required to get out of your car. While you are sitting in the car, your seatbelt should be fastened (passengers too!). Ideally, there should be at least one witness present at every exchange with an officer.[19]

The ensuing discussion of these and other rules, which were posted prior to a protest scheduled for January 28, 2006, lasted nine days and included eighty-three separate posts. These, in turn, were divided just about evenly into two groups. The first dealt with the image and impression the protest was meant to create. Participants were asked to wash their cars (not a pleasant task in January in Moscow) and to affix to them homemade signs with Svoboda Vybora logos and slogans, Russian flags, and orange ribbons. A large portion of the discussion concerned the best way to get these items to adhere to cars in cold weather. Information was also posted regarding where and when television cameras would be filming and how to create the most effective images for television (drive slowly, flash your lights, and sound your horns). The second group concerned how to deal with the traffic police. Participants were encouraged to bring video and still cameras and tape recorders to dissuade officers from pursuing fictitious infractions. To a certain extent, advice in this category contradicted the image-conscious advice given in other posts, as participants suggested that slow driving, flashing lights, and honking horns could be interpreted as disrupting traffic and disturbing the peace. In the end, though, most of the forum came to the conclusion that, however participants behaved, the police would harass them. This was seen as inevitable and, to the extent that it could attract media attention, even desirable.

The Authorities' Reaction

As far as the authorities were concerned, the police were on hand at every event, and none of the protests went by without at least some drivers being fined. The severity with which the police reacted, however, seemed to be left up to local police chiefs to determine; in Moscow, fines and confiscation of licenses were ubiquitous, and the police seemed determined to disperse each protest as quickly as possible. In each case, however, the politicians gave in to the protesters' demands quickly, generally on the same day as the protest.

The law enforcement reaction to Svoboda Vybora's protests seemed designed to achieve two aims: first, to disrupt the protest; and, second, to discourage drivers from participating in further protests. Neither of these aims was achieved.

From the start, Svoboda Vybora's tactics presented a peculiar challenge for the police. Generally, Russian law enforcement agencies have little trouble putting a quick end to protests. Russian law requires that protest organizers "inform" municipal authorities of their plans, after which the authorities may ban the protest on various technical grounds, including the scheduling of another event in the same place at the same time, a threat to public security, the necessity of conducting urgent repair work to the pavement, and so on. As a result, very few opposition protests receive permission, despite the fact that the law does not actually require permission. Citing their constitutional rights to free assembly, many organizers go ahead with their plans regardless of the official ban, as a result of which they are usually rounded up by riot police, detained, questioned, fined, and released.

Svoboda Vybora's chosen form of protest—driving cars through public thoroughfares—does not lend itself to this sort of disruption. For one, because the protest would be in motion and did not require that any space be cordoned off, there was no legal need to request permission, and thus the protest could not be banned. Moreover, because the protesters would be driving rather than blocking the roads, they could not be accused of disrupting public order. And, should the authorities nonetheless decide to break up the protest forcefully, it is not immediately clear how easily riot police with shields and clubs could clear several hundred cars off the roads without causing significantly more public disruption than the protest itself.

Nevertheless, the traffic police eventually developed a tactic that met with some success. First, they employed various means to break up the protest column into small groups and then to stop the drivers in each small group for one infraction or another. A particular favorite of the police was to take manual control of traffic lights, switching them rapidly to red as soon as a portion of the column crossed into the intersection. All of the drivers caught on the wrong side of the red light could thus easily be pulled over for failing to heed a traffic signal. The second aspect of their tactic was aimed at deterrence. Once stopped through whatever means, protesting drivers generally had their licenses confiscated and—if there were no other licensed drivers among the passengers—their cars impounded.[20] That, however, is the full extent of retaliation, and with the exception of the initial protest, none of the movement's members has been jailed or even detained, unlike participants in many human rights–oriented protests. Encounters with the police are reported on the movement's Internet forum, collected in a central database, and made available as press releases. Where necessary, volunteers—including lawyers—assisted protestors in reclaiming their licenses and automobiles; in Moscow, Lysakov himself makes the rounds of police stations after protests and has been uniformly successful in reclaiming licenses and cars, usually without hassle.[21] Thus, while it is impossible to know the police's exact orders and motives, they seem to have established a tactic that involves dispersing any protest as quickly as possible, coupled with mild and generally ineffectual discouragement of further participation in such protests.

Interim Conclusions

In the initial phase of Svoboda Vybora's emergence we see the genesis of a classic social movement, answering to all of the basic theoretical expectations. Sustained contention arises within an injustice frame that provides all of the necessary prerequisites: an imminent threat of irrevocable loss, a clearly identified human target of blame, and the ability to tap into a broader sociocultural current. More pertinent to our thesis, the fact that this injustice frame develops how and when it does supports the theoretical argument presented here. General dissatisfaction erupts into action only after the government makes a concerted and coherent intrusion that affects an entire group of people identically. And action is repeated only when provoked by consistent state intrusion. Thus, a pattern of interaction begins to emerge, driven primarily by the state, which intrudes, retreats, and intrudes again, allowing Svoboda Vybora to develop a repertoire of protest and a track record of interaction (and successful interaction, at that) with its adversary.

Svoboda Vybora: Development

New Challenges

A key turning point for Svoboda Vybora came in early 2006. Several months earlier, in August 2005, Altai Governor Mikhail Evdokimov and his driver were killed when their Mercedes flew off a two-lane rural road while attempting to pass another car at a speed of approximately 200 kilometers per hour. In the oncoming lane was Oleg Shcherbinskii, who failed to get out of the way of Evdokimov's car, forcing the latter to swerve and leave the road, after which it hit a tree (Sedel'nikov, Marchuk, et al. 2006). In February 2006, for failing to yield to a car he barely had time to notice, Shcherbinskii was sentenced to four years in a labor colony (Moshkin and Mel'man 2006). A month later, after massive protests organized primarily by Svoboda Vybora, the verdict was overturned by a higher court (Tepliakov and Kaspirshin 2006).

Svoboda Vybora adopted a two-pronged approach to this affair. Creating a new section of their website dedicated exclusively to defending Shcherbinskii,[22] the movement announced a rolling series of protests, the largest of which were held in late February and early March 2006, in Moscow, St. Petersburg, Ekaterinburg, Vladivostok, Cheliabinsk, Magadan, Krasnoiarsk, Novosibirsk, Iakutsk, and Barnaul (Chebotarev and Kostenko 2006; Chebotarev, Varshavchik, et al. 2006; Shramenko 2006). At the protest in Barnaul on the day Shcherbinskii's verdict was due to be read out, some 2,000 people gathered, symbolically, on Sakharov Square (Tepliakov 2006). As before, the protests were not overtly political, although—with the prominent slogan of "We could all be the next Shcherbinskii"—they at least hinted at a goal that went beyond ensuring Shcherbinskii's acquittal (Butorina 2006). Parallel to the Shcherbinskii campaign, Svoboda Vybora launched another campaign against so-called *migalki*, the flashing blue lights that bureaucrats in Russia use to allow them to break traffic rules.

The second part of the campaign was to provide direct material support to Shcherbinskii and his family. Because the organization was still not officially registered, Lysakov provided his own bank account as a repository for funds, which could be wired in from all over the country, as did another activist from the Svoboda Vybora community in Barnaul. In all, the campaign raised some $8,000 over two months, approximately half of which flowed into Lysakov's account in Moscow and half into the account in Barnaul; $2,000 of the money raised covered the travel costs and other expenses of Shcherbinskii's attorney, who was working pro bono, while the rest was given to Shcherbinskii's wife.[23]

In defending Shcherbinskii, Svoboda Vybora hit on an issue that had tremendous public resonance. Some 216 articles were written in the nationwide Russian press about Shcherbinskii, and there was broad coverage on television, both of his trial (although it was closed to the press) and of the protests. According to a poll conducted in March 2006, prior to the overturning of Shcherbinskii's conviction, 70 percent of Russians were aware of the case, and of those 90 percent felt that the verdict was unfair.[24] During the affair, Svoboda Vybora's Shcherbinskii site reached the number two spot for hits in the Russian-language Internet.[25]

In developing its response to the Shcherbinskii case, the movement had to further refine the parameters of its "injustice frame." Thus, if in previous protests it was fairly easy to determine whom to blame—the lawmakers who were attempting to ban right-side-drive cars and pass other "unfriendly" regulations—in the Shcherbinskii case blame was less clear. Evdokimov, the governor whose death the authorities appeared to be avenging, was dead. Moreover, the authorities themselves seemed to be pursuing Shcherbinskii at least in part out of inertia, essentially because it felt like the logical thing to do. Thus, movement members began to feel that "the system" was at fault more than individuals. And this, in turn, gave rise to unending debates as to root causes and how to address them.

Thus, in planning a protest on the Shcherbinskii case, Lysakov—under the nickname Moskvich—wrote on the movement's forum:

> Because Oleg[26] was the victim of a car with a *migalka*, the victim of inequality on the roads, of unearned privileges, which would seem outrageous in civilized countries, it would make sense to hold our protest not only in defense of Oleg; he is one of the victims, and any one of us, our friends and those close to us, could be in the same position. In defending Oleg and showing what we think of this unjust verdict, let's place the main emphasis on our demands to get rid of all *migalki* altogether on Russia's roads, except for ambulances, the police, and fire trucks. I think this has grown into a nationwide problem, when we as drivers (and not only as drivers) have been divided into two groups, two castes—"untouchables" and "trash."[27] That is why Oleg was given his sentence—the untouchability of *migalki* dictates the rules of behavior, forms the psychology of the traffic cop on the road and the judge behind the courtroom desk. Oleg's fate is the result of these circumstances. If we demand that they change, then Oleg's fate will change as well, and many other fates in the future will not be broken so impudently, carelessly, defiantly.[28]

In response, a core activist using the nickname Sanych writes:

> Getting rid of *blat* is a good goal. But are the central authorities to blame? It happens at all levels of the bureaucracy. And a hit at any level is a battle with today's authorities. I'm all *for* it. You?[29]

To which Lysakov responds:

> Sanych, let's not get into global politics. We are talking about the concrete fate of a concrete individual, who was a victim of lawlessness in the courts. The cause lies in inequality on the *roads*; we're talking about that now. We don't want ourselves or our friends or those close to us to end up in the same situation. Let's start by demanding that the law be enforced or changed, rather than global political changes. No offence, but everything that goes beyond the discussion of this protest of *drivers* against this unjust judicial verdict, involving the fate of a concrete person and the existence of "untouchables" on the roads will be deleted from this forum. Otherwise we'll get lost in endless discussions. I ask for everybody's understanding.[30]

Another activist, nicknamed Badiboy, interjects:

> I don't entirely agree. In this case Oleg actually *is not* a victim of *migalki*. He is alive and almost unhurt. Oleg is a victim of a *dependent* investigative and especially judicial system—one that is biased and that takes orders from above. Would it not be logical, probably, to protest against that?[31]

Lysakov replies:

> I ask again and for the last time that we leave all of the systems be except the roads. We'll start putting the *roads* in order, and not in Mr. Ustinov's office.[32] The first we can achieve, while the second will end up as hot air. In the best case . . .[33]

An activist using the nickname IZh2126 wrote:

> I don't entirely agree with the emphases. Shcherbinskii was the victim of unfortunate circumstances and the victim of the authorities' readiness to destroy an ordinary citizen to justify themselves. *Migalki* and whistles are only one of the symptoms of how the authorities relate to their people and to themselves. . . . Our protest, in my view, might better be summed up as "We are all Shcherbinskiis" (regardless of whether you have an automobile).[34]

Some despaired. For example, Advokat:

> The paradox of the situation in our country is that the caste of untouchables emerged a long time ago (it was present in Soviet times, at least!), and it's difficult to say whether it will ever end! So, even if all of a sudden they ban *migalki* and special number plates, nothing will change. We need to change people's mentality.[35]

In the end, the general opinion coalesced around the defense of Shcherbinskii and drivers in general, rather than a more generalized political agenda. The protests broadly adopted the slogan proposed by IZh2126, "We are all Shcherbinskiis." One activist, nicknamed Bushmaster, summed up the position as follows:

> People are fed up with all this chatter of "down [for example, with the tsar]"[36] and "for how long [for example, will we put up with this]?"[37] Let's leave the pretty slogans about justice in the world to those who make their career and money on such things. Our task (if I'm not mistaken?) is to achieve equality of citizens before the law, rather than to get Oleg out of prison by any means necessary. . . . Doubtless, if we get a bunch of people out into the streets with slogans like "No to *migalki*!" we'll be shown on TV; they'll do interviews with us and maybe even invite us to the Public Chamber. But let's be realistic. *Migalki* aren't going to disappear from the roads as a result, nor will ordinary drivers cease to be "obstacles" in the path of their owners. As

a result, people will get the impression (and they already are) that SV is just another movement of "democrats," and the word *democrat* for some time now has been a synonym for "hot air"—all the more so because the state media will put maximum effort into making sure that this image is cemented as fast as possible. So, imho,[38] we need to focus on a concrete case, that is, Oleg's case, and get a fair verdict at least (!) in this concrete episode, and from there we can develop further attacks. As they say, it's better to have a small victory than a big, loud loss.[39]

What the movement decided, then, was to broaden its stance and its approach to the state without biting off more than it felt it could chew, to oppose the state's actions in an area at least tangentially connected to the movement's initial grievance, but not to become an opposition movement as such, taking on the state on all fronts simultaneously.

Thus, Svoboda Vybora's mobilization in the Shcherbinskii case had the effect of broadening the movement's injustice frame—what Snow and Rochford refer to as "frame bridging," "the linkage of two or more ideologically congruent but structurally unconnected frames regarding a partiular issue or problem" (Snow and Rochford 1986)—but only to a degree. Although acknowledging systemic blame and calling into question the general issues of inequality and unfairness stemming from *nomenklatura* privilege, the movement would not expand its concrete demands beyond the removal of the specific irritants provided by the authorities: the Shcherbinskii verdict and the use of *migalki*. To some extent, this reflects Lysakov's anxiety that the movement would fracture if it moved too far beyond the specific issues that brought it together in the first place. But Lysakov himself was not in full control of the debate over how to approach the Shcherbinskii campaign, and the conversation on the forum was dominated by other participants. In the end, participants seemed to recognize the potentially threatening diversity of their own viewpoints and chose instead to stick to common ground, even if that meant delaying the voicing of the broader political demands that many of them felt to be pressing.

Nonetheless, the process brought two key results. First, it conceptually recentered the movement on an issue—inequality before the law—that was both highly contentious and unlikely to go away any time soon. This would increase the movement's staying power, even if the government capitulated on specific demands such as the right-side-drive law and the Shcherbinskii verdict. And second, the Shcherbinskii case added a degree of solidarism to the movement. Prior to the Shcherbinskii protests, movement members had been either defending themselves directly against an imminent loss or else had reason to believe that a similar loss was likely to afflict them in the future. However, it is statistically highly unlikely that many Russians will ever be accused of causing the death of a governor (or any other high official, for that matter) in a traffic accident. Representing a shared sense of both vulnerability and of outrage over the fate of one man, with whom many movement members could evidently identify, the slogan "We could all be the next Shcherbinskii," then, is a classic example of the ethos of Gamson's "solidary groups," whose members "feel that they are in some way personally affected by what happens to the aggregate" (Gamson 1968: 35).

Movement Identity

The Shcherbinskii episode illustrates the difficulties that Svoboda Vybora underwent in shifting its targets from individuals to the system. As mentioned earlier, the movement consistently fell back on a narrow framing, with contention focusing on specific sins committed by the authorities, even if the definition of those sins gradually broadened. This internal discussion, however, led to another debate on how or whether to address broader sources of dissatisfaction. The activists of Svoboda Vybora, after all, are not only motorists. They are also voters, taxpayers, workers, and so on, and in their daily lives anger over road-related irritants inevitably mingles with anger over numerous other issues, including reforms of state subsidy and benefit systems; state-mandated increases to gas, heating, and other utility bills; and so on.

A typical example of this dynamic is a January 2006 exchange on the Svoboda Vybora forum between three activists, nicknamed PaNick, Sanych, and Agdam, in which the question of targeting spills out into a broader political debate. PaNick starts it off:

> One of the priorities of our protest should be as follows:
> 1. *No* to abuse by the GAI/GIBDD/DPS!!!![40]
> 2. Accountability for the GAI!!! We demand investigations, that the guilty be punished, and that people be compensated for their losses!!!
> 3. We demand the dismissal of Kir'ianov,[41] who is incapable of putting his impudent and greedy ranks in order!!![42]

In response, Sanych writes:

> I share your justified anger at the traffic police and so on. But look deeper. *They* are using all of this to distract us from the real problems. Have you received your utility

bills yet? How do you like the reforms? That's what we need to concentrate on now. Purely IMHO.[43]

And PaNick's reply:

Sanych, you didn't understand me. I understand what you're saying. But understand this: "The authorities"[44] are faceless. Let's punish one individual for a start. Especially because his guilt is incontrovertible, his face is fat,[45] and his underlings are real bandits in uniform. Then (if we punish this one) the next chief traffic cop will keep a stronger thumb on his underlings and will be more careful in his dealings with the people.[46]

Sanych:

Kol'ia! I agree that we can start with any bureaucrat. I'd be happy to. But the system is to blame. And until we rip up the roots of the weeds, *they* will keep coming back up. And we need to get out of just automotive problems. I think everybody already understands that until we get rid of the root cause, we won't be able to deal with its effects.[47]

Agdam interjects:

2 Sanych. . . . Let's not work toward any world revolutions. We haven't even solved our automotive problems. If, for example, right-handers had come out on May 19 with slogans like "Down with the tsar—all power to the people!!" there's no way we would have been able to defend our right-side steering wheels. Our demands need to be a little more concrete.[48]

Finally, PaNick comes up with some common ground:

Let's send one little bureaucrat into retirement. Let them be afraid. Right now they're not afraid of a thing because we haven't set clear targets. And next time it'll be the minister in charge of utilities reforms. And from there, things might go all the way up to Vovochka,[49] the chief werewolf.[50,51]

After some further debate involving other participants, Agdam summarized the general consensus:

We shouldn't forget that we are an *automotive* movement. And the problems that we raise are *automotive*. All of the rest, of course, also concerns us as citizens. But we are not going to take the bread of the great number of "general profile" political parties and social organizations. Which, by the way, are unable to achieve their grand goals and get able-bodied people out onto the streets without paying them. If we follow the trail they've cut, we'll dissolve in the fog.[52]

This sort of dynamic, common throughout much of the movement's Internet forum, keeps Svoboda Vybora close to its roots. If, as described in the previous section, the movement had tended to mobilize generally in reaction to specific irritants created by the state, the exchange presented in the preceding paragraphs suggests that the movement's own repertoire, and history becomes a guiding—if not constraining—factor. The movement's reluctance to address nonautomotive issues head-on does not stem from a lack of concern with those issues. Rather, it seems to arise from a fear of getting too far away from the factor that created the movement in the first place: cars. Cars—and, in particular, the use of cars as a vehicle of protest—made the movement visibly unique, and that fact is clearly perceived by participants as crucial to their success in forcing government concessions. But cars are also key to the movement's collective identity. Indeed, movement activists may share myriad concerns, running the full gamut of Russian public and political life, but it was cars—and only cars—that brought them together.

Shared concerns, however, do not mean that the movement is free from internal ideological conflict. There are significant differences among members in terms of how to relate to and, if possible, reform the current Russian regime. Thus, an activist using the nickname Advokat wrote:

> I support dialogue with the authorities rather than their violent overthrow![53]

To which another participant, tat'iana, replied:

> And what slogans would you propose for those who have a normal political orientation, and not some sort of sadomasochism? People just don't understand this sort of love from the authorities anymore. We recently had a pensioner drown himself. In his suicide note he wrote: "I have no money for medicine, nothing to pay my rent; I see no point in life." How long are you planning to negotiate?[54]

And Tolan writes:

> How long can we keep changing our leaders? Things were bad under Gorbachev, they were bad under Yeltsin, and under Putin they're still bad. They bring new faces into the government with them, and things for us are still bad.
>
> The conclusion? There is *no point* in a change of the guard up top. So, instead of changing our leadership, we need to force it to live up to its obligations to improve our country.[55]

And Alex53 writes:

In recent times our laws have changed to such a degree that people who don't have connections in the government simply can't protest publicly without breaking the law. There aren't yet any laws about automotive marches, and it would be pretty hard to do so, because we're not asking for space, and that's the basic excuse for all sorts of bans. It's pointless to negotiate with today's authorities—you can only fight and protest. These authorities don't have any moral principles and so will lie and lie again, ad infinitum. It seems that SV should be the kind of organization that doesn't negotiate but that presents the authorities with reasonable solutions to emergent problems that would suit the majority of motorists in the country (and in the future not only motorists), and, in the event of refusal, protest as much as possible.[56]

And Plotnik writes:

Personally, I've been able to adapt, plus, my work doesn't depend on the government. But that doesn't mean that it (the government) takes care of me. It means that it has forgotten about me, which makes me quite happy. Because, as soon as it remembered me, it immediately demanded my garage as a gift! It's pointless to change the people in power, just as it is to change the system. None of that will change their mentality. But we have to come up with effective levers of pressure. The only thing they understand is force . . . A protest is one such lever. So let's come up with slogans that our rulers will not just understand but that have real bite. Not "8 *migalki*," but "*Migalki* only for the special services"; not "For a just court," but "Prosecutor, get your soap"; not "Put the Guarantor[57] in a helicopter," but "let the parliamentarians take the metro."[58]

These differences, clearly, grow out of varying interpretations not of automotive issues but of broader sociopolitical issues. No one in the movement's forum seems satisfied with the current state of affairs in Russia or with the country's political leadership, Vladimir Putin included. But the movement's broad geographic, demographic, and socioeconomic base inevitably means that members will have very different experiences and outlooks. This simultaneously reinforces and is ameliorated by the movement's reluctance to stray too far from automotive issues.

What's more, as the movement developed it seemed to be held together by an increasing sense of solidarity—both within the movement and in a broader social context. Thus, in at least two cases the activity of participants in the organization's Internet forum has led it to get involved in issues that it might not have otherwise addressed. First, according to Lysakov:

We've gotten involved in a case in Voronezh. On our site, someone wrote about a five-year-old story, about an accident, in which a drunk driver ran up on the sidewalk and killed two teenaged boys. They died instantly. Another girl died later, in the hospital. The lawyer of the perpetrator is the son-in-law of the chief judge, and for five years this guy has avoided conviction. We have arranged for legal help and informational support for the parents of the children who were killed. It's ironic, but we're defending the rights of pedestrians and trying to put a driver in jail. Our lawyer has volunteered his time; a journalist from *Vedomosti* donated money, and so did the drivers' union. I called the Republican Party, and they called their local city duma deputy, who is now working with the parents. And the editor of *Novaia Gazeta* got the story into the paper.[59]

And second:

We got a post in our forum about a woman who had twins, a boy and a girl, and the boy was sick. When the mother was well enough, she left the hospital with the girl but left behind the sick boy. Someone who had been in the hospital with her and seen this happen started writing about it in the Internet, and it made it into our forum. Everyone was writing in, wanting to adopt the boy. The threat got 32,000 hits and 300 comments. We had responses from all over the world, even from Boston. It turned out that the story wasn't quite true, that the mother came back later and got the boy, who had stayed in the hospital for treatment. But because we had seen such an emotional outpouring, we decided to create two new parts of the forum. The first is called "Help Children," and it's for transporting aid and donations from one place to another. It's a way for people who have something to send to find a driver who might be able to take the package. And the second is called, "Let's Talk about Children," for emotional discussion.[60]

Thus, while broad politically oriented mobilization is problematic, the movement has proved itself capable of solidaristic action outside the realm of its traditional concerns. Demanding that a driver be jailed for a crime on the road is not what one might initially expect from a movement created to defend drivers. Nor is the distribution of charitable donations to poor children clearly linked to automotive issues. Of course, neither of these is ideologically contentious, and that makes mobilization less risky. But neither are these activities direct responses to state intrusion. Rather, they are small steps toward proactive engagement by the movement, generated by a sense of solidarity and common purpose, which itself was generated through the gradual development of a successful repertoire of reactive engagement. The emergence of this solidarity is noteworthy, particularly because it is on such a philosophical level. Theory and hypothesis had already predicted that the cohesive and coherent nature of the initial intrusion—the right-side-drive ban—would provoke a collective response because a single policy decision threatened a large group of people by virtue of their membership in that group. What is remarkable here is that, having come to see themselves as a class, the members of the movement were able to develop a collective response to just the sort of law enforcement abuses that Public Verdict struggled with in Chapter 5. In other words, the movement's identity was born and weaned in reaction, and once weaned that identity begins to take on a life of its own.

Patterns of State Reaction: Co-Opt, Control, Concede

As predicted in social movement theory (Tarrow 1998), various other political forces began trying to attach themselves to the movement. Thus, at the rally for Shcherbinskii in Barnaul, Svoboda Vybora was joined by the Republican Party (a liberal opposition party led by Vladimir Ryzhkov, a State Duma deputy from Barnaul), The Movement in Support of the Army (a populist/nationalist fraction of the Communist Party, associated with the outspoken anti-Semite Viktor Iliukhin) and Edinaia Rossiia, the Kremlin's "party of power" (Tiazhlov 2006). None of these groups was invited by the protest's organizers.[61]

In fact, the Kremlin's interest in Svoboda Vybora began much earlier than the Shcherbinskii affair. Within two months of the first protest, Lysakov was called in for a meeting at the presidential administration, where it was strongly suggested that he get "in with the vertical," a suggestion he rejected (Martova-lieva 2005a). In response, the administration appeared to adopt a strategy of making it look as though the movement and the ruling party were working in tandem. Local Edinaia Rossiia party leaders in Vladivostok glommed onto the protest against new customs rules organized there in October 2005 by Svoboda Vybora (Klimov 2005). After initially keeping silent about the Shcherbinskii case—the deceased governor had been a party member—as the protests grew Edinaia Rossiia also joined in, reportedly at the urging of the local party leadership in Barnaul (Nagornykh, Buranov, et al. 2006). In response to the anti-*migalki* campaign and the related protests, the government offered to create a commission to look into the movement's concerns (Chebotarev 2006). Government ideologues, however, attacked opposition parties for latching onto the movement and again tried to claim Svoboda Vybora as its own (Solovykh 2006).

The administration likewise worked through unofficial channels, primarily through the journalist Vladimir Solov'ev, who hosts political talk programs on NTV television and Silver Rain radio, both loyal to the Kremlin. The radio

station launched its own campaign in defense of Shcherbinskii, calling for bureaucrats to be deprived of *migalki* and distributing white ribbons to be tied
onto car radio antennas, in contrast to *Svoboda Vybora*'s orange ribbons. In a
series of radio and television broadcasts, Solov'ev accused Svoboda Vybora of
being unprofessional stooges of hidden interests, while portraying as the true
protest the campaign organized by Silver Rain with the evident backing of Edinaia Rossiia.[62]

It was not only progovernment forces that tried to glom onto the movement, however. Representatives of Garri Kasparov's United Civic Front—a
key organizer of the campaign to ensure that President Putin is not given a
third term in office—told newspapers that the Front had been working in close
cooperation with Svoboda Vybora from the beginning (Chebotarev and Kostenko 2006). Lysakov acknowledged having meetings with Kasparov and his
assistants, but said he had decided from the beginning that it would be best to
avoid any association: "We're not going in the same direction," he said.[63] Nonetheless, when he was arrested during the first protest, Lysakov was defended
by a lawyer from the oppositional Union of Right-Wing Forces political party
(Martovalieva 2005b).

As mentioned early in this chapter, the government also made consistent—
though consistently ineffectual—efforts to suppress the movement's protests.
Unlike with other opposition movements, though, Russian law enforcement
agencies avoided heavy-handed confrontations with Svoboda Vybora, and
the repercussions for movement members rarely extended beyond the merely
annoying and inconvenient. Also unlike with other opposition movements,
meanwhile, the government has given in to most of the movement's demands:
The ban on right-side-drive cars was repealed, changes to the rules of the
road and the criminal code were scrapped, Shcherbinskii was released, and at
least some movement has been made toward limiting the number of cars with
migalki.

Conducting contemporary political research, particularly in authoritarian
contexts, is always to a certain degree impeded by the fact that we can never
know with any real degree of certainty why the authorities adopt one course
of action over another. In Russia in particular, the relevant decision makers
are not available for interview; even if they were, the honesty of their answers
would be colored by political exigencies. And so we are left guessing as to why
the ruling elite in Russia held on so long to its *migalki*, provoking so much
anger along the way.[64] It should be noted, though, that elite privilege on the

roads in Russia dates back to the days of the *nomenklatura*. In his seminal deconstruction of the life of the Soviet elite, first published in samizdat, Mikhail Voslenskii devoted a section to the *nomenklatura* fleet of cars, with their special license plates, chauffeurs, and privileged access to gasoline and other necessities (Voslenskii [1990] 2005: 317–318). With few cars on the roads, traffic then was sparse, and *migalki* were not needed to speed passage. These have been added by the post-Soviet Russian elite, for whom personal chauffeur-driven cars with special number plates ensuring unhindered passage through traffic police checkpoints are evidently not sufficient. Again, we do not know why *migalki* are so dear to the Russian elite. But their reluctance to give them up, even in the face of overwhelming public disdain, suggests that a higher value is placed on privilege than on public politics. As in the Public Verdict case, when the authorities showed themselves unwilling to introduce accountability into law enforcement systems despite the high cost of losses in the European Court of Human Rights, here again the elite display a staunch unwillingness to surrender even a small measure of their impunity, such as the freedom that *migalki* give them on the road. But because this unwillingness is consistent, and because Svoboda Vybora has succeeded in incorporating it into a collective injustice frame, the movement has been able to turn it into a salient political issue.

Consolidation: Who's in the Driver's Seat?

Crystallization of Conflict Lines

In early 2006, Lysakov began looking ahead to May of that year, when Svoboda Vybora would celebrate its first birthday. What had been conceived of on a whim as a protest lasting at most several hours had evolved into a fully fledged social movement, with hundreds if not thousands of participants throughout the country. It had developed its own identity and solidarity. It had forced the authorities to retreat again and again. And it showed no signs of dissipating any time soon. Svoboda Vybora's first birthday, Lysakov decided, was an event worth celebrating. And what better way to mark the day than with another big protest?

Thus, in planning a protest for May 2006, Lysakov wrote the following wide-ranging letter to the forum, reproduced here almost in its entirety:

We're asking everybody to give us their ideas for holding a protest on May 20 (form, scenario, route, concerts, and so on). Your ideas will be systematized, evaluated by the Coordinating Committee, and the best will be developed and used.

From what has already been said, it's clear that the majority cannot accept the general tightening of the Administrative Codex, as concerns motorists, without a symmetrical tightening of control over the traffic police and a fundamental change in the way they function (providing safety for everyone on the road, and not just the a chosen few, with personal responsibility for an officer's section of road and with the officer's career development depending on that basic factor).

It is unacceptable to have a system of punitive "points" that do not expire, which is double punishment and an ideal means of forcing bribes. . . .

It is unacceptable to try to lower the number of accidents exclusively by putting pressure on drivers, without an adequate plan for radically improving the financing of construction and maintenance of the roads. The road infrastructure is bankrupt.

The state's impotence is shameful in terms of controlling the quality of fuel, oils, and other technical liquids (if tests in Moscow found 30 percent counterfeit, then what must be happening in the provinces; specialists say that 50 percent of motor oil in Russia is fake).

The biggest problem is total corruption in law enforcement in general and the traffic police in particular. Giving an even sharper knife to someone who is less a surgeon than a highway robber is just to create even worse chaos on the roads. Why threaten law-abiding citizens with fifteen days in prison, if it still won't get the real bastards off the streets? In order to have absolute power, especially in the periphery, where getting to the truth is often impossible and almost any criminal case can be openly fabricated? Why should we make life easier for the "werewolves"?

But for driving through a red light or a pedestrian crossing, people should be punished, to the tune of 5,000 or 6,000, like they do in Latvia ($200 for crossing a "zebra").

In other words, we're *for* a packet of document that would make the roads safer, but we are not for amendments to the Administrative Codex. Otherwise, the traffic police—or, looking higher, the government—will achieve it (road safety) the easiest way possible—through total terror on the roads, technical bans on imports and on inspections, ridiculous prices for fuel (given its awful quality), and other great ideas for getting the likes of you and me off the road.

And lastly: The protest on the 20th is planned to support, first and foremost, the "eight *migalki*" bill.[65] We were asked to do this by the bill's authors in the State Duma. But we won't forget the Administrative Codex; otherwise they'll soon be locking us away.

They already are.[66]

Lysakov's call for ideas met with broad support. Indeed, forum participants unanimously agreed that the movement needed to be more proactive, raising issues of importance to its members without waiting for a provocation from the state. Thus, while it was decided that the May 2006 protest should maintain the focus on core Svoboda Vybora issues such as *migalki*, the consensus shifted toward making it clear to the authorities that the movement had a broader reformist agenda at heart, that it was seeking not just redress for motorists but a qualitative change in the way governance is conducted. One leading activist, using the nickname Maxim22, summarized this consensus as follows:

> We need a preemptive protest. "*Migalki*" and the dispute about them is in large part a creation of SV, and we need to hold the line here. . . .
>
> On the second point, it's more complicated. It seems to me that we must not combine what SV does with what others are doing with SV, with the way they are trying to fence us in. Specifically: the so-called amendments . . . on raising fines, creating punitive points, and tow trucks and everything else, are simply "fodder" for SV. They are forcing SV to react to the news, for the benefit of the "puppet masters." They have no doubt that the logic of SV's response will provoke a constant tussle over nonexistent issues, such as, for example, the size of fines, whether to allow arrests, and so on. SV is being dragged into an inferno of local conflicts, pushing it away from the issues that really matter. Should SV allow itself to be led like this?
>
> It would be more proper to raise their level of understanding, to make the bureaucrats scratch their heads. The protest could, for example, draw attention to the need to weed out the fatal principle of passing laws that increase corruption in society, to introduce the concept of an "immoral" law, uncover the meaning of "democracy," the essence of higher, conceptual power. Let them see their place clearly. Let them think.[67]

Despite an official ban, Svoboda Vybora held a small protest on May 27, 2006, together with the Interregional Union of Professional Drivers, drawing some 200 cars and trucks (Buranov 2006a,b). The turnout was lower than in prior protests, perhaps reflecting some strain from the movement's expanding range of issue areas, but it was also a proactive event, without a strong irritant to provoke a larger mobilization. On the same day, rallies were also held in Neriungri, Iakutsk, Magadan, and Kirov, with support from the Union, as well as the Republican Party and the Communist Party (Chebotarev 2006). The rallies focused on a collection of issues that have come to the fore through the movement's forum. Lysakov said:

Our main slogan now is "No to *Migalki*." The *migalka* is the symbol of inequality before the law; it's an insult to civil society. We need to get rid of it. We are also asking for a review of the administrative code. It includes a major increase in fines and mandates: fifteen days in prison if you fail to see a traffic cop's hand signal or if you get ten points on your driver's license. What's worse, the points never expire. This is just a personal feeding trough for the traffic police. First, we want a law on corruption and a reform of the traffic police, and then you can raise fines. Give us normal roads, normal lighting, and so on.[68]

Notably, Lysakov and others—both inside and outside the movement—started more frequently to use the term *civil society*. Asked about how he saw the meaning of the term and its relation to Svoboda Vybora, Lysakov said:

The West overestimates the activities of the human rights organizations, with all their legal and financial and other support for them. There is a lack of balance. The general human rights organizations today in Russia have become divorced from real Russian civil society. The grassroots organizations, created by society from below and not political parties, are the pieces of the puzzle of the new Russian civil society. Groups like us, like the ecological movements, which are starting to get in contact with us. All the Western aid is going only to the old organizations, and although we are not calling ourselves rights defenders, it is what we are doing.[69]

The "general human rights organizations," meanwhile, appear to recognize Lysakov's argument. In an interview given to a Moscow newspaper in May 2006, Liudmila Alekseeva, head of the Moscow Helsinki Group, said:

Right now in our country the bulk of the population is inert, and active citizens are coming together in a very large number of small organizations. . . . But we are seeing a new kind of activism, "from below," for example, the drivers' movement. They don't have an office, a charter; they agree on their activities on the Internet. And when Shcherbinskii was in court, they held demonstrations in several cities all at once, and our independent court woke up quickly. Or some other ham-fisted decree comes around, like the one about red taillights, and they protest, unified, in different cities simultaneously, and the authorities annul the decree. Because it's not a small group, but a popular movement. (Kolesnichenko 2006)

The fact that Svoboda Vybora began looking toward more proactive engagement, coupled with its new civil society ideology, is evidence of an effort by the movement to develop a more consolidated role for itself than simply reacting to the state's intrusion. As we saw throughout the development of the movement's identity and strategy, after an extended series of intrusions and protests, the movement's members knew more or less what they could expect from the state, felt that they understood the ruling elite's agenda, and clearly saw some benefit from collective action. Thus, at this stage—again, as predicted by our theory in this project—the importance of state intrusion begins to fade, and the relationship itself takes on more significance.

Alliances

As Svoboda Vybora grew and became a more evidently permanent operation, the necessity of seeking support and alliances became increasingly pressing. In February 2006, in the heat of the Shcherbinskii battle, Lysakov was pessimistic about the opportunities for sponsorship and, in any case, did not want to seek Western grant funding.[70] Still working without a salary, Lysakov said at the time:

> I'm trying to get people to register and to broach the idea of membership dues of at least 200 rubles per month. In the meantime, we're living off small donations. The people who have come together are surprisingly decent people, surprisingly spiritual. People have put money on the organizers' mobile phone accounts . . . We have a lawyer working pro bono. One member donated $3,000 to buy a professional video camera. I'm looking for a sponsor who won't dictate our actions. I was approached by the organization Russia Without Narcotics, who offered to help with office supplies. The most important thing is not to get involved with political parties.[71]

On April 5, 2006, Svoboda Vybora was officially registered as an "interregional public organization," with membership dues of $100 per year, close to Lysakov's initial estimate. The headquarters are in Moscow, with regional branches registered in Cheliabinsk, Magadan, and Iakutiia, joined later by affiliates in Krasnoiarsk, Izhevsk, and Barnaul. Still, the organization had no rented office and no paid staff, and, as of late April 2006, no dues had yet been collected. Lysakov explained:

> We're starting from a blank slate, taking in new regional sections, new members. We're asking local coordinating councils to get organized and delegate someone to the federal council. We do everything on-line. We're constantly in contact, almost daily discussing various issues. Every month we have an official meeting, not physically, but on-line. We have to have an annual conference by law. That will be difficult for us. The distances are huge, and it will be very expensive. But it is a legal requirement. We are opening an account for membership dues and donations. But we're flexible. Pensioners, people with disabilities, parents with large families can join free or with a discount, or we can extend their payments over a longer period. Activists who volunteer their time can also join without paying dues. About five people will

be working full time—myself, an assistant, our site manager, our accountant, and our lawyer. They all will need salaries.[72]

So far, however, the real support for the organization remains informal. During the Shcherbinskii campaign, Lysakov befriended Aleksandr Kotov, chairman of the Interregional Union of Professional Drivers, a trade union representing long-distance truck drivers. The two agreed on a strategic alliance between the union and Svoboda Vybora, and Lysakov was given the position of deputy chairman of the union, a small salary and limited financial support for Svoboda Vybora.[73] In addition, Lysakov wrote regular columns for the newspapers *Novaia Gazeta* and *Vedomosti* and was paid honoraria for giving interviews to international organizations such as the Cato Institute. Taken together, that allows Lysakov to work full-time for Svoboda Vybora. At the time this was written, all of the other activists maintained full- or part-time jobs.

Growth has not come without growing pains. Two of the initial movement's largest regional sections—in Novosibirsk and Vladikavkaz—have fallen away. Lysakov explains:

> Novosibirsk and the Pacific Marities have gone their separate ways. Novosibirsk in particular is trying to kick me out of my post and break up the organization. Our relationship with Novosibirsk has been ruined. We believe that the FSB was involved. In the Maritimes, the local leader wanted to become a deputy in the local legislature and used the organization for his campaign. The organization is now dying slowly. We hope the activists will come back to us.[74]

In its current campaign—the fight against *migalki*—Svoboda Vybora has softened its stance on working with political parties. Indeed, by mid-April 2006, the relationship between Svoboda Vybora and two opposition parties— the Communists and the Republican Party—was made public. Together, they proposed a law to reduce the number of *migalki* to from approximately 4,500 to eight. Republican Party leader Ryzhkov summed up the argument as follows: "If a citizen is on his way to his wife who is giving birth, or to his father who has had a heart attack, or if he is late for his plane, that's his problem. But if a bureaucrat has to tear his rear end out of his chair and rush off to his boss, he can fly through the oncoming lanes and break all the rules. That's the logic of our bureaucracy" (Zakatnova 2006). Lysakov explained the change of strategy as follows:

> The political parties have started dancing in circles around us. We have been cooperating some with the Communist Party and the Republican Party, regarding our

campaign against *migalki*. Because we are working with more than one party, and because we are the initiators, we are able to keep our independence and leadership.[75]

Early in the summer of 2006, Lysakov received an invitation to participate on behalf of Svoboda Vybora in a conference called "The Other Russia." Convened by a broad spectrum of opposition groups—ranging from Soviet-era human rights defenders to post-Soviet nationalists—"The Other Russia" was designed to show the world leaders descending on Russia for the G8 summit that a significant portion of Russian society did not approve of the way Vladimir Putin's government was running the country. Up until this point, as mentioned earlier, Lysakov had tried to keep Svoboda Vybora out of direct political engagement, except where it was necessary to lobby for or against a law of particular interest, such as in the *migalki* campaign. Svoboda Vybora was thus positioned as a motorists' movement, not an opposition movement. Participating in "The Other Russia" would inevitably change that.

In justifying his decision to participate in the movement—and to the Coordinating Committee in particular, which approved his decision—Lysakov cited two groups of factors. The first was that the conference was being supported by several people and organizations whose goals and ideals Lysakov saw as being in line with the movement's own. These included the newspaper *Novaya Gazeta*, for which Lysakov writes a regular column: the INDEM Foundation, run by anticorruption campaigner Georgii Satarov; and the Moscow Helsinki Group.[76] The second factor Lysakov cited was that, from the very first meeting he had with the presidential administration in May 2005, the Kremlin had clearly considered the movement to be oppositional; thus, in his estimation, there was nothing to be lost from participating.[77]

The issue of whether to participate in "The Other Russia" sparked a considerable amount of debate in the movement's forum. Strikingly, however, none of the comments opposed the decision for ideological reasons. Indeed, most of the participants voiced their approval; a posting by On-liner is typical:

> We really are another Russia—those who aren't among the 8,000,000 people needed to service the oil sector and Gazprom. "They" don't need us. And now they're even planning on doing without us at elections. So, we're going to have to find our own way out.[78]

The overall track record of success led to a considerable degree of confidence among the movement's activists, reflecting two things that are uncommon in

Russia: a lack of fear of reprisal and the belief that protest can bring results. Thus, Alex53 writes:

> To hell with the traffic police! What can they really do to us? So they can take our licenses, but they'll give them back anyway. So they can fine us. So what else? They won't confiscate our cars; they won't put us in jail (and if they do, only for three hours); they won't exile us to Kolyma! How long can we keep on being afraid? Thankfully we're no longer living under Stalin. The Russian Federation has signed so many international laws that the authorities should be afraid of our every fart, and here we are still being afraid of them. To hell with them . . . Let's build civil society and get rid of these monsters. Only one "but": Everyone has to be involved, and all for one![79]

Similarly, Peter Tiger writes:

> A quick thought. Our current authorities are deathly afraid of *any* demonstration. A year ago, a few hundred people blocked Leningradskoe Shosse and the result: revision of the benefit monetization law . . . If there will be a lot of cars, IMHO the authorities will turn tail . . . They'll simply be *frightened*.[80]

And an activist going by the nickname SerGT writes:

> A single traffic jam on the way into the center of the city is a lot more effective than making rings around the beltway! Closing off all the exits from the Garden Ring for an hour—that would resonate! But only the beltway, you can ride around all day, and the only person who will notice are people who happen to be driving by (if they even notice) and invited (!) journalists, while the bureaucrats and the government couldn't care less about such "joyrides" . . . And the journalists too are soon going to get sick of covering our traditional ring races . . .
>
> The impact and resonance of our protests must grow, so that even the intention of holding a protest would be enough to make the bureaucrats stop and think. And if all of our protests are going to be of the traditional "ring around the sausage" variety, the authorities will learn how to slice the salami in such a way that no matter how long it is, the pieces will be ever smaller and harder to see . . . imho . . .[81]

However, as Svoboda Vybora and Lysakov moved closer to the opposition, some participants, including Alex53, voiced reservations about what it might mean for the movement's future:

Good evening, Vladislav.

This is an issue you're going to have to think about like no other. You're being invited on an international level into the opposition to the existing regime. And, most likely, after taking part in this event they will close *all* of your channels of legitimate influence on the government. The results are fairly predictable—either you can work with the government commissions, or you can go into strict opposition. The only question is, what are you ready for?[82]

Lysakov replied to Alex53 in a lengthy posting that laid out a new, more openly oppositional stance for the movement. He wrote:

Good evening!

. . . Why should we, civic organizations, be afraid of civic activity? Ecologists, Soldiers' Mothers, citizens of Russia beaten and lied to and unified into communities, and now us, motorists—what, are we all supposed to supplicate ourselves before the official ideology, taking on bended knee all of our social realities and ideological strictures from the hands of people, many of whom are nothing more than carpetbaggers? The era of totalitarianism is irreversibly slipping away, and it is slipping away because of the contributions that we all have made. We are the free citizens of a free country, and we simply must not forget that.

And finally: My speech at this event was more than balanced and sets us apart from the revolutionaries and radicals, confirming that the only acceptable way forward for us is evolutionary development but nonetheless announcing our fundamental goal: control by civil society over the state—which, actually, we have been trying to achieve since May 19, 2005, remaining with in the interests of drivers, that is, the whole range of problems and questions that concern us.

And we are going to continue to do this, whether anyone likes it or not.[83]

After the conference, Lysakov reported:

The decision to participate in the Conference justified itself a hundred times over.

And so. I made contact with sixteen not entirely unknown people, which surprised me. Whenever I handed out my card, saying "I'm Lysakov . . .", everyone answered, "I know you." ☺)))[84]

His contacts at the conference included a number of prominent members of the liberal opposition, such as Alekseeva, Satarov, *Ekho Moskvy* radio journalist Evgeniia Al'bats, and former Putin economic advisor Andrei Illarionov.

∾

It was never a foregone conclusion that Svoboda Vybora would end up in this company. From the beginning, Lysakov had sought to avoid outright opposition to the regime, and he said repeatedly during interviews that he felt the human rights defenders to be out of touch with reality and wasting donors' money. While his affinity for *Novaya Gazeta* and his support—though not broadly publicized—for Ukraine's "Orange Revolution" fairly clearly delineate his personal political leanings, he also recognized from the beginning that acting on his own preferences would be detrimental to the unity of the movement. Indeed, the available evidence suggests that Svoboda Vybora aligned itself with "The Other Russia"—which later became a permanent opposition movement—as the result of a general consensus. The lack of internal objections to Lysakov's participation certainly points in this direction. But even more important, participating in "The Other Russia" seemed a natural extension of the movement's compromise between broadly held feelings of dissatisfaction and the desire to stick to campaigning on automotive issues. In its own activities, Svoboda Vybora thus sought to remain true to its roots without diluting the core identity that held it together. It would not last.

Epilogue: The Rise of the Blue Bucket Brigades

Sergei Parkhomenko, a prominent opposition-minded journalist, radio commentator, and book publisher, thought that the video of the man with the blue bucket on his car was amusing.

Years after the Oleg Shcherbinskii murder trial made headlines and galvanized public opposition to *migalki*—those flashing blue lights on the tops of so many public officials' cars, which evidently empower them to barrel down public thoroughfares, endangering and enraging others—the problem was still there. One gentleman, it appeared, decided to have a bit of fun. He purloined his young son's little blue sandbox pail and affixed it to the top of his own car. And then, with a passenger recording everything on a video camera, he went for a ride. Traffic police, noticing the blue bucket and apparently guessing that it wasn't a real *migalka*, pulled him over to investigate. Repeatedly. Not having violated any laws, he was let go. Hilarity ensued.

Parkhomenko found the resulting video on YouTube and wrote about it in his blog (Parkhomenko 2010). "I think this could be the start of a new mass movement," he wrote. "I can imagine thousands and thousands of members of the Blue Bucket Society, leaving for work in the morning. And the sorry, frightened owners of blue sirens, crawling along in that traffic, to the laughter and honks of their neighbors."

If anyone needed proof of the power of suggestion (or the power of the Internet, for that matter), it was quick in coming. Within days, Petr Shkumatov, an activist at the Federation of Car-Owners of Russia (whose Russian acronym, FAR, also means headlight), an organization that had split several years earlier from Viacheslav Lysakov's Svoboda Vybora, created "Sinie Vederki"—the Blue Bucket Society—as a subgroup within the movement. It was an experiment in public satire, and although it didn't reduce the number of real *migalki* on the streets, it was a mobilizational and ideational success. The blue buckets became a ubiquitous symbol not only of the fight against *migalki* but more broadly of the inequality those *migalki* represented. Russia's ruling elite, after all, could inhabit its own rarified world, separated by security, high walls, and the barriers of extreme affluence from ordinary citizens almost everywhere—but not on the roads. On the roads, space is inevitably shared, and when the elite seek to maintain their privilege, friction follows. Within a year, the blue buckets evolved from a symbol of the automotive movement into an emblem of emergent urban opposition as a whole. Again, the evidence is in the humor. In the spring of 2011, a satirical comic strip featuring Putin as a judo-fighting superhero went viral on the Internet. Putin's enemies? Armies of zombies, with blue buckets on their heads.[85]

It is noteworthy that Lysakov, the man who had started this fight, was no longer around to finish it. Fissures in the automotive movement had been there almost since the beginning, but they began to grow more serious by 2008 or so. It was then that two things happened. First, Lysakov began taking the organization he had launched, Svoboda Vybora, in a direction of increasing formalization and centralization, an idea many in the movement rejected. Second, Lysakov was offered an increasingly cozy relationship with the government. The man who once hobnobbed with old-school antiregime activists such as Liudmila Alekseeva was now invited to serve as a permanent expert on parliamentary and ministerial committees and to consult on the drafting of laws and was eventually nominated for a position in the newly created Public Chamber, a government-backed body of civil society organizations. To many, this looked like co-optation. That feeling was only cemented by Lysakov's announcement that he would be among the cochairs of the Kremlin-backed All-Russian Popular Front, created to mobilize support ahead of the 2011 parliamentary elections, and that he would stand in those elections on the list of Putin's United Russia party.

And so, while Svoboda Vybora continued to press forward with many of the same agenda items—including *migalki*, taxes, road safety, and regulations—FAR emerged as a less formalized and more openly confrontational alternative. Among the earliest activists was Sergei Kanaev, the commercial director of a meatpacking plant in Kemerovo, who had seen his close friend killed at a crosswalk by a speeding car—bearing, of course, a blue light and a siren—right before his eyes. The experience led him to join the then nascent automotive movement, particularly the national defense of Oleg Shcherbinskii, who had been accused of causing the traffic death of Altai region Governor Evdokimov (Gulenok 2009) and whose case became something of a siren call for the movement. First in Kemerovo, and later in Moscow, he was among the activists who galvanized local automotive groups opposed to Lysakov's course into the FAR. And, by 2010, the protest heat that had once been generated by Svoboda Vybora was now being kindled by FAR and the Blue Bucket brigades. In the terms of social movement theory, the movement itself had thus escaped its initial institutional trappings to follow the frame, the sense of injustice, and identity of grievance that had led to the mobilization in the first place. Kanaev, Shkumatov, and others were now speaking the language that Lysakov had spoken a few years prior.

Conclusions

The Russian automotive rebellion, one of an exceedingly small number of civil society organizations in Russia capable of mobilizing true grassroots support and of putting effective pressure on the state, began as a protest by motorists afraid of having their cars taken away from them and grew into a social movement fighting for government accountability, equal rights, and the limiting of elite privilege. That a movement could have arisen in response to the initial intrusion—the attempt to ban cars imported from Japan—is predicted by classical social movement theory and the movement's initial development follows all the laws of social mobilization and injustice frames. That the movement's further development would take the course described in the preceding pages, however, was less obvious. That is not to say, however, that it was accidental.

My hypothesis argues that civic activism arises in response to concerted and coherent state engagement, regardless of the nature of that engagement. As discussed in previous chapters, the Russian state has broadly disengaged from the populous, demanding neither political participation nor ideological conformity, nor even much in the way of taxes. In the two preceding chapters on human rights and housing, we have seen the haphazard, "privatized" use of power and the atomization of policymaking stymie other attempts at civic mobilization, despite the salience of the issues and the depth of the grievances. In this case, the intrusion—on behalf of an industry lobby, first by attempting to ban Japanese cars, then by placing severe limitations on imports from America, and so on—seems almost trivial in comparison. But it was sufficient, and sufficiently cohesive and coherent, to provoke massive protest.

What caused the challenge to emerge and consolidate as a social movement is revealed in the pattern of interaction between the movement and the state. The state, in effect, plays a dual game with the movement, being at once confrontational and accommodating. Unwilling to risk a spiral of protest, the state consistently gives in to the movement's specific demands. But the state cannot appear to be giving in, and so it makes a public show of repressing the protests (though without severe consequences for participants), minimizes the movement's media coverage, and spins the movement's achievements as its own. Thus, no one wins, and the battle becomes indefinite. There is a definite loser, however: the state. At the beginning of the process, the state was in the driver's seat, able at least in theory to cut off oxygen to the movement by ending its provocative intrusions. But by the time Svoboda Vybora joined "The Other Russia," the situation was out of the state's control; when Svoboda Vybora abandoned the opposition and Lysakov joined the ranks of the ruling elite, the movement itself abandoned its leader and took on a new form. By continuing to engage, the state allowed the formation of a consolidated relationship between itself and the movement, on which the movement in turn could build an identity and develop a self-sustaining agenda. Russian motorists as a social movement—as a sustained interaction between dissatisfied citizens and the state—had become an established feature of the political landscape, one with which the regime was now obliged to contend. At least in one policy area, the state lost its autonomy.

What is most interesting is how the elite chooses when to give in and when to keep fighting. The state gives in almost immediately to demands that the import bans be lifted, despite the fact that these bans were lobbied by a powerful industry. On the other hand, it drags out the battle over *migalki*, suggesting that elite privilege trumps even corporate interests in the Russian political equation. (Incidentally, loyalty here is not an issue. The government controls the largest Russian automakers.) Correspondingly, without departing from its automotive roots, the movement evolves into a full constituent of the Russian opposition, demanding equality, accountability, and the rule of law. And this happened not because the movement was populated by dissidents but because, as it turned out, it is impossible to defend the rights of Russian motorists without establishing equality, accountability, and the rule of law.

8

Seizing the Moment

У каждого мгновенья свой резон
Свои колокола, своя отметина.
Мгновенья раздают кому позор,
Кому бесславие, а кому бессмертие!

—Роберт Рождественский

Each moment follows its own logic
Tolls its own bells, makes its own mark.
Moments bring shame to some,
To others infamy, and, to a few, immortality!

—Robert Rozhdestvenskii

On December 6, 2011, Alexei Navalnyi descended from a stage outside Moscow's Chistye Prudy metro station and into a crowd of some 5,000 to 6,000 protesters. Cajoling, pushing, shouting "Forward!," he urged them on, down Miasnitskaia street, toward Lubianka and the headquarters of the Federal Security Service, or FSB. That Navalnyi, a popular blogger and anticorruption activist, would find himself surrounded by a few dozen of Russia's most ardent oppositionists was not surprising. More unexpected was the fact that the crowd numbered several thousand, including much of the capital's intellectual elite and creative class. As they marched toward Lubianka and a phalanx of riot police, chanting for Putin's resignation, their numbers only grew.

On one level, the sequence of events leading up to December 6, 2011, to the months of escalating protest and standoff that ensued, and to the shifted political landscape that characterized Russia at the time of this writing, began a little more than two months earlier, on September 24, 2011. It was on that day that Vladimir Putin, who had followed two four-year presidential terms with a four-year stint as prime minister, announced he would return to the country's highest office. That announcement, it seems certain, set in motion the political calculations and miscalculations that led to electoral fraud, public indignation, and a spiral of sociopolitical conflict.

But on another level, the story begins much earlier, perhaps back in 2005, when the first sustained grassroots protest movements in Putin's Russia began to emerge and consolidate, to formulate agendas and points of view, and to pursue a confrontational yet purposive relationship with an unresponsive state. Those stories have been told, in large part, in the preceding chapters. There is, I argue, a very real link between the social movements described earlier and the massive mobilization that accompanied Putin's return to the Kremlin. It is a link that is much bigger than just people. It is ideas that are linked, frames, ways of seeing the social space and one's own place in it.

In this chapter, I will trace the arc of the more immediate narrative, beginning in September 2011 and running into the fall of 2013. We will see the power of accidental coordination and organization that is so often observed in social movements and the struggle to maintain an uncomfortable balance between the idea of leadership and the leadership of ideas. Finally, I will sketch the new landscape of power and opposition in what continues, however tenuously, to be Putin's Russia.

The Internet Hamsters and the Office Plankton

In the 1930s, the Soviet government began a project that would lead to one of the most significant outpourings of Russian voluntarism—some eighty years later. The project was a search for fuel, and the answer Stalin's Kremlin found was peat, partly decayed plant matter compressed in the soil over centuries. Thankfully, the stuff was abundant, as massive peat bogs could be found in large numbers throughout central Russia, including in the areas surrounding Moscow. The only problem was, the bogs—as bogs tend to be—were filled with water. So the government drained them, allowing them to harvest the peat, which, once dried, burns quite nicely. And that is precisely what the peat proceeded to do: burn.

Most summers, peat fires are a part of life in the central part of European Russia. Peat burns so well that it is almost impossible to extinguish. A fire, once started, can burn for years, smoldering deep under the surface, imperceptible under a winter snowfall, but ready to reignite in the dry, hot continental summer. The summer of 2010 was particularly hot in Moscow and most of the surrounding regions, with temperatures holding for weeks at 40 degrees Celsius as a stubborn high-pressure system kept the rain away. In June, July, and August, the smoke that blanketed the capital made it impossible even to see across the street ("Torfianye pozhary" 2010). Between the fires themselves, which engulfed whole villages in the countryside, and the ill effects of heat exposure and smoke inhalation, 55,736 people were estimated to have been killed ("2010 Disasters in Numbers" 2010).

As Russia's firefighters and Emergency Situations Ministry struggled to contain the fires and help victims, a small group of young amateur computer programmers, led by Grigorii Asmolov and Alexei Sidorenko, launched their own effort. Called the Help Map (*Karta pomoshchi*), the system they devised—at a total cost of $50 to rent space on a server—adapted a tool called Ushahidi, which itself had been developed by activists in Nairobi, Kenya, to help deal with election-related violence there, and has since been used to help coordinate volunteer efforts after natural disasters in Haiti, Chile, and elsewhere. Ushahidi relies on what its proponents call "crowd sourcing," allowing large numbers of participants to interact through a single, simple interface to create a project without an overriding role for central leadership.[1] In the case of the Help Map, users were invited to submit information about the location of fires, as well as help needed (volunteer firefighters, transportation, blankets, water, food, and so on), and help available, through the website or via mobile phone text messages. The results were posted in real time to a map, allowing those who could give help to see where, when, and how help was needed.[2] Some 60,000 people used the system during the fires, and although no one knows exactly how many volunteers took part, their efforts are widely credited with having saved thousands of lives and homes (Machleder and Asmolov 2011).

In the summer of 2010, 38 percent of Russians went online at least monthly, 33 percent weekly, and 25 percent daily, all up from under 5 percent when Putin first took office in 2000. By the winter of 2011, all of the figures had risen still further, to 50 percent monthly, 47 percent weekly, and 38 percent daily.[3] Who exactly these people were was and is still a matter of some controversy: They are, of course, more likely to be urban, young, and well educated and to work in white-collar jobs, and many of that daily audience get most or all of their news from on-line sources (Toepfl 2013). But the broader social meaning of this online community is a matter of interpretation, and, as usual in Russia, interpretations abound. Many of these were vaguely zoological and broadly derogatory. Surfing blogs, nursing cell phones with their lattes in Moscow's increasingly fashionable cafés—Les Amis de Jean-Jacques, a Parisian-style bistro on Moscow's boulevard ring is and was a particularly popular hangout—with time and money to spare, these, some wrote, were Russia's new class of "office plankton," young, white-collar workers whose self-worth was presumed to exceed their societal worth (Oleinik 2011). Others began to refer to them as "network hamsters," running to and fro in the on-line hamster wheels but going nowhere in particular (Sidorenko 2011).

However others saw them, through the summer of 2010 this cohort of technologically adept, socially integrated, and economically successful Russians had proven—at least to themselves—that they could have an impact. And so, by early 2011, as the Kremlin inched toward its announcement on the resuccession, some sociologists began warning that it was time for the government to take the network hamsters seriously, as well. In the spring of 2011, Sergei Belanovskii and Mikhail Dmitriev of Moscow's Center for Strategic Developments—a Moscow think tank best known for writing reform proposals for the Ministry of Economic Development—warned that the ubiquitous leitmotif in focus groups with young to middle-aged Russian professionals was, "People are tired of being treated like cattle"; unless the Kremlin learned to listen to these people, who almost unanimously felt that the country was on the wrong track, Putin, Medvedev, and United Russia could face a catastrophic loss of legitimacy (Belanovskii and Dmitriev 2011).

September 24, or Ten Basketball Players Walk into a Shower

September 24, 2011, was not a day of surprises. In the smaller arena of Moscow's massive Luzhniki sports complex, United Russia—Russia's ruling party, and the only "party of power" to survive multiple election cycles in post-Soviet history—met for its preelection convention. In two and a half months' time, the party would stand for elections to the State Duma; three months after that, it would seek to get its candidate elected president. The only question, ostensibly, was who that candidate would be—Vladimir Putin, an eight-year veteran of that particular office, or the incumbent Dmitrii Medvedev, who was widely presumed to be keeping Putin's seat warm. In reality, of course, few if any were truly in doubt.

However, unanimity of expectation should not be mistaken for unanimity of opinion. While Putin remained the most popular politician in the country by a wide margin, his popularity had come well off its 2007 peak, hovering, in various polls, in the mid-50s; the popularity of United Russia had sunk even further, and the party was commonly referred to by the moniker devised by Navalnyi, "the party of swindlers and thieves"[4] (Greene 2012a). In fact, by mid-2011 a search on the Internet for the Russian version of that phrase generally turned up the official United Russia website as the top result. As Belanovskii and Dmitriev (2011) had noted six months prior, both Putin and Medvedev had lost a large measure of legitimacy among a public who felt that the regime was no longer pushing the country forward.

Disaffection had infected the elite, too. The Institute for Contemporary Development, a public policy think tank sponsored by the Kremlin and backed by many of Russia's business leaders, published in the summer a platform for the "next president," outlining a spate of necessary reforms, including political and economic liberalization (Gontmakher, Denisenko, et al. 2011). While the document was mum as to who the next president should be, the Institute's director, Igor Iurgens, made it clear in a number of public statements that the platform was one Putin would be incapable of implementing (Samarina 2011).

And so, when Medvedev announced to his party that he wished to nominate his predecessor to succeed him, even if no one could have been surprised, many still allowed themselves a measure of disappointment (Kolesnikov 2011). Iurgens and his colleagues were only the most visible of a section of the Russian elite who imagined a better future for themselves if Medvedev's influence grew and Putin's waned. Even Arkadii Dvorkovich, Medvedev's chief economic adviser, tweeted in frustration that it would have been better if they had gathered to play hockey at Luzhniki, rather than politics ("Pomoshchnik prezidenta Dvorkovich" 2011). The Putin–Medvedev tandem, however tentatively, had allowed some Russians who could not bring themselves to support Putin to continue supporting the regime. On September 24, 2011, that vanished.

The decision to return Putin to the Kremlin also deprived the regime of flexibility. The division between formal and informal power that existed while Medevedev was president and Putin was prime minister had arguably served both to cushion Putin against the deleterious effects of financial crisis (for which Medvedev could plausibly be blamed) and to provide room for political and ideational maneuver. With the different parts of the tandem staking out political territory across the spectrum, most elites and masses alike could find plausible reasons to lend their support, or not to drop it in the face of adversity. But September 24 gave the political system a single focus and a single objective: to return the leader to formal power, ideally in a resounding manner. From that day until March 4, 2012, every action by every actor in the regime could serve only that one purpose.

If, as I have argued in previous chapters, Russian social movements and civic opposition to the state had been stymied by the latter's refusal to engage in a cohesive, coherent, and institutional manner with citizens, then this sudden crystallization of the regime might be expected to lead to a consolidation of oppositional mobilization: Citizens now faced a hard target, not a nebulous and diffuse one, and one whose actions could be predicted with a great degree of certainty. That expectation is further strengthened by the fact that the regime elected to add insult to injury. Among the many things said by Putin and Medvedev on September 24 was a statement by the once and future president, perhaps not terribly well thought through, that he and Medvedev had "come to an agreement years ago" regarding the reverse succession (Kolesnikov 2011). After more than three years of telling Russian voters that, when the time came, the he would sit down with Medvedev and they would decide together who would stand in 2012, Putin's matter-of-fact reversal felt to many like a slap in the face (Fishman 2011).

On December 4, election day, journalist Antonina Samsonova was on duty in the newsroom of Slon.ru, a popular Russian news and blogging website. A month or so before the election, Slon.ru—along with a handful of other news-oriented websites—had begun running advertisements for Golos, an election-monitoring organization, which was encouraging voters to volunteer as election monitors, formally or informally, using crowd-sourcing techniques similar to those that had been so successful during the 2010 fires. In the run-up to the vote, Golos had been the subject of unfriendly attention from state-run television channels, as well as from law enforcement, and many of the websites that had agreed to run Golos's ads had been subject to "distributed denial of service" (DDoS) attacks. Slon.ru was among those attacked repeatedly, but despite a large DDoS attack on election day, they managed to keep the site up and running.

And so it was that Samsonova began receiving e-mails, text messages, and phone calls from voters and volunteer election monitors:

> Despite the DDoS attack on our site, we managed to keep publishing about the voting, and we started getting a huge number of messages from observers. We had no idea where these people were coming from. It turned out that these were people I knew; they were researchers from the Higher School of Economics, authors of articles about abstract subjects; and it turned out that these people were monitoring the elections. They started sending me their materials and observations from the voting and even journalistic reports. And even though we did not have a large network of

journalists covering events in Moscow, I always publish my phone number, and I got tons of messages and calls. "Look what's happening!" "This is what's happening here." "Come quick, it's total lawlessness here." And everybody who called to tell about what he or she had seen thought it was unique. They thought what they were witnessing was only happening where they were. I had to explain to them that there were only two of us in the newsroom, that I was getting forty calls an hour with exactly the same messages. I told them that we were making a record of everything. And all of those people—they were the ones who came out to the protest at Chistye Prudy, and later on Bolotnaia and Sakharova.[5]

Vladimir Ryzhkov, an opposition politician whose Republican Party of Russia had been disbanded by court order, was the first to speak at the rally at Chistye Prudy on December 6. His presence, like the rally itself, had long been planned. A month earlier, a permit to hold the rally had been sought and received by a long-standing group of activists—including politicians Ryzhkov and Boris Nemtsov, human rights activists Liudmila Alekseeva and Lev Ponomarev, and others—loosely grouped into the Solidarnost' (Solidarity) and Strategy 31 political movements. For more than two years, Strategy 31 had held rallies under the statue of Maiakovskii on Triumfal'naia square, on the 31st day of every month that has one, to call on the government to respect Article 31 of the Russian Constitution, which guarantees the right of peaceful protest. More often than not, the Strategy 31 protests were banned, and riot police easily dispersed the few dozen or so activists who came out regardless.

For whatever reason, the city authorities had granted permission to the Strategy 31/Solidarnost' group to hold a rally at Chistye Prudy on December 6, and so a stage was erected, audio equipment installed, and a space cordoned off. Still, few expected a strong turnout. In particular, those—like Samsonova or Ryzhkov—who had been used to learning of such protests through individual contacts with the organizers, whether in person or on the phone, had all but written it off. "That afternoon, I had no idea what would happen in the evening," Samsonova recalled.[6]

Had they looked on-line—particularly at the social networking site Facebook—they might have gained a different impression. That, said Sergei Parkhomenko, is how he knew what was coming:

Because I have Facebook, and because I have kids, I had these two channels of information. On the one hand, my friends on Facebook told me I should go [to Chistye Prudy]. On the other hand, my kids told me I should go. A lot of people had one of these channels telling them they should go, and I had two.[7]

The people who came out to deliver United Russia a record-low vote tally on December 4, who contributed their observations to Slon.ru, Golos and other initiatives that same day, and then turned out to the rally on December 6 are, conceptually, the same people who took part in the peat bog fire mobilization of 2010, the "network hamsters" and "office plankton" and technologically progressive (or progressed) urban middle class about which Belanovskii and Dmitriev wrote in the spring of 2011. The events of September 24, which had encouraged electoral (and, evidently, fraudulent) overstretching on December 4, had brought them to the same place on December 6 with the opposition activists who had been there all along. Parkhomenko describes the effect as follows:

> It seems to me that the best analogy for explaining what happened is a story about what happens when ten basketball players walk into the shower room after practice. They're all standing there in their ten shower stalls, turning the faucets, and the water comes out hot, then cold, then hot, and so on. Because they're doing it chaotically, they can't get the temperature right. But at some point, they all do the same thing. It just happens that they all turn the faucet to the cold side, and they all get cold water, and then they carefully start turning the faucets to the warm side, and they eventually get to the right temperature and can finally take a normal shower.[8]

After Navalnyi descended from the stage and the protestors began the march toward Lubianka, he, Ryzhkov, Parkhomenko, Kanaev, Romanova, Chirikova, and others found each other in the crowd. "It was almost an accident, the way we came together," Ryzhkov said.[9] Their brief discussion in the dark and snow led to further conversations, in person and online, and then led to a protest that brought some 50,000 people to Bolotnaia Square on December 10 and to a rally of as many as 100,000 on Prospekt Sakharova on December 24—three months, to the day, after Putin had announced his return to the Kremlin.

The Regime Reacts: If You're Not with Us, You're with Them

If the protest on December 6 was never expected to be a massive event—held on a workday evening, with very little publicity—the December 10 rally on Bolotnaia Square was an entirely different story. Held on a Saturday afternoon, in what passes for sunlight in mid-December in Moscow, the event was meant to be big, and it was—50,000 to 60,000 people turned out for the biggest opposition protest Moscow had seen in years (though not the biggest it would see that season). And this time, the list of speakers grew. While Navalnyi and leftist leader Sergei Udaltsov were absent due to a fifteen-day jail sentence following their arrest outside Lubianka on December 6, their place was taken by Udaltsov's wife, Anastasiia Udaltsova; Just Russia Duma deputies Gennadii Gudkov and Il'ia Ponomarev; journalist Leonid Parfenov; writers Boris Akunin and Zakhar Prilepin; and all of those who had spoken on the 6th—Romanova, Chirikova, Ryzhkov, Nemtsov, and others (Savina, Smirnov, et al. 2011).

At the end of the rally, two announcements were made: first, that the organizers would deliver a petition to the Kremlin demanding the release of Navalnyi, Udaltsov, and other political and economic prisoners (including many of those for whom Romanova and *Rus Sidiashchaia* fought); and second, that the protestors would come out again, on December 24, and would continue to mobilize until the parliamentary elections were annulled and new elections called. The Kremlin thus had two days to consider its strategy.

Holding to form, the Kremlin neither sought confrontation nor offered conciliation. City authorities issued a permit for the December 24 rally, just as they had for those on the 5th and the 10th. Riot police stood idly by. But the Central Election Commission certified the results of the vote, and there were few signs of impending compromise when Putin prepared for his annual "Direct Line with the Nation," a lengthy question-and-answer session with journalists, public figures, and ordinary Russians around the country, scheduled for December 15.

When Putin did take to the air, he offered limited ground for compromise (Cherkasov 2011). Governors, who had been appointed by the president since 2004, could be elected again, he said, although there would have to be some kind of "presidential filter" to ensure that the "wrong people" didn't get into power. Parliamentary elections would not be revisited, but reforms in the future might make it easier to register opposition parties, and web cameras would be installed at all voting stations around the country in time for the presidential ballot. But he also went on the attack, using his trademark deprecating humor to denigrate the protestors. The white ribbons that had become the symbol of the movement reminded him of condoms, he said. And the protestors, perhaps unwittingly, were working on behalf of foreign interests—like the leaderless Bandar Log of Kipling's *Jungle Book*, they needed to be brought back into the fold. The country, he said, needed a séance of collective psychotherapy.

Putin's four-hour-long "direct line" was perhaps the single largest source of inspiration for opposition memes ahead of the December 24 rally. Within hours, what Ryzhkov called "the Party of Jean-Jacques" (referring to the popular café) swung into action, filling the Internet with mash-ups and parodies on Putin's phrases, splicing video of the "direct line" together with images of the python Kaa from cartoons of the *Jungle Book*, for instance. A popular YouTube video featured a young woman holding a condom in one hand and a white ribbon in the other. "If you can tell the difference," she said, "join us on December 24." Pavel Bargin and Vladimir Mirzoev, two of Russia's most prominent filmmakers, produced 100 minute-long clips of famous Russians, writing their names on white ribbons and explaining why they were planning to join the rally. They included such prominent TV personalities as Vladimir Pozner, Leonid Parfenov, Mikhail Shats, Tat'iana Lazareva, and Kseniia Sobchak; writers Boris Akunin and Dmitrii Bykov; and musician Iurii Shevchuk.[10] A group of young, Internet-facile journalists, including Il'ia Klishin, Il'ia Faibisovich, and the brothers Tikhon, Filipp, and Timofei Dziadko, organized online communities in Facebook and the Russian social networking site VKontakte to disseminate information and coordinate activities.

All of these people and more flowed into an open-door organizing committee, which swelled at various points to as many as 200 participants. Meeting in Moscow cafés, bookstores, and anywhere else they could find space, and with meetings broadcast live to as many as 300,000 viewers through the Russian video streaming site Setevizor, they set about assigning roles and determining the agenda for the December 24 rally. The brothers Dziadko managed the online public relations; Parkhomenko, Gudkov, and Ryzhkov were put in charge of negotiating with the police and other authorities; Iurii Saprykin, editor of *Afisha*, Moscow's leading culture magazine, took charge of the stagecraft for the rally itself. There was, of course, conflict between long-time opposition politicians and the newer wave of activists and between the political and cultural elites, according to Olga Romanova, who was invited by Boris Akunin and Leonid Parfenov to moderate the meetings and handle the budget:

> Everyone understood that for us, for the members of the organizing committee, this was one of life's big chances. For some, this was the last chance to come to power, and for others the last chance to change something, something in themselves, in the country, for their children—to try really hard not to leave [the country]. After sitting on my suitcases for the last five years, I understood that it's easier for me to try to do something here, than to start all over again [somewhere else]. . . . For me, it's honest work and the last chance to stay in the country. For Nemtsov, of course, it's the last chance to come to power, for example. And so it is all very serious; a lot of people have forgotten all their grudges, because there are more important things than arguing. We're all well aware that we'll have plenty of time later to blame each other for everything that goes wrong.[11]

With as many as 120,000 participants, the December 24 rally on Prospekt Sakharova was the largest Moscow had seen since 1991. Opposition-minded Russians of all stripes came out—liberals from inside and outside the system, including recently resigned finance minister Aleksei Kudrin; nationalists; environmentalists; the automotive movements; feminists; and the traditionally marginalized LGBT movement—and representatives from all major groups had a chance to speak. Broadly speaking, the makeup was the same it had been on December 6 and 10, only larger: upper-middle class, well-educated urban intellectuals, broadly sympathizing with Russia's liberal opposition (*Opros na prospekte* 2011). But the demands had changed since December 10: No longer content to call for a rerun of the parliamentary elections, the protestors were calling for Putin's resignation.

If Putin had hoped that his give-and-take "direct line" on December 15 would defuse the protest movement, he was disappointed. Instead, the protests had only escalated, and his own words had added fuel to the fire, as the protests grew both in size and in radicalism. And so when the organizing committee proposed the next protest—a march from Kaluzhskaia Square to Bolotnaia Square on February 4, 2012—the authorities at first balked, banning it thirty-six hours before it was to be held, only to reverse their decision hours later. Parkhomenko, as before, led the negotiations on behalf of the organizing committee:

> I tried to show them that street protests are their problem. They have an interest in making sure that they happen and happen without conflict. It was important to avoid a situation in which it's important to me to hold a protest, and they don't want it, and so I have to find some way to sell my goals to them. It was important to me to explain to them that they have an interest in this. Because there are people, I told them, who have certain intentions and feelings, and they're going to act in accordance with those intentions. We don't know how, but we know that a person is angry, that he is consumed by a desire to do something, and neither we [the committee] nor you [the authorities] know what [that person will do]. And so it is your problem, and you have to find some form, some reservoir, that you can propose to these people and that they will find acceptable, in accordance with the feelings that are tearing them apart.
>
> And the second thing I explained to them is that I'm not in control. That's a very paradoxical thing, which I didn't immediately understand, because it contradicts the usual understanding of how negotiations work. Usually, negotiations are built on one person trying to demonstrate to his partner his power and competence. . . . But

these negotiations were totally different. I don't control anything. I told them: You can come to an agreement with me about anything you like, you can convince me of anything at all, you can force me, you can outsmart me, but you have to understand that that won't guarantee you anything. If you convince me that we should hold this protest out at Sheremet'evo Airport, then all you'll achieve is that I'll come back and say, "Friends, I've agreed that we're going to hold the rally at Sheremet'evo." And the people will call me an idiot, and that will be that, and then you'll have to negotiate with someone else. So, don't try to convince me; let's try together to come up with something that the people will accept.[12]

The police and Moscow city authorities, Parkhomenko believes, understood his logic and sought, wherever possible, to avoid conflict. The February 4 protest brought out another 100,000 or so participants, peacefully. But Putin and his political team, evidently, saw things differently. On February 23, just ten days before the presidential vote, Putin rallied the faithful in the large soccer stadium at Luzhniki, just next door to the smaller arena where his candidacy had been announced. February 23 is also Defender of the Fatherland Day, Russia's annual "men's day," and Putin's rhetoric was suitably militaristic:

Putin: We are all ready, together, to work for the good of our great Motherland. Ready not only to work, but to defend her. To defend her always. And we will not allow anyone to interfere in our internal affairs. We will not allow anyone to force their will on us, because we have our own will. Our will has always helped us to triumph. We are the people of victory. It's in our genes, in our genetic code. It is passed down from generation to generation. And we will triumph. I ask you, will we triumph?

Crowd: Yes!

Putin: Yes, we will triumph, but it is not enough for us to win only in these elections. . . . We ask everyone not to glance over the horizon, not to run off to the left, to the side, not to betray their Motherland, but to be together with us, to work for her and her people, to love her as we do, with all our hearts. . . . We will remember our greatness and remember these words: *We will die at Moscow/As our brothers died/And to die we promised/And our oath of loyalty we kept.*[13] The battle for Russia goes on, and we will be victorious! (Vystuplenie Vladimira Putina 2012)

In theory, the "revolutionary spiral" of conflict between a social movement and a regime generally involves a ratcheting up of both protest and repression (Goldstone and Tilly 2001: 190–191). In this case, however, a spiral of rhetoric seemed to suffice.

The New Landscape of Power and Opposition in Russia

On March 4, 2012, Vladimir Putin was elected to the Russian presidency for the third time and for the first two six-year terms he is now constitutionally allowed to serve. Although Russian and international election observers noted a significant degree of fraud, few argued that it was sufficient to call his victory into question. That could have been the end of the movement, but it was not. "I'm in a good mood," said Sergei Parkhomenko, interviewed in May of 2012:

> Because in December, it seemed to me that we had to be in a hurry, that if we don't hurry, we'll either bring the whole place crashing down or everything will quiet down, stop, go into hibernation. But now I feel differently; now things are developing slowly, gradually. Of course, it goes in waves like a sine curve, but it clear that each wave does not dip back down to the previous trough, that the general trend is upward. Of course, each dip brings some desperation, and then each rise brings exaggerated optimism. But you can get used to that over time. There was a time when everything that happened was good for Putin. We even won at football. Oil prices went in the right direction. But now the opposite is true. We're winning at hockey, but it's not his victory. Now, everything that happens works in our favor. It's funny. Girls go back to school with their white bows in their hair; it's good for us. White nights in St. Petersburg; that's also our victory.[14]

The period since Putin's reelection, however, has been anything but easy. The regime's rhetorical counterattack continued, including a number of "investigative" documentary films shown on state-run television, portraying the protest leaders as corrupt agents of the West. Interest in the protests themselves has gradually waned. The March 5 protest on Pushkinskaya Square brought out only an estimated 30,000 people—still very large by pre-2011 standards but much smaller than the December rallies. Ensuing protests were smaller still, until May 6, 2012, when a nationwide day of protest was called to coincide with Putin's inauguration. Estimates of turnout range from 50,000 to 120,000, with the bulk marching from Kaluzhskaia Square to Bolotnaia Square. As the marchers crossed the bridge to Bolotnaia Square, they were confronted by a battalion of riot police. In the ensuing violence, some forty people were injured, and between 400 and 700 were arrested (Feldman, Grechina, et al. 2012). It was the first incident of violence since the movement began.

The organizing committee that had put together all of the previous protests played no part in the May 6 march, which was led primarily by Udaltsov and Navalnyi, but the movement was not over. The election monitoring organiza-

tions Golos, Liga Izbiratelei (League of Voters), and Grazhdanin Nabliudatel'
(Citizen Observer), the latter two of which had been formed since December
2011, continued to appeal contested local elections in cities, including Astrakhan, and monitored local and regional elections through the spring and summer of 2012. Those involved in the Moscow street protests began gathering
regularly at the statue of the Kazakh poet Abay Qunanbayuli and other points
around the city, forming the Occupy Abay group and gathering, weather per-
mitting, for open-air lectures and strategy sessions modeled on the Occupy
Wall Street movement in the United States ("Okkupai Abai prodolzhaetsia"
2012). In October, some 80,000 people voted in elections to a forty-member
Opposition Coordinating Committee, tasked with developing strategies for
new protests, election-related activities, and the general development of the
movement (Elifanova 2012).

A new structure had emerged, too, underpinning the new oppositional
movement. A young generation of journalists and bloggers, particularly working with Internet news outlets such as Lenta.ru, Gazeta.ru, Slon.ru, and Dozhd,
were central to the aggregation and dissemination of mobilizational information and memes throughout the peak protest period and had, by the summer of 2012, developed personal relationships and identities associated with
the movement (Greene 2012b). What is more, preexisting social movements,
NGOs, and protest groups that had prior to December 2011 focused on their
thematically or geographically localized conflicts were now woven into a much
broader civic network, which, in turn, recruited a much broader constituency
to the movement as a whole (Greene 2013). As a result, as the heat of election-
related protest began to subside, activists such as Kanaev, Chirikova, Navalnyi,
or Romanova—whose husband, Aleksei Kozlov, was reconvicted and returned
to jail on March 15, ten days after Putin's reelection—returned to their initial
conflicts not only with new ideas and new energy, but with new friends, followers, and mobilizational resources. So, too, do the individual protestors return to
daily life with a new set of experiences and understandings. Expecting Putin to
be reelected, Sergei Kanaev said just prior to the presidential vote:

> I think people will understand the positive direction. Look at the [election] ob-
> servers, or at projects like Navalnyi's. . . . Go, participate. These people will begin
> to seek their own development, their minutes of fame in these civic organizations.
> There will be more and more of these people. That is where they will direct their
> energies.[15]

The regime, meanwhile, has chosen a combination of repression and rhetoric. In the immediate aftermath of Putin's inauguration, a number of laws made their way through the Duma aimed in one way or another at the opposition: a law increasing the penalties for violations during street protests; a law requiring all NGOs receiving funding from abroad to register as "foreign agents"; a law allowing tighter control over the Internet. Criminal cases have been opened into several of those arrested on May 6, on charges of inciting mass unrest. State-run television has run further "exposés" of the protest leaders, which have in turn led to the opening of criminal cases against Udaltsov and others; one suspect, Leonid Razvozzhaev, was reportedly kidnapped by Russian secret servicemen in Kiev and delivered to Moscow for interrogation ("ONK" 2012). Official and state-media rhetoric has continued to associate the opposition with the West, with extremist ideologies and—following the Pussy Riot scandal, in which a feminist punk band was sentenced to two years in prison after singing about Putin in Moscow's Christ the Savior Cathedral—with blasphemy and "nontraditional" values. The object, to the extent that the object is possible to discern, seems to be to isolate the opposition while galvanizing the regime's core conservative constituency.

An early test of both the regime and the newly structured opposition came in the summer of 2013. Sergei Sobianin, appointed mayor of Moscow after Luzhkov was forced out by then-President Medvedev in October 2010, resigned his appointment in June 2013 and called snap elections for September of that year, in which he would stand as candidate (and acting mayor). The Opposition Coordinating Committee nominated Navalnyi to stand. The resulting campaign was short, fraught, and confused. Navalnyi was forced to spend much of the summer in the provincial city of Kirov, where he was battling charges that he had embezzled money from a forestry company owned by the regional government, for which he had briefly been a consultant. Despite the belief by many observers that the charges had been fabricated, Navalnyi and his codefendant, Petr Ofitserov, were convicted and sentenced to five and four years in prison, respectively, on July 18, 2013 ("Delo o khishchenii imushchestva" 2013).

That Navalnyi might be prevented from running was not a surprise to most observers; the real surprise came the next day, on July 19, 2013, when the prosecution itself filed a motion requesting that Navalnyi's sentence be suspended pending appeal, thus releasing him from jail and freeing him to run against Sobianin. The ensuing campaign saw Navalnyi—with the broad but not unanimous support of many of those who stood with him during the 2011–2012 protests—raise as much as 70 million rubles (approximately $2.1 million) through small on-line donations and mobilize as many as 14,000 volunteers (by the campaign's own estimate), distributing leaflets and stickers, bombarding Muscovites with phone calls and on-line social media messages, and staffing "cubes" that the campaign set up outside metro stations throughout the city, where potential voters could interact with Navalnyi supporters (Feldman 2013). In the end, on September 8, 2013, Navalnyi garnered 27.24 percent of the vote, while Sobianin narrowly evaded a second round, with 51.37 percent.[16] Opposition candidates did better elsewhere, winning mayoral races in Ekaterinburg and Petrozavodsk.

The result is a stalemate. The opposition is not strong or large enough to upend the regime, and, with the next Duma and presidential elections scheduled for 2016 and 2018 respectively, they are not likely to have an opportunity to do so anytime soon. But, absent the will to pursue outright and large-scale repression, neither is the regime able to dislodge the opposition. The ideas that underpinned the mobilization—ideas of dignity, justice, and right, stemming from localized offense but extended almost immediately to a sense of infringed citizenship—were present, indeed widespread, long before 2011. Now, however, there appears to be a greater recognition among the movements' activists that those ideas, senses, and interests are shared; that they inhabit a single political field; and that common cause can be pursued through common effort.

What, then, have we learned? When events occur that surprise us, it is always easiest to carry that surprise forward, readjusting our expectations of the future. It is often more important, however, to carry that surprise backward in time, reevaluating the assumptions we had of the past. If we assumed that the lack of civic and political mobilization in Russia was due to a lack of social capital, trust, or adherence to the values of democratic participation, then the events of 2011 and 2012 might cause us to wonder what could have changed so rapidly in Russian society to make this sort of mass mobilization possible. But societies do not change in a matter of months, and social capital takes time to accumulate.

The Russian social movements explored in this book, however, tell a different story. Theirs is a story in which trust is relatively easy to come by, in which positive experiences of mobilization are quickly disseminated and assimilated, and in which the gap between particularized grievance and generalized injustice is rapidly bridged. The difficulties these movements faced stemmed not from themselves or their participants but from their institutional environment, from the amorphous nature of the state with which they were fated by geography to interact. This deinstitutionalized state atomized the experiences of its citizens and thus yielded little traction to collective mobilization. In the rarer instances when it acted institutionally, it immediately faced opposition, and it often lost.

What changed, then, was not Russian society, but the Russian state. On September 24, the state crystallized, presenting citizens with a view of the future— or, at least, twelve years of the future—that could easily be predicted to look very much like the recent past. It tied that view to a single goal that centered on the reelection of a single man, with none of the both-sides-of-the-coin flexibility and managed uncertainty that had allowed the hedging of bets in previous cycles. Faced with opposition, it crystallized still further, pursuing rhetorical and then coercive confrontation of the kind that almost always supports the building of collective identities in social movements. By making the state more tractable, the regime has succeeded in creating an intractable opposition.

9   Conclusions

This book began with a few hundred Russian protestors sitting, cross-legged and isolated, behind an iron fence at the end of an island in St. Petersburg in a self-conscious illustration of their own futility. It ends with hundreds of thousands of Russian citizens in the streets of Moscow and other major cities, protesting an election they felt was stolen and launching the country's most significant wave of political contestation since the early 1990s. Sustained through Vladimir Putin's third presidential inauguration in May 2012, this mobilization—while unsuccessful in its attempt to force political liberalization in Russia—has crystallized into an entrenched political opposition that the regime is either unwilling or unable to dislodge. The result, while short of a revolution, is a real and lasting shift in Russia's political landscape.

Prior to December 2011, the consensus among analysts and observers of Russian political life held that Russian civil society was weak, undermined by an ingrained lack of trust and a host of debilitating maladies inherited from the Soviet past, beset by an oppressive state, fractured by divisive and inept leadership and co-opted at turns by the West and the Kremlin. Such a civil society was seen as impotent in the face of authoritarian retrenchment, systematically unable to rouse a passive population in the defense of democratic rights.

The natural instinct of an analyst caught off guard by events as they unfold is to think about the future; to assume that something important has changed, upending a prior order; and thus to seek to understand the new order as it emerges. This has been the dominant approach as scholars have begun to explore the events of 2011 and 2012 in Russia. But understanding where we're going requires understanding where we stand and how we got here. Unless we take a hard look at the past, reevaluating our earlier conclusions and questioning our prior assumptions, our next set of conclusions will prove no more robust than the last one.

That is the puzzle at the heart of this book: What do we need to understand about the relationship between Russian citizens and their state prior to December 2011 in order to get a grip on how that relationship is changing? A closer look at Russia's recent past—in this case, the period of Putin's rule—reveals a citizenry capable of pressing demands against the state and, in some cases, winning; a citizenry capable of trust and mobilization; and a citizenry fully aware of the political realities in which it exists. In short, Russia's election protests did not emerge from nowhere. They had roots, and those roots are the subject of this book.

The title of this volume—*Moscow in Movement*—suggests the thrust and origins of its argument. In approaching the study of state–society engagement in Russia, I draw on the insights of Sidney Tarrow, author of *Power in Movement*, and others, who understood the state and civil society as mutually constituting. From this perspective, civil society itself is a mirror held up to the state, the contours and content of civic action and mobilization reflecting the content and contours of ruling elites' intrusions into the private and social lives of citizens.

Throughout most of Putin's rule, the Russian state has developed a form of hybrid authoritarianism that is both disengaged and deinstitutionalized, seeking to minimize points of contact between the state and its citizens and, where contact is necessary, failing to structure that engagement along coherent, predictable patterns. The result, I argue, is a political and civic landscape that privileges individual coping mechanisms over collective action. But when, on rare occasions, the state does intervene in the lives of its citizens in a concerted manner, allowing them to sense a collective injustice and identify themselves as aggrieved, Russians prove eminently capable of mounting a coherent and often successful response.

The question that should arise after December 2011, then, is not what changed in Russian society, but what changed in the Russian state. If power and opposition are seen as mutually constituting, then we begin to understand that it was shifts in the elite's strategies—specifically, the replacement of flexible political brinksmanship with a rigid and narrowly construed strategy of authoritarian retrenchment—that gave rise to the current regime's strongest political challenge since its inception. And if that is the case, then Russian citizens are best understood not as passive, untrusting, and hide-bound individualists but as adept navigators of a shifting and uncertain sociopolitical landscape that they nonetheless understand exceedingly well.

~

Throughout this volume I have tried to tell the stories of ordinary Russians faced with injustice and their failures and occasional successes in seeking redress. They have fought abuses of human rights; violations of their civil, political, and economic rights; and threats to their very livelihood. They have shown themselves to be in possession of solidarity and trust and more than capable of drawing conclusions—even democratically informed conclusions—about their predicaments. They see a deeply uninstitutionalized environment, in which laws are neither binding nor empowering and in which the state is usurious, rather than useable. Russians are acutely aware of their political surroundings and of the opportunities and limitations those surroundings create for fruitful collective action. It is precisely because of that awareness, and not despite it, that Russian civil society seems so weak to a Western observer. Opposition, then, reflects the power structure that provokes it: individualized, ad hoc, opportunistic, and unstructured. The cases presented in this thesis show that when, for whatever reason, the power structure behaves differently, opposition responds in kind.

Indeed, the Russian state presents a rare combination of tremendous power and tremendously little institutionalization. Numerous writers have underscored the need to pay attention to institutions and the fact that states must be strong to function (see, for example: Fukuyama 2004). Weak states, accordingly, cannot be functioning democracies, and the desire of a state to become stronger is not necessarily a sign of authoritarian tendencies. But however weakly institutionalized Russia may be, the regime is not weak. Deinstitutionalization, paradoxically, is the source of the regime's strength. Having ensconced themselves in the residual apparatus of what used to be a highly institutionalized state, the new Russian ruling elite enjoy a remarkable degree of power and privilege, to a degree greater than in any democratic regime and even than in most authoritarian regimes. And they do so not despite but because of deinstitutionalization: the regime's ability to control the rules of the game makes its position virtually unassailable. But the maintenance of power and privilege, both in current and potential terms, requires at least a degree of solidarity among a divided and competitive elite. They must act on the understanding that their personal power and privilege will persist only as long as the club persists; although they may compete, in the end they either sink together or swim together. Yet the creation of any institutional mechanisms that would enforce this solidarity would inevitably diminish the elite's power and privilege, by making rules and outcomes predictable and, in so doing, decreasing the elite's competitive advantage over other social groups and those who might leave the club to attack its position from outside. Thus, such institutions are rejected, and solidarity is enforced through deinstitutionalization, which creates a degree of uncertainly sufficient to keep the elite in line. It is through the manufacture and management of uncertainty that the regime produces and reproduces power.

Prior to the ascent of Putin, Russian elites had access to a broad spectrum of competitive resources: private business, the media, independent political parties participating in unpredictable elections, and, of course, access to the bureaucratic apparatus. As we explored in Chapter 3, Russia's political, economic, and bureaucratic elites began to reconsolidate in 1999, essentially reconstituting a version of the "club" that had controlled access to power and privilege under the Soviet system and adapting it to Russia's new circumstances. The members of this "club" sought to maintain their unencumbered and unchallenged access to power and privilege in a system more stable and less risky than the all-out competition of the 1990s. This was accomplished by affecting a monopoly over all perceived potential sources of power. Thus, in Putin's Russia, the state has monopolized the media and the political space, and business "owners" have little more than a tenuous leasehold on their property. All of these resources pertain to the club and may not be removed from the club; departure of an individual from the club implies the forfeiture of his or her resources. Competition for control over these resources within the club is conducted exclusively within and by means of the administrative apparatus. Competitors were persuaded to give up their prior freedom of maneuver in return for an implicit guarantee that all well-behaved members of the elite would enjoy power and privilege for as long as the regime stood.

In this context, a politics that is responsive to the public is not merely superfluous: It is antithetical to the spirit of the club and threatens the cohesion of the system. This both shapes and is reflected by the way that Russian citizens experience their state. It leads to maximized rent seeking by public officials, for whom the law is first and foremost a tool of personal power. It also makes these "civil servants" (though the term seems particularly perverse in the Russian context) impervious to considerations of public accountability, to a rather shocking degree: It takes an extraordinary (for the Russian context) outpouring of protest to force the system to respond to demands from below and a tremendous amount of pressure to generate anything resembling institutional change. And this inevitably redounds to the development of civil society. Atomized, unstructured relationships between citizens and the state do not favor collective solutions, as problems are perceived as being primarily individual in nature. The evidence presented here shows that these perceptions change when the state, for one reason or another, departs from its usual repertoire. And then arises collective action, often in the form of protosocial movements. These movements (or, rather, movement organizations) then face the difficult task of preventing the state from reverting back to its preferred stance of disengagement and ad hoc policy making, which would otherwise undermine the movement. Or they must hope that the state, for whatever reason, itself stays the course of coherent and concerted intrusion into the lives of its citizens in such a way that those citizens are able to form injustice frames and movement identities.

As I review in Chapter 2, civil society, by virtually all accounts, exists in the space between individuals and the state, with at least some expectation that it will mediate the interaction between the two. Much of modern political thought, and the core of liberal theory, has been dedicated to proving the idea that the state–society relationship is a zero-sum game: The stronger one side becomes, the weaker becomes the other. Those concerned with failing states have begun to suggest that this may not actually be the case, that strong societies require strong states. Indeed, theorists of civil society who have looked beyond modern, Gramscian notions of the concept back to its roots in earlier political philosophy note that the nature of civil society depends first and foremost on the nature of the state. Thus, Krishan Kumar writes: "De Tocqueville, we may remember, noted that it was politics that spreads 'the general habit and taste for association.' In other words, politics precedes civil society" (Kumar 1993: 391). It is this politics-centered viewpoint, rather than the apolitical focus on horizontal social relations, that dominates much of the normative literature, that I have found useful here.

If we return the focus of study to the state–society relationship and the practice of politics and political engagement, it becomes clear that the weakness of Russian civil society is not solely explained by issues of trust, social capital, or the Soviet legacy. I do not mean to suggest that such issues play no role in Russia. And this is not to say that there have been no obstacles. But the key obstacles faced by Russian citizens have been of a different nature, the result of a disengagement by the state. Russia's aggressively deinstitutionalized political space leads inherently to an atomized civic space. It is considerations of utility that stymie Russian civil society; they cannot and do not often identify with one another as a group, capable and motivated to act, not because of an aversion to groups, to action, or to each other but because of a calculation that such action would generally be useless. This assertion can be tested to a certain degree by seeking exceptions to the rule, the sorts of exceptions presented here. And in those exceptions we see clearly that, when the state does engage in a way that allows Russian citizens to form collective identities, collective action is both possible and potent.

Linz and Stepan (1996) and others have argued that postauthoritarian civil society needs to adapt itself to new, democratic modes of interaction. But even given the failure of democracy to develop, even if we remain within an authoritarian context, civil society must recognize shifts within authoritarian rule and find ways to engage with the state along those front lines where the state continues to engage its citizens.

It is at some of those points of engagement that this book has found its cases. In the first instance, in Chapter 5, we have seen an attempt by a highly professional group of activists to reshape the system that currently allows Russian law enforcement to abuse the civil and human rights of citizens. In one of its goals—defending citizens who have been abused—the activists have been remarkably successful. But they have been utterly unable to affect any systemic change. Police, prosecutors, and judges act as free agents, pursuing their interests in an institutional (or deinstitutionalized) environment that allows them to privatize the law, with little or no upward or downward accountability. Citizens recognize the chaos inherent in this arrangement, and no collective response arises to address a problem that is, in the end, highly individualized.

In the second instance, in Chapter 6, we have seen spontaneous protests grow into sustained resistance against various acts by state and private actors that put at risk Russian citizens' housing and property rights. Faced with clear and immediate adversity, the citizens involved prove eminently capable of self-organization, solidarity, and trust, quickly recognizing the collective nature of the threat and putting together a response that is successful in repelling specific threats. The state, however, refuses to perceive the diverse protest movements as reflecting a systemic problem—one that stems from corruption, weak property rights, and the lack of political accountability—and, instead, treats protestors either as small groups or as individuals, resolving conflicts on an ad hoc basis. As a result, the protestors themselves fail to consolidate into a horizontally integrated movement, and even the local movements begin to disintegrate.

The success and solidarity of the automotive rebellion, explored in Chapter 7, is remarkable not only against the backdrop of contemporary Russia, but when compared to the other cases in this book as well. Neither Public Verdict nor the housing movements were abject failures; the former has succeeded in obtaining justice for many of its "clients," while the latter produced a degree of solidarity where none had existed before and won temporary victories against the state. Still, the protagonists in both cases failed, I argue, not because of their own mistakes, or even for a lack of resources, but because of the failure of the state to provide the sociopolitical and institutional context in which citizens could begin to conceive of and develop strategies of collective action. If the reader were to approach these chapters from back to front, reading the stories from the end, numerous differences would emerge: The automotive movement has a stronger ideological component, a more robust media component, a more flexible organizational structure, a larger support network, and so on and so forth. But causality does not work backwards through history, and we need to read the stories from the beginning. And, in the beginning, the only thing that truly separates these cases is the nature of the state's interaction. In the Public Verdict case, the state afflicted people individually, and collective action failed. In the housing case, the state afflicted people as a group but responded to them individually, and collective action faltered. But in the automotive case, the state afflicted people as a group and responded to them as a group, and collective action succeeded.

∽

This volume may provide a useful corrective to the study of "democratization in waves" that returned to the forefront of political science first in the aftermath of the so-called color revolutions that swept through the postcommunist space (Ukraine, Georgia, and Kyrgyzstan were the most prominent cases), and again following the "Arab Spring" that ended (at least temporarily) autocratic rule in Tunisia, Egypt, and Libya. Writing on the "color revolutions" but expressing a sentiment that could just as easily be applied to the Arab Spring, Lucan Way cautioned against assuming that a series of events occurring in relatively quick succession implies a logic of contagion or diffusion: "A succession of cars may pull into a gas station because the drivers are emulating the cars in front of them, but it is more likely because each has run out of gas" (Way 2008: 57).

In their seminal work on "competitive authoritarianism"—hybrid regimes "in which formal democratic institutions exist . . . but in which incumbents' abuse of the state places them at a significant advantage vis-à-vis their opponents"—Steven Levitsky and Lucan Way posit that the apparent durability of these regimes, which many had formerly assumed would be unstable, moving quickly either to democracy or full authoritarianism, was a factor of "vulnerability to Western democratizing pressure" and the regime's own "organizational power" (Levitsky and Way 2010: 5, 23–24). Similarly, Jason Brownlee posits dominant political parties as the key variable, suggesting that they provide the coordination mechanisms needed to keep elites in line and on board (Brownlee 2007). This helps us understand that authoritarian regimes fall as a result of breakdowns in their own internal dynamics, including autocrats' effective control over wealth and the institutions (often informal) of elite coordination and coercion (Way 2008).

This clarity, perhaps, allows us not to be surprised when the failure of an authoritarian regime does not lead to the establishment of a democratic one— as, indeed, few if any of the "color" or Arab revolutions has yielded democratic governance, with the possible exception of Tunisia at the time of this writing. And yet by returning the focus to the macrolevel, these formalistic, top-down approaches to the study of politics in authoritarianism prevent us from seeing much more fundamental change.

While finding very little evidence of democratic durability in the aftermath of the Arab Spring, Alfred Stepan and Juan Linz note that:

> Neither the Hungarian Revolution of 1956, the Prague Spring of 1968, nor Poland's Soldiarity in 1981 succeeded in immediately creating a democracy. Yet each of these historic movements eroded forever the legitimacy of the dictatorial regime that it challenged. We think that the events of the Arab Spring at the very least have made Arab "presidents for life" increasingly unacceptable, and the dignity of citizens increasingly desired. (Stepan and Linz 2013: 29)

Dignity, too, was a common refrain of the protests on Bolotnaia Square and Prospekt Sakharova. It was a refrain among the motorists and among those who struggled to save their neighborhoods, their homes, their lives.

If this book makes a contribution to our understanding of autocratic power and social movements more broadly, I hope that it will be to underscore the importance of understanding authoritarianism as a lived social experience rather than as an aggregation of macrolevel conditions and structures. Indeed, this sort of approach is gaining ground in the study of other countries, and the contrasts are instructive. In China, Ching Kwan Lee and Yonghong Zhang, in an endeavor strikingly similar to what this book has sought to achieve for the Russian case, turn to the study of "microfoundations," by which the authors refer "to the microapparatuses of the state that have direct interaction with aggrieved citizens and protesters" (Lee and Zhang 2013: 1477).

They find that Chinese authorities use three key mechanisms effectively to manage, contain, and channel dissent: "logics of market exchange," "interpersonal bonds" and "rule-bound games" (Lee and Zhang 2013). In Russia, by contrast, we do find a reliance on the "logics of market exchange" and "interpersonal bonds" but an aversion, by the state and its representatives, to "rule-bound games," tending instead to use the lack of rules (and thus the unpredictability of state behavior) as a means of discouraging collective challenges. The result is that, while the peace is often (though not always) kept, the underlying grievances themselves are rarely resolved, and would-be challengers are not turned into proponents of the system. To borrow Lee and Zhang's formulation, the experience of Russian authoritarian domination appears to be much more of a zero-sum game than in China.

A focus on the microlevel likewise helps us understand change over time. In an earlier study of protest in Russia, Graeme Robertson found that labor mobilization—which dominated the Russian protest scene in the 1990s—was elite-led and manipulated, which is not to say that the grievances weren't real (they were), but that mobilization was useful to certain politicians (regional governors, mostly) in their battles against others (mostly in the Kremlin) (Robertson 2011). This, Robertson wrote, argues for understanding protest in hybrid regimes such as Russia's as dependent on three factors: "organizational ecology"; "state mobilization strategies"; and "patterns of elite competition." However, he writes:

> The relationship between regime and contention is not unidirectional; patterns of contention affect how regimes develop too. The analysis illustrates that large numbers of protesters in the streets are usually the result of fissures in the incumbent elite coalition but are not necessarily a sign of the kind of civil society organization that promotes longer-term democratic development. The long-term effect of crowds depends on the organizations that underlie them. Where independent organizations capable of holding elites and the state accountable emerge in the process of contention, movement in the direction of democracy is more likely. However, neither spontaneous wild-cat protests nor elite-managed demonstrations often leave behind strong, independent organizations, so we can see a lot of protest without much progress toward democratization. (Robertson 2011: 4)

Many things have shifted since the period about which Robertson wrote. For one, the Kremlin succeeded in consolidating its control over regional power structures, culminating in the shift to appointed governors (Sharafutdinova 2013). At first, as Robertson writes, this leads to a dramatic decline in the prevalence of protest in general and labor mobilization in particular, supporting Robertson's hypothesis. But, by 2007, a new strike wave emerged, led by independent unions and with newly framed grievances, following a logic distinct from that Robertson observed in the pre-Putin period (Greene and Robertson 2010). To that we can add the evidence presented in this volume, and we arrive at a picture of a society that is developing, tentatively, its own "organizational ecology," independently of the mobilizational strategies of the regime and the elite.

At the very least, we now know where to look if we want to understand where Russian society and politics may be headed.

Notes

Chapter 1

1. In Russian, *"Prava ne daiut, prava berut!"* and *"Nam nuzhna drugaia Rossiia!,"* respectively.

2. The foregoing narrative was compiled from firsthand observation.

3. While Kitschelt and Smyth's argument in this case is specifically about political parties, there is nothing to suggest that their logic would not apply equally to nonparty and civic actors as well.

4. Incidentally, more has been done in this area in Latin America. See, for example, Wampler and Avritzer 2004.

5. In this discussion, an institution is understood in the classic sociological sense as an ingrained set of generally accepted norms governing an aspect of social behavior and allowing actors to make predictions about the consequences of their actions with a reasonable degree of certainty. In this view, institutions are consolidated over time, as rules are established and transformed into norms through their repeated application by different participants in the given social relationship. In a complex social system such as the modern state, there exists a multilayered web of institutions that interact with and build on each other. Social relationships will rest on the highest level of consolidated institutions; if a particular institution is not consolidated, the relationship will settle one level lower. Thus, for example, if the institution of state–society relations is unconsolidated, the relationship between state and individual will be preeminent. Likewise, if the formal structures of state power are unconsolidated, the prerogative will fall to corporate or even individual interests within the governing elite.

Chapter 2

1. From Cicero's *The Republic*, quoted in Islamoglu 2001: 1891.

Chapter 3

1. The foregoing narrative was reconstructed from the author's interview with Anna, the participant described, on July 12, 2008. The subject requested that her

surname not be revealed. Quotations are reconstructed, as reported by the interview subject, and are meant to be illustrative, rather than exact.

2. The term, popular in Russian academic thought, is less common in English. From the *Oxford English Dictionary*: "aiming at a union or reconciliation of diverse beliefs, practices or systems." The connotation is that syncretic system attempts to combine elements that are inherently in tension with each other, in this case market relations and a political hierarchy.

3. All translations from Kordonskii 2000 are my own.

4. In their categorization, Helmke and Levitsky identify *blat* and its attendant phenomena as "accommodating informal institutions" that "contradict the spirit, but not the letter of the formal rules" to increase efficiency. It may be more appropriate, however, to classify them as "competing informal institutions" that "structure incentives in ways that are incompatible with the formal rules" (Helmke and Levitsky 2004: 729). The informal economy in the Soviet Union clearly contradicted the strictures of socialism and most associated activities were punishable by law. The question, then, becomes why the regime largely ignored such violations.

5. "Stagnation."

6. "Black-marketeers."

7. "Currency-men."

8. "Dealers."

9. "Pushers."

10. How this was carried out will be explored in more detail in the following sections of this chapter.

11. All translations from Kodin 1998 are my own.

12. Many observers at the time speculated that the initial law was written deliberately so that Putin could revise it, appearing liberal while maintaining a robust new set of rules.

Chapter 5

1. Public Verdict, www.publicverdict.org

2. This number is based on a search for the organization's name in the EastView database of Russian newspaper archives.

3. Interview with an anonymous representative of a Western donor, Moscow, January 23, 2007.

4. S. B. Rashupkin, "Zakliuchenie sluzhebnoi proverki v otnoshenii sotrudnikov Kanavinskogo ROVD Frolova M. F. i Khor'iakova N. A.," December 15, 2000, photocopy in the archives of Public Verdict, Case File No. 6.

5. O. V. Kiriukhov, "Postanovlenie o prekrashenii ugolovnogo dela No. 522616," May 27, 2001, photocopy in the archives of Public Verdict, Case File No. 6.

6. G. I. Khavroshechkin, sworn affidavit to the Committee Against Torture, May 29, 2001, photocopy in the archives of Public Verdict, Case File No. 6.

7. Information drawn from the archives of Public Verdict, Case File No. 62, 2007.

8. Information drawn from the archives of Public Verdict, Case File No. 15, 2007.

9. Information drawn from the archives of Public Verdict, "Delo Khalilova" (no case file number), 2007.

10. Information drawn from the archives of Public Verdict, Case File No. 06/30, 2007.

11. Basmannaia mezhraionnaia prokuratura g. Moskvy, "Postanovlenie of priznanii poterpevshim," from the archives of Public Verdict, Case File No. 06/30, 2007.

12. Interview with Oleg Novikov, deputy director of Public Verdict, Moscow, May 10, 2007.

13. *Druzhba*, ironically, means "friendship" in Russian.

14. Information drawn from the archives of Public Verdict, Case File No. 06/57, 2007. See also Perova 2007.

15. O. I. Khabibrakhmanov, "Zakliucheniia predvaritel'noi proverki po informatsii o massovykh narusheniiakh prav cheloveka, imevshikh mesto v noch' s 18-go na 19-e iiulia 2006 goda v poselke Nizhnee Makopse Lazarevskogo raiona g. Sochi," July 25, 2006, from the archives of Public Verdict, Case File No. 06/57.

16. O. I. Khabibrakhmanov, "Sluzhebnaia zapiska," sent to N. Taubina, August 2, 2006, from the archives of Public Verdict, Case File No. 06/57.

17. Interview with Oleg Novikov, deputy director of Public Verdict, Moscow, May 10, 2007.

18. Ibid.

19. N. Iu. Serdiuk, "Soobshchenie o prestuplenii v poriadke st. 144 UPK RF," sent to the prosecutor of the Lazarevskii district, Sochi, photocopy in the archives of Public Verdict, Case File No. 06/57, 2007.

20. O. I. Khabibrakhmanov, "Zakliucheniia predvaritel'noi proverki."

21. Interview with Oleg Novikov, deputy director of Public Verdict, Moscow, May 10, 2007.

22. Information drawn from the archives of Public Verdict, Case File No. 144, and "Delo o 'zachistke' v Bezhetske," no case file number, 2007; see also Sapozhnikova 2005.

23. A. Kokorin, e-mail to N. Taubina, September 2, 2005, printout, in the archives of Public Verdict, Case File no. 144.

24. Tverskaya Oblast' Prosecutor's Office, Case No. 065049, "Postanovlenie o priostanovlenii predvaritel'nogo sledstviia v sviazi s neustanovleniem litsa,

podlezhashchego privlecheniiu v kachestve obviniaemogo," photocopy in the archives of Public Verdict, Case File No. 144, 2007.

25. Articles reviewed on the Sochi case: Elkov 2006; Glanin 2006a,b,c, 2007; Ivanov 2006; Lebedeva 2006a,b; Perova 2007; Titov 2007.

26. Articles reviewed on the Gladyshev case: "Delo ob izbitom podrostke" 2006; (2006b). "Militsionerov posadili za izbienie shkol'nika" 2006; "Militsionery, izbivshie 12-letnego shkol'nika, poluchili po tri goda" 2006; Alekseev and Urban 2006; Lokotetskaia 2006; Rogacheva 2006; Zorin 2006.

27. Articles reviewed on the Bezhetsk case: "Mesto Sobytii" 2005; "Politika-Ekonomika" 2005; Khairullin 2005; Kondrat'eva 2005; Konygina 2005; Konygina and Spirin 2005; Mandrik 2005; Sapozhnikova 2005; Sas and Ukolov 2005; Sergeev 2005.

28. Articles reviewed on the Oleinik case: "Novosti. Proisshestviia" 2003; "Protsessy" 2003; Chelysheva 2003); "Militsionery, sdelavshie zaderzhannogo invalidom, poluchili uslovnye sroki" 2004; Goncharova 2004; Shamburova 2004; Anisimov 2006.

29. *Brigada* was a popular television series in Russia about organized crime on the police, containing a notorious amount of violence.

30. The picture might have been somewhat different if television were also included, given the general reluctance of the national networks to cover such incidents. However, due to the lack of systematic archives of the transcripts of television news broadcasts, the sample was inevitably limited to newspapers.

31. Interview with Oleg Novikov, deputy director of Public Verdict, Moscow, May 10, 2007.

32. I would not, of course, go so far as to assert that this logic figured into the calculations made by journalists. It is more likely that pogroms, which are fewer, seem more alike each other than individual beatings, which happen more frequently. Nonetheless, the relative utility of the information remains unchanged.

33. Interview with Natalia Taubina, director of Public Verdict, Moscow, August 1, 2006.

34. See Iakovleva 2008.

Chapter 6

1. From the Russian word *l'goty*, "benefits"; literally, receivers of benefits.

2. From the Russian word *dolia*, "share," referring to what is known as *dolevoe stroitel'stvo*, or "share construction," in which an apartment project is built on money collected up front from the future homeowners.

3. Many Russian surnames are gender specific, with feminine names often ending in the letter *a*; thus, Iuliia's last name is Prokof'eva, while her son is Prokof'ev.

Standard practice is to use the masculine variant as the generic name for the family unit.

4. The foregoing narrative was reconstructed from the author's observation, including of the media, and interviews with Butovo residents. For a summary of events, see "V Iuzhnom Butovo" 2008.

5. Protester interview No. 3, South Butovo, Moscow, June 22, 2006.

6. Protester interview No. 2, South Butovo, Moscow, June 22, 2006.

7. Protester interview No. 3, South Butovo, Moscow, June 22, 2006.

8. Protester interview No. 4, South Butovo, Moscow, June 22, 2006.

9. Protester interview No. 4, South Butovo, Moscow, June 22, 2006.

10. Protester interview No. 3, South Butovo, Moscow, June 22, 2006.

11. Protester interview No. 1, South Butovo, Moscow, June 22, 2006.

12. In Russian, "tochechnoe stroitel'stvo."

13. Interview with Larisa Solomatina, South Butovo, Moscow, June 22, 2006.

14. http://ikd.ru/Campaign/Housing/ and www.siforum.fastbb.ru/

15. www.pismo-vlasti.ru/prjamoi-dialog-s-prezidentom-okc.html, last accessed July 19, 2007.

16. In fact, Putin said that the crisis had been created by irresponsible policies put in place in the 1990s, under Boris Yeltsin, which had opened the loopholes that developers later used to defraud buyers. See "Priamaia liniia s Prezidentom" 2007.

17. See http://pismo-vlasti.ru/forum/viewtopic.php?t=19, last accessed 19 July 19, 2007.

18. Interview with Larisa Solomatina, South Butovo, Moscow, June 22, 2006.

19. Protester interview No. 4, South Butovo, Moscow, June 22, 2006.

20. Interview with Larisa Solomatina, South Butovo, Moscow, June 22, 2006.

21. See http://pismo-vlasti.ru/forum/, last accessed July 19, 2007.

Chapter 7

1. *Duraki i dorogi.* Whether Gogol actually wrote this is disputed, but this is the most widely held view. In any case, the phrase is common.

2. Originally on the web forum www.auto.vl.ru. Unfortunately, the administrators of the site have deleted the relevant discussions from their archive, reportedly under pressure from the government.

3. Interview with Viacheslav Lysakov, February 20, 2006, Moscow.

4. Ibid.

5. A Russian automobile brand.

6. Ibid.

7. This is the force charged with defending the government facilities, including the White House.

8. These are the internal secret services, one of the successors of the KGB.

9. Ibid.

10. Svoboda Vybora website, www.19may.ru

11. Interview with Viacheslav Lysakov, February 20, 2006, Moscow.

12. Ibid.

13. Ibid.

14. Ibid.

15. These results add up to more than 100 percent because some households have more than one car. See "Avtomobil' dlia rossiianina" 2006.

16. All data on site visits are from http://top.mail.ru and refer to the month of October 2006. Data were last accessed on November 15, 2006.

17. Interview with Viacheslav Lysakov, February 20, 2006, Moscow.

18. Ibid.

19. Svoboda Vybora forum, posted on January 18, 2006; retrieved on August 18, 2006, from http://19may.ru/forum/printthread.php?t=4033&pp=40

20. Svoboda Vybora forum, various posts from January 28 through May 29, 2006; retrieved on August 18, 2006, from http://19may.ru/forum/printthread.php?t=4186&pp=40.

21. Svoboda Vybora forum, post from February 3, 2006; retrieved on August 18, 2006, from http://19may.ru/forum/printthreat.php?t=4186&pp=40.

22. Shcherbinskii campaign website, Oleg.19may.ru

23. Interview with Viacheslav Lysakov, April 28, 2006, Moscow.

24. See "Sotsial'no-politicheskaia situatsiia" 2006. www.levada.ru/press/2006041104.html.

25. Interview with Viacheslav Lysakov, April 28, 2006, Moscow.

26. Oleg was Shcherbinskii's given name.

27. Lysakov misuses the combination of "caste" and "untouchable"; he is referring not to an underclass, as in the Indian sense, but to a group of people who are above the law. The word translated as "trash" in Russian is *bydlo*, which can also be translated as "cattle," "herd," or "mob" and is meant to refer to the conception of the bulk of the population as expendable, unimportant, and mindless.

28. Svoboda Vybora forum, posted 4 February 4, 2006; retrieved on August 18, 2006, from www.19may.ru/forum/printthread.php?t=4372&pp=40.

29. Ibid.

30. Ibid.

31. Ibid.

32. Ustinov at the time was prosecutor general. He was later made minister of justice.

33. Svoboda Vybora forum, posted 4 February 4, 2006; retrieved on August 18, 2006, from www.19may.ru/forum/printthread.php?t=4372&pp=40.

34. Ibid.

35. Ibid.

36. *Doloi*, in Russian.

37. *Dokole*, in Russian.

38. "Imho" is a common abbreviation used on Internet forums and in other electronic media to mean "in my humble opinion."

39. Svoboda Vybora forum, posted 4 February 4, 2006; retrieved on August 18, 2006, from www.19may.ru/forum/printthread.php?t=4372&pp=40.

40. These are various abbreviations for the Russian traffic police.

41. Kir'ianov was head of the Russian traffic police.

42. Svoboda Vybora forum, posted 13 January 13, 2006; retrieved on August 18, 2006, from www.19may.ru/forum/printthread.php?t=3950&pp=40.

43. Ibid.

44. He uses the Russian word *vlasti*, which could also be translated as "power" or "the powers that be."

45. The phrase "his face is fat" is translated from the Russian *riakha zhirna*, which itself is a bastardization of the phrase *zhirnaia riakha* or *zhirnaia riazhka*, literally "fat face" but using an unpleasant colloquialism for "face." The phrase is commonly used in relation to police officers, who are assumed to "get fat" on bribes and extortion.

46. Svoboda Vybora forum, posted January 13, 2006; retrieved on August 18, 2006, from www.19may.ru/forum/printthread.php?t=3950&pp=40.

47. Ibid.

48. Ibid.

49. *Vovochka* is a diminutive for Vladimir. PaNick is clearly referring to Vladimir Putin.

50. Werewolf—*oboroten'* in Russian—comes from the Russian phrase *oboroten' v pogonakh* (literally, werewolf in epaulets), widely used in the media to refer to law enforcement and military officers who use their official positions to commit crimes, particularly extortion.

51. Svoboda Vybora forum, posted January 13, 2006; retrieved on August 18, 2006, from www.19may.ru/forum/printthread.php?t=3950&pp=40.

52. Svoboda Vybora forum, posted on January 14, 2006; retrieved on August 18, 2006, www.19may.ru/forum/printthread.php?t=3950&pp=40.

53. Svoboda Vybora forum, posted on January 16, 2006; retrieved on August 18, 2006, from www.19may.ru/forum/printthread.php?t=3950&pp=40.

54. Ibid.

55. Svoboda Vybora forum, posted on April 27, 2006; retrieved on August 18, 2006, from www.19may.ru/forum/printthread.php?t=5690&pp=40.

56. Svoboda Vybora forum, posted on April 18, 2006; retrieved on August 18, 2006, from www.19may.ru/forum/printthread.php?t=5690&pp=40.

57. A reference to the president, who is referred to in the Russian constitution as "guarantor of the constitution."

58. Svoboda Vybora forum, , posted on April 27, 2006; retrieved on August 18, 2006, from www.19may.ru/forum/printthread.php?t=5690&pp=40.

59. Interview with Viacheslav Lysakov; April 28, 2006, Moscow.

60. Ibid.

61. Ibid.

62. Ibid.

63. Interview with Viacheslav Lysakov, February 20, 2006, Moscow.

64. At the time this was written, but after the research period had ended, the ruling party, Edinaia Rossiia, had finally given in and backed a law limiting *migalki* to 1,000 cars nationwide, plus police, ambulances, and fire brigades. In a show of populism, Edinaia Rossiia members handed their own *migalki* over to the police on national television, while party leader Boris Gryzlov announced: "If you see a politician on the road with a *migalka*, it can only be a member of the opposition."

65. Lysakov is referring to a bill introduced by the movement's opposition allies in the Duma that would have limited the number of *migalki* in the country to eight; this is as opposed to the bill supported by Edinaia Rossiia, which would have limited the number of *migalki* to 1,000. Neither bill passed.

66. Svoboda Vybora forum, posted on April 14, 2006; retrieved on August 18, 2006, from www.19may.ru/forum/printthread.php?t=5690&pp=40.

67. Svoboda Vybora forum, posted on April 15, 2006; retrieved on August 18, 2006, from www.19may.ru/forum/printthread.php?t=5690&pp=40.

68. Interview with Viacheslav Lysakov, April 28, 2006, Moscow.

69. Interview with Viacheslav Lysakov, February 20, 2006, Moscow.

70. Ibid. Just a month earlier, the national television channels had launched a high-profile campaign in which foreign governments and private foundations were accused of being covers for espionage; Putin likewise criticized Russian NGOs for being insufficiently selective in their sources of financing.

71. Ibid.

72. Interview with Viacheslav Lysakov, April 28, 2006.

73. Ibid.

74. Ibid.

75. Ibid.

76. Vybora forum, posted on July 4, 2006; retrieved on August 18, 2006, from www.19may.ru/forum/printthread.php?t=6372&pp=40.

77. Svoboda Vybora forum, posted on July 6, 2006; retrieved on August 18, 2006, from www.19may.ru/forum/printthread.php?t=6372&pp=40.

78. Svoboda Vybora forum, posted on July 5, 2006; retrieved on August 18, 2006, from www.19may.ru/forum/printthread.php?t=6372&pp=40.

79. Svoboda Vybora forum, posted on April 25, 2006; retrieved on August 18, 2006, from www.19may.ru/forum/printthread.php?t=5690&pp=40.

80. Svoboda Vybora forum, posted on January 16, 2006; retrieved on August 18, 2006, from www.19may.ru/forum/printthread.php?t=3950&pp=40.

81. Svoboda Vybora forum, posted on April 18, 2006; retrieved on August 18, 2006, from www.19may.ru/forum/printthread.php?t=5690&pp=40.

82. Svoboda Vybora forum, posted on July 6, 2006; retrieved on August 18, 2006, from www.19may.ru/forum/printthread.php?t=6372&pp=40.

83. Ibid.

84. Svoboda Vybora forum, posted on July 12, 2006; retrieved on August 18, 2006, from www.19may.ru/forum/printthread.php?t=6372&pp=40.

85. See "Epizod I: Skrytaia ugroza" 2011.

Chapter 8

1. Ushahidi website; retrieved on November 26, 2012, from www.ushahidi.com/.

2. Retrieved on November 26, 2012, from www.russian-fires.ru.

3. See "Internet v Rossii" 2012.

4. "*Partiia zhulikov i vorov.*"

5. Interview with Antonina Samsonova, Moscow, December 27, 2011.

6. Ibid.

7. Interview with Sergei Parkhomenko, Moscow, May 21, 2012.

8. Ibid.

9. Interview with Vladimir Ryzhkov, Moscow, December 26, 2011.

10. See "Miting za chestnye vybory," YouTube channel, www.youtube.com/user/WakeUpR?feature=watch.

11. Interview with Olga Romanova and Aleksei Kozlov, Moscow, December 27, 2011.

12. Interview with Sergei Parkhomenko, Moscow, May 21, 2012.

13. See Lermontov 1983."

14. Interview with Sergei Parkhomenko, Moscow, May 21, 2012.

15. Interview with Sergei Kanaev, Moscow, March 1, 2012.

16. Retrieved from www.moscow_city.vybory.izbirkom.ru/region/region/moscow_city?action=show&root=1&tvd=27720001368293&vrn=27720001368289&region=77&global=&sub_region=0&prver=0&pronetvd=null&vibid=27720001368293&type=234.

Works Cited

Adjani, M. (2006). *Ethnic Profiling in the Moscow Metro*. New York: Open Society Institute.

Afanas'ev, I. N. (2001). *Opasnaia Rossiia. Traditsii Samovlast'ia Segodnia*. Moscow: RGGU.

Afanasiev, M. N. (1996). *Praviashchie elity i gosudarstvennost' posttotalitarnoi rossii*. Moscow: Izdatel'stvo "Institut prakticheskoi psikhologii."

Al'bats, E. (2004). "Bureaucrats and the Russian Transition: The Politics of Accommodation, 1991–2003." PhD dissertation. Cambridge, MA: Harvard University.

———. (2011). "Edinstvennoe, chego u menia net,—normal'noi blagopoluchnoi strany." *The New Times*. October 3.

Alekseev, I., D. Chernov, et al. (2004). "Okhota na izbiratelia." *Vremia novostei*, Moscow, March 15: 2.

Alekseev, M., and K. Urban (2006). "Desiat' del otnogo goda." *Kommersant. Vlast'* (51): 26–30.

Alekseeva, L. (1984). *Istoriia inakomysliia v SSSR. Noveishii period*. Benson, VT: Khronika Press.

Alekseeva, N. (2005). "'Kak mozhno bol'she iarkikh liudei'. Putin s senatorami ishchet oshibki monetizatsii." *Izvestiia*, Moscow, February 4.

Almond, G. A., and S. Verba. (1963). *The Civic Culture. Political Attitudes and Democracy in Five Nations*. Princeton, NJ: Princeton University Press.

"Amnistiia predprinimatelei." (2011). Moscow: Legal and Economic Studies Center, Higher School of Economics.

Anderson, R. D. Jr., M. S. Fish, et al. (2001). *Postcommunism and the Theory of Democracy*. Princeton, NJ: Princeton University Press.

Anheier, H. K., and J. Kendall (2000). Trust and Voluntary Organisations: Three Theoretical Approaches. *Civil Society Working Papers*. London: Centre for Civil Society, London School of Economics.

Anisimov, S. (2006). "Zhitel' Nizhnego Novgoroda piat' let dobivalsia material'noi kompensatsii." *Novye Izvestiia*, Moscow, March 1: 2.

Aptekar', P. (2004). "'Protiv vsekh' ne schitaetsia." *Gazeta*, Moscow, November 30: 1.

Aptekar', P. (2005). "K urne. Kreml' opredililsia s novymi pravilami vyborov." *Gazeta*, Moscow, April 15: 4.

Arato, A. (2000). *Civil Society, Constitution, and Legitimacy*. Lanham, MD: Rowman & Littlefield Publishers.

Arrow, K. J. (1974). *The Limits of Organization*. New York: W. W. Norton & Co.

Ashwin, S. (1996). "Forms of Collectivity in a Non-Monetary Society." *Sociology* 30(1): 21–39.

Ashwin, S. (1998). "Endless Patience: Explaining Soviet and Post-Soviet Social Stability." *Communist and Post-Communist Studies* 31(2): 187–198.

Auyero, J. (2001). *Poor People's Politics. Peronist Survival Networks and the Legacy of Evita*. Durham, NC: Duke University Press.

Averkiev, I. (2003). "Zachem cheloveku prava cheloveka." *Civitas* 2003(1): 17–30.

"Avtoklub. Pravyi bunt." *Rossiiskaia Gazeta*, Moscow, June 10, 2005.

"Avtomobil' dlia rossiianina—uzhe ne roskosh'. A chto?" (2006). Press-vypusk No. 512, August 23. Moscow: WCIOM.

Barnes, A. (2003). "Comparative Theft: Context and Choice in the Hungarian, Czech, and Russian Transformations, 1989–2000." *East European Politics and Societies* 17(3): 533–565.

Belanovskii, S., and M. Dmitriev. (2011). *Politicheskii krizis v Rossii i vozmozhnye mekhanizny ego razvitiia*. Moscow: Center for Strategic Development.

Belin, L. (2002). "The Russian Media in the 1990s." *Journal of Communist Studies and Transition Politics* 18(1): 139–160.

Belyaeva, N., and L. Proskuryakova (2008). *Civil Society Diamond: Civicus Civil Society Index Shortened Asessment Tool. Report for the Russian Federation*. Moscow: Interlegal Foundation.

Berglas, E. (1976). "On the Theory of Clubs." *American Economic Review* 66(2): 116–121.

Berglas, E., and D. Pines. (1981). "Clubs, Local Public Goods and Transportation Models." *Journal of Public Economics* 15: 141–162.

Berkowitz, D., and W. Li. (2000). "Tax Rights in Transition Economies: A Tragedy of the Commons?" *Journal of Public Economics* 76: 369–397.

Beshlei, O. (2011). "Rus' sidiashchaia. Zheny osuchdennykh boriutsia za svoikh muzhei." *The New Times*. November 14.

Bobbio, N. (1988). Gramsci and the Concept of Civil Society. In *Civil Society and the State: New European Perspectives*, J. Keane, ed. London: Verso.

Bondarenko, A., and S. Migalin. (2005). "Pensionery razuverilis' v dobroi vlasti. Na mitingakh v regionakh vse chashche zvuchat politicheskie trebovaniia." *Nezavisimaia Gazeta*, Moscow, February 1.

Borooah, V. K., and M. Paldam. (2007). "Why Is the World Short of Democracy? A Cross-Country Analysis of Barriers to Representative Government." *European Journal of Political Economy* 23: 582–604.

Broadway, R. (1980). "A Note on the Market Provision of Club Goods." *Journal of Public Economics* 13: 131–137.

Brownlee, J. (2007). *Authoritarianism in an Age of Democratization.* Cambridge, UK: Cambridge University Press.

Buchanan, J. M. (1965). "An Economic Theory of Clubs." *Economica* 32(125): 1–14.

Bunce, V. (1983). "The Political Economy of the Brezhnev Era: The Rise and Fall of Corporatism." *British Journal of Political Science* 13(2): 129–158.

———. (1999). *Subversive Institutions: The Design and the Destruction of Socialism and the State.* Cambridge, UK: Cambridge University Press.

Buranov, I. (2005). "Aktsiia protesta: Rulevye igry." *Kommersant*, Moscow, May 20.

———. (2006a). "Aktsiia protesta: Avtomobilisty udarili po migalkam probkami." *Kommersant*, Moscow, May 29.

———. (2006b). "Probki na dorogakh: Avtomobilisty vybrali MKAD vzletnoi ploshchadkoi." *Kommersant*, Moscow, May 26.

Buranov, I., N. Iablonskii, et al. (2006). "Mitingi protiv novykh PDD." *Kommersant*, Moscow, January 30.

Burawoy, M., P. Krotov, et al. (2000). "Involution and Destitution in Capitalist Russia." *Ethnography* 1(1): 43–65.

Butorina, E. (2006). "V tsentre vnimaniia: 'My vse mozhem okazat'sia Shcherbinskimi.'" *Vremia Novostei*, Moscow, March 24.

Carothers, T. (1999). "Western Civil-Society Aid to Eastern Europe and the Former Soviet Union." *East European Constitutional Review* 8(3).

Carothers, T., and M. Ottaway. (2000). "The Burgeoning World of Civil Society Aid." In *Funding Virtue: Civil Society Aid and Democracy Promotion*, M. Ottaway and T. Carothers, eds. Washington, DC: Carnegie Endowment for International Peace.

Chebotarev, A. (2006). "Dal'noboishchiki ugrozhaiut perekryt' Rublevku." *Nezavisimaia Gazeta*, Moscow, May 22.

Chebotarev, A., and N. i. Kostenko. (2006). "Massovye aktsii teriaiut sviaz' s politikoi." *Nezavisimaia Gazeta*, Moscow, February 7.

Chebotarev, A., S. Varshavchik, et al. (2006). "Klassovaia bor'ba pokatilas' na kolesakh: Aktsii v zashchitu altaiskogo voditelia Olega Shcherbinskogo okazalis' bespretsedentno massovymi, khorosho podgotovlennymi i demonstrativno apolitichnymi." *Nezavisimaia Gazeta*, Moscow, February 13.

Chelysheva, O. (2003). "Sustav prestupleniia: Uslovnym zashchitnikam—uslovnoe nakazanie." *Novaia Gazeta*, Moscow, April 17: 15.

Cherkasov, G. (2011). "Neizmennyi." *Kommersant*, December 15.

Chernega, I., and V. Khamraev. (2006). "Glas Naroda: Rossiianam vse chashche khochetsia protestovat." *Kommersant*, Moscow, April 5.

Clement, C. (2008). "Ot obyvatelia k aktivistu (na primere dvizheniia zhilishch-nogo samoupravleniia v Astrakhani)." In *Grazhdanskoe obshchestvo sovremennoi Rossii. Sotsiologicheskie zarisovki s natury*, E. S. Petrenko, ed. Moscow: Institut Fonda "Obshchestennoe mnenie."

Coleman, J. S. (1990). *Foundations of Social Theory*. Cambridge, MA: Harvard University Press.

Colton, T. J., and H. E. Hale. (2009). "The Putin Vote: Presidential Electorates in a Hybrid Regime." *Slavic Review* 68(3): 473–503.

Crozier, M. (2001). "Bureaucracy, Sociology of." In *International Encyclopedia of the Social and Behavioral Sciences*, N. J. Smelser and P. B. Baltes, eds. London: Elsevier.

Curkowski, J. (2004). "Russian Oil: The Role of the Sector in Russia's Economy." *Post-Communist Economies* 16(3): 285–296.

Dahl, R. A. (1971). *Polyarchy. Participation and Opposition*. New Haven, CT: Yale University Press.

Davydov, O. B., Ed. (2000). *Rossiiskaia elita: psikhologicheskie portrety*. Moscow: Laromir.

de Tocqueville, A. ([1835] 1994). *Democracy in America, First Part*. London: Everyman's Library.

———. ([1840] 1994). *Democracy in America, Second Part*. London: Everyman's Library.

"Delo biznesmena Alekseia Kozlova. Spravka." (2011). *RIA Novosti*, September 20.

"Delo ob izbitom podrostke." (2006). Moskovskii Komsomolets, Moscow, October 13: 2.

"Delo o khishchenii imushchestva KOGUP 'Kirovles.' Spravka." (2013). *RIA Novosti*, July 18.

"Delo Svetlany Petrovny Bakhminoi. Spravka." (2008). *RIA Novosti*, September 24.

Diamond, L. (1994). "Rethinking Civil Society: Toward Democratic Consolidation." *Journal of Democracy* 5(3): 4–17.

Dogan, M., and J. Higley. (1998). Elites, Crises, and Regimes in Comparative Analysis. In *Elites, Crises, and the Origins of Regimes*, eds. M. Dogan and J. Higley. New York: Rowman & Littlefield.

Domrin, A. N. (2003). "Ten Years Later: Society, 'Civil Society,' and the Russian State." *Russian Review* 62(2): 193–211.

Drankina, E. (2004). "'Politkonsul'tanty vynuzhdeny rabotat' v vol'ere' (Interview with Marat Gel'man)." *Kommersant Den'gi* (502): 54–55.

Dubin, B., and L. Gudkov. (2005). "Privatizatsiia politsii." In *Indeks proizvola pravookhranitel'nykh organov*, A. Novikova, ed. Moscow: Obshchestvennyi Verdikt.

Durkheim, E. ([1893] 1984). *The Division of Labour in Society*. Houndsmills, UK: Macmillan Press.

Duverger, M. (1972). *The Study of Politics*. London, Nelson.

———. (1974). *Modern Democracies: Economic Power versus Political Power*. Hinsdale, IL: Dryden Press.

Easter, G. M. (2002). "Politics of Revenue Extraction in Post-Communist States: Poland and Russia Compared." *Politics and Society* 30(4): 599–627.

Ehrenberg, J. (1999). *Civil Society: The Critical History of an Idea*. New York: New York University Press.

Elifanova, M. (2012). "Tsentral'nyi vybornyi komitet obnarodoval itogi vyborov v Koordinatsionnyi sovet oppozitsii." *Novaia Gazeta*, October 22.

Elkov, I. (2006). "OMON na narakh." *Rossiiskaia Gazeta*, Moscow, August 9: 7.

"Epizod I: Skrytaia ugroza." (2011). Available at www.superputin.ru.

Etzioni-Halevy, E. (1993). *The Elite Connection. Problems and Potential of Western Democracy*. Cambridge, UK: Polity Press.

Evans, A. B. Jr. (2008). "The First Steps of Russia's Public Chamber: Representation or Coordination?" *Demokratizatsiya* 16(4): 345–362.

Fedorin, V. (2008). "Biznes pod pressom." *Forbes Russia*.

Feldbrugge, F. J. M. (1975). *Samizdat and Political Dissent in the Soviet Union*. Leyden, Netherlands: A. W. Sijthoff.

Feldman, E. (2013). "Aleksei Naval'nyi: 'My vozrodili politiku. I eto kruto.'" *New Times*.

Feldman, E., V. Grechina, et al. (2012). "6 maia: Marsh millionov zavershilsia massovymi zaderzhaniiami i ulichnoi voinoi s politsiei." *Novaia Gazeta*, May 6.

Ferguson, A. ([1767] 1966). *An Essay on the History of Civil Society*. Edinburgh, UK: University of Edinburgh Press.

Fish, M. S. (1995). *Democracy from Scratch: Opposition and Regime in the New Russian Revolution*. Princeton, NJ: Princeton University Press.

———. (2005). *Democracy Derailed in Russia: The Failure of Open Politics*. Cambridge, UK: Cambridge University Press.

Fishman, M. (2011). "Tsena odnoi tainoi sdelki." *Forbes Russia*.

Flynn, M. (2006). "Formal and Informal Strategies of Migrant Populations: Migrant Activity in Post-Soviet Russia." In *Russian Civil Society: A Critical Assessment*, A. B. Evans Jr., L. A. Henry, and L. M. Sundstrom, eds. Armonk, NY: M. E. Sharpe.

Folger, R., ed. (1984). *The Sense of Injustice: Social Psychological Perspectives*. New York: Plenum Press.

Fromm, E. (1963). *Marx's Concept of Man*. New York: Frederick Ungar Publishing Co.

Frye, T. (2002). "The Two Faces of Russian Courts: Evidence from a Survey of Company Managers." *East European Constitutional Review* 11(1/2).

Frye, T., and A. Shleifer. (1997). "The Invisible Hand and the Grabbing Hand." *American Economic Review* 87(2): 354–358.

Fukuyama, F. (2000). "Social Capital and Civil Society." *IMF Working Papers*. Washington, DC: IMF Institute.

———. (2004). "The Imperative of State-Building." *Journal of Democracy* 15(2): 17–31.

Gaidar, Y. ([1994] 2003). *State and Evolution. Russia's Search for a Free Market*. Seattle: University of Washington Press.

Gamarnikow, E., and A. Green. (2005). "Citizenship, Education and Social Capital." In *Education for Citizenship*, D. Lawton, J. Cairns, and R. Gardner, eds. London: Continuum.

Gamson, W. A. (1968). *Power and Discontent*. Homewood, IL: Dorsey Press.

Ganev, V. I. (2001). "The Dorian Gray Effect: Winners as State Breakers in Postcommunism." *Communist and Post-Communist Studies* 34: 1–25.

Garcelon, M. (2005). *Revolutionary Passage: From Soviet to Post-Soviet Russia, 1985–2000*. Philadelphia: Temple University Press.

Gellner, E. (1994). *Conditions of Liberty: Civil Society and Its Rivals*. London: Hamish Hamilton.

Gibson, J. L. (2001). "Social Networks, Civil Society, and the Prospects for Consolidating Russia's Democratic Transition." *American Journal of Political Science* 45(1): 51–68.

———. (2003). "Social Networks, Civil Society, and the Prospects for Consolidating Russia's Democratic Transition." In *Social Capital and the Transition to Democracy*, G. Badescu and E. M. Uslaner, eds. London: Routledge.

Giddens, A. (1984). *The Constitution of Society: Outline of the Theory of Structuration*. Berkeley: University of California Press.

Glaeser, E., J. Scheinkman, et al. (2003). "The Injustice of Inequality." *Journal of Monetary Economics* 50: 199–222.

Glanin, I. (2006a). "Kriminal. Mest' pokhmel'nogo OMONa." *Vremia Novostei*, Moscow, July 27: 2.

———. (2006b). "OMON protiv detei." *Vremia Novostei*, Moscow, July 21: 3.

———. (2006c). "Skandal. Zhertvy deshevoi provokatsii." *Vremia Novostei*, Moscow, July 25: 3.

———. (2007). "Ne dlia ekrana." *Vremia Novostei*, Moscow, March 23: 3.

Glinski, D., and P. Reddaway. (1999). "The Ravages of 'Market Bolshevism.'" *Journal of Democracy* 10(2): 19–34.

Goldman, M. I. (1980). *The Enigma of Soviet Petroleum: Half-Full or Half-Empty?* London: George Allen & Unwin.

——. (2003a). *The Piratization of Russia. Russian Reform Goes Awry.* London: Routledge.

——. (2003b). "Render unto Caesar: Putin and the Oligarchs." *Current History* 102(666).

Goldstone, J. A., and C. Tilly. (2001). "Threat (and Opportunity): Popular Action and State Response in the Dynamics of Contentious Action." In *Silence and Voice in the Study of Contentious Politics*, R. R. Aminzade, J. A. Goldstone, D. McAdam, et al., eds. Cambridge, UK: Cambridge University Press.

Goncharova, N. (2004). "Militsioneru dali uslovno." *Nizhegorodskie Novosi*, Nizhnii Novgorod, August 28.

Gontmakher, E., M. Denisenko, et al. (2011). Obretenie budushchego: Strategiia 2012. Moscow: Institute for Contemporary Development.

Granina, N. i. (2005). "Dol'shchikov Podmoskov'ia obmanuli na $240 mln." *Izvestiia*, Moscow, December 28.

Greene, S. A. (2012a). "Citizenship and the Social Contract in Post-Soviet Russia: Twenty Years Late?" *Demokratizatsiya* 20(2): 72–80.

——. (2012b). "Twitter and the Russian Street: Memes, Networks and Mobilization." CNMS Working Paper. Moscow: Center for the Study of New Media & Society, New Economic School.

——. (2013). "Beyond Bolotnaia: Bridging Old and New in Russia's Election Protest Movement." *Problems of Post-Communism* 60(2): 40–52.

Greene, S. A., and G. B. Robertson. (2010). "Politics, Justice and the New Russian Strike." *Communist and Post-Communist Studies* 43(1): 73–95.

Grishin, A., and S. Tsikulina. (2006). "Sego Dnia. Nastoiashchikh buinykh malo." *Moskovskii Komsomolets*, Moscow, May 23.

Grivach, A., N. Gorelov, et al. (2004). "Sekret dlia bol'shoi kompanii. Tsenu 'Iuganskneftegaza' ustanoviat chetyre chlena soveta direktorov 'Gazproma.'" *Vremia Novostei*, Moscow, December 3: 7.

Grozovskii, B., and S. Ivanova. (2005). "Den'gi/Vlast'. Zurabov ne gotov." *Vedomosti*, Moscow, April 11.

Grzymala-Busse, A. (2008). "Beyond Clientelism : Incumbent State Capture and State Formation." *Comparative Political Studies* 41(4/5): 638–673.

Grzymala-Busse, A., and P. J. Luong (2002). "Reconceptualizing the State: Lessons from Post-Communism." *Politics and Society* 30(4): 529–554.

Gulenok, O. (2009). "Ne soglasen—predlagai." *Kasparov.ru*, January 16.

Guseva, D. i. (2004). "Narod—pofigist. Rossiiane bezrazlichny k skandal'nomu zakonu o mitingakh." *Vremia novostei*, Moscow, April 29: 4.

——. (2006). "Iavka neobiazatel'na." *Vremia novostei*, Moscow, November 9: 4.

Gustafson, T. (2012). *Wheel of Fortune: The Battle for Oil and Power in Russia.* Cambridge, MA: Harvard University Press.

Habermas, J. ([1962] 1995). *The Structural Transformation of the Public Sphere: An Inquiry into a Category of Bourgeois Society.* Cambridge, MA: MIT Press.

Hale, H. E. (1999). "The Party's On: The Impact of Political Organizations in Russia's Duma Elections." *Working Papers.* Cambridge, MA: Harvard University.

———. (2006). "Democracy or Autocracy on the March? The Colored Revolutions as Normal Dynamics of Patronal Presidentialism." *Communist and Post-Communist Studies* 39: 305–329.

Hann, C., and E. Dunn, eds. (1996). *Civil Society: Challenging Western Models.* London: Routledge.

Hanson, P., and E. Teague. (2005). "Big Business and the State in Russia." *Europe-Asia Studies* 57(5): 657–680.

Hanson, S. E. (2001a). "Defining Democratic Consolidation." In *Postcommunism and the Theory of Democracy,* R. D. Anderson Jr., M. S. Fish, S. E. Hanson, and P. G. Roeder, eds. Princeton, NJ: Princeton University Press.

Hanson, S. E. (2001b). "The Dilemmas of Russia's Anti-Revolutionary Revolution." *Current History* 100(648): 330–335.

Havel, V. (1988). Anti-Political Politics. In *Civil Society and the State: New European Perspectives,* J. Keane, ed. London: Verso.

Hayoz, N., and V. Sergeyev. (2003). "Social Networks in Russian Politics." In *Social Capital and the Transition to Democracy,* G. Badescu and E. M. Uslaner, eds. London: Routledge.

Hegel ([1820] 1896). "The Philosophy of Right." In *Hegel's Philosophy of Right,* S. W. Dyde, ed. London: George Bell and Sons.

Hellman, J. S. (1998). "Winners Take All: The Politics of Partial Reform in Postcommunist Transitions." *World Politics* 50(2): 203–234.

Hellman, J. S., G. Jones, et al. (2003). "Seize the State, Seize the Day: State Capture and Influence in Transition Economies." *Journal of Comparative Economics* 31: 751–773.

Hellman, J. S., and M. Schankerman. (2000). "Intervention, Corruption and Capture. The Nexus between Enterprises and the State." *Economics of Transition* 8(3): 545–576.

Helmke, G., and S. Levitsky. (2004). "Informal Institutions and Comparative Politics: A Research Agenda." *Perspectives on Politics* 2(4): 725–740.

Henderson, S. L. (2003). *Building Democracy in Russia: Western Support for Grassroots Organizations.* Ithaca, NY: Cornell University Press.

Hendley, K. (1999). "Rewriting the Rules of the Game in Russia: The Neglected Issue of the Demand for Law." *East European Constitutional Review* 8(4).

Henry, L. A. (2006). Russian Environmentalists and Civil Society. In *Russian Civil Society: A Critical Assessment*, A. B. Evans Jr., L. A. Henry, and L. M. Sundstrom, eds. Armonk, NY: M. E. Sharpe.

Herb, M. (2005). "No Representation without Taxation? Rents, Development, and Democracy." *Comparative Politics* 37(3): 297–316.

Higley, J., and M. G. Burton. (1989). "The Elite Variable in Democratic Transitions and Breakdowns." *American Sociological Review* 51(1): 17–32.

Hoffman, D. E. (2002). *The Oligarchs. Wealth and Power in the New Russia.* New York: Public Affairs.

Hopkin, J. (2006). "Conceptualizing Political Clientelism: Political Exchange and Democratic Theory." Annual Meeting of the American Political Science Association. Philadelphia.

Horowitz, D. (1990). "Comparing Democratic Systems." *Journal of Democracy* 1(4): 73–79.

Hough, J. F. (1976). "The Brezhnev Era: The Man and the System." *Problems of Communism* 25(2): 1–17.

———. (2001). *The Logic of Economic Reform in Russia.* Washington, DC: Brookings Institution Press.

Howard, M. M. (2002). "The Weakness of Postcommunist Civil Society." *Journal of Democracy* 13(1): 157–169.

———. (2003). *The Weakness of Civil Society in Post-Communist Europe.* Cambridge, UK: Cambridge University Press.

Hughes, J. (2002). "Managing Secession Potential in the Russian Federation." In *Ethnicity and Territory in the Former Soviet Union. Regions in Conflict*, J. Hughes and G. Sasse, eds. London: Frank Cass & Co.

Hughes, J., P. John, et al. (2002). "From Plan to Network: Urban Elites and the Post-Communist Organisational State in Russia." *European Journal of Political Research* 41(3): 395–420.

Hume, D. ([1772] 1994a). "Of Civil Liberty." In *Political Essays*, K. Hankonssen, ed. Cambridge, UK: Cambridge University Press.

———. ([1772] 1994b). "Of the First Principles of Government." In *Political Essays*, K. Hankonssen, ed. Cambridge, UK: Cambridge University Press.

———. ([1772] 1994c). "Of the Liberty of the Press. In *Political Essays*, K. Hankonssen, ed. Cambridge, UK: Cambridge University Press.

Iakovleva, I. (2008). "Missiia Biznes Solidarnosti: razvitie kapitalizma v Rossii." Moscow: Business Solidarity. Retrieved on November 22, 2012, from www.kapitalisty.ru/path/print/003/.

Iasin, E. G. (2002). *Rossiiskaia ekonomika. Istoki i panorama rynochnykh reform.* Moscow: GU-VShE.

Ignat'eva, I., and K. Finaeva. (2005). "Zakon o dolevom stroitel'stve: grazhdane vooryzheny i dazhe opasny." *Izvestiia*, Moscow, April 1.

Innes, A. (2002). "Party Competition in Post-Communist Europe: The Great Electoral Lottery." *Comparative Politics* 35(1).

International Monetary Fund. (2013). Current Government Finance Statistics. Washington, DC: International Monetary Fund.

"Internet v Rossii: dinamika proniknoveniia. Leto 2012." (2012). Moscow: FOM.

Islamoglu, H. (2001). "Civil Society, Concept and History of," In *International Encyclopedia of the Social and Behavioral Sciences*, N. J. Smelser and P. B. Baltes, eds. London: Elsevier.

Ivanov, S. (2006). "Rassledovanie. Sochinskii OMON prevysil polnomochiia." *Kommersant*, Moscow, July 24: 4.

Ivanova, A., M. Keen, et al. (2005). *The Russian Flat Tax Reform*. Washington, DC: IMF.

Jackson, W. D. (2004). "Russia and the Council of Europe: The Perils of Premature Admission." *Problems of Post-Communism* 51(5): 23–33.

Jasper, J. M. (1998). "The Emotions of Protest: Affective and Reactive Emotions in and around Social Movements." *Sociological Forum* 13(3): 397–424.

Jenkins, J. C. (1995). "Social Movements, Political Representation, and the State: An Agenda and Comparative Framework." In *Politics of Social Protest. Comparative Perspectives on States and Social Movements*, J. C. Jenkins and B. Klandermans, eds. London: UCL Press.

Jowitt, K. (2008). "Rus United." *Journal of Communist Studies and Transition Politics* 24(4): 480–511.

"Kak pravilis' zakony o vyborakh." (2007). *Kommersant*, Moscow, November 12: 4.

Kaldor, M. (2003). *Global Civil Society: An Answer to War*. Cambridge, UK: Polity Press.

Kaul, I., P. Conceicau, et al., eds. (2003). *Providing Global Public Goods: Managing Globalization*. Oxford, UK: Oxford University Press.

Keane, J., ed. (1988). *Civil Society and the State: New European Perspectives*. London: Verso.

Khairullin, M. (2005). "Demonstratsiia sily: Uzhe polgoda siloviki derzhat v strakhe Tverskuiu oblast." *Novaia Gazeta*, Moscow, March 21: 18.

Kharkhordin, O. (1998). "First Europe-Asia Lecture:. Civil Society and Orthodox Christianity." *Europe-Asia Studies* 50(6): 949–968.

Khmelev, M. (2006). "Deputaty vstupilis' za obmanutykh dol'shchikov." *Izvestiia*, Moscow, May 25.

Kis, J. (1989). *Politics in Hungary: For a Democratic Alternative*. Boulder, CO: Social Science Monographs.

Kitschelt, H. (2000). "Linkages between Citizens and Politicians in Democratic Polities." *Comparative Political Studies* 33(6/7): 845–879.

Kitschelt, H., and R. Smyth (2002). "Programmatic Party Cohesion in Emerging Postcommunist Democracies: Russia in Comparative Context." *Comparative Political Studies* 35(10): 1228–1256.

Klimov, D. (2005). "'Edinaia Rossiia' podderzhala oranzhevykh." *Novye Izvestiia*, Moscow, October 11.

Klimov, I. (2008). "Permanentnyi bunt: reforma sotsial'nykh l'got 2004–2005 godov i novye formy protestnoi aktivnosti." In *Grazhdanskoe obshchestvo sovremennoi Rossii. Sotsiologicheskie zarisovki s natury*, E. S. Petrenko, ed. Moscow: Institut Fonda "Obshchestvennoe Mnenie."

Knox, Z., P. Lentini, et al. (2006). "Parties of Power and Russian Politics. A Victory of the State over Civil Society?" *Problems of Post-Communism* 53(1): 3–14.

Kodin, M. I. (1998). *Obshchestvenno-politicheskie ob'edineniia i formirovanie politicheskoi elity v Rossii (1990–1997)*. Moscow: Fond sodeistviia razvitiiu sotsial'nykh i politicheskikh nauk.

Kolesnichenko, A. (2006). "Predsedatel' Moskovskoi Khel'sinkskoi Gruppy Liudmila Alekseeva: 'Menia ni razu ne nazvali shpionkoi.'" *Novye Izvestiia*, Moscow, May 12.

Kolesnikov, A. (2011). "Kandidatskii maksimum: Vladimir Putin i Dmitrii Medvedev obmenialis' predlozheniiami o novykh dolzhnostiakh." *Kommersant*, September 26.

Kondrat'eva, M. (2005). "Vnutrennie organy: Karandash v nos." *Gazeta*, Moscow, March 16: 4.

Konitzer-Smirnov, A. (2005). "Serving Different Masters: Regional Executives and Accountability in Ukraine and Russia." *Europe-Asia Studies* 57(1): 3–33.

Konygina, N. i. (2005). "'Rossiia izbitaia' razoblachit 'oborotnei.'" *Izvestiia*, Moscow, July 29: 2.

Konygina, N. i., and I. Spirin. (2005). "Prokuratura vozbudila delo protiv narkopolitseiskikh." *Izvestiia*, Moscow, March 25: 7.

Kordonskii, S. (2000). *Rynki vlasti. Administrativnye rynki SSSR i Rossii*. Moscow: OGI.

Kornai, J. (1992). *The Socialist System*. Oxford, UK: Oxford University Press.

Kozenko, A. (2006). "Kvartirnyi vopros. Soinvestorov razvel Gorbatyi most." *Kommersant*, Moscow, May 23.

Kryshtanovskaia, O. V. (2002). "Biznes-elita i oligarkhi: itogi desiatiletiia." *Mir Rossii* 2002(4): 1–57.

———. (2008). "The Russian Elite in Transition." *Journal of Communist Studies and Transition Politics* 24(4): 585–603.

Kryshtanovskaia, O. V., and S. White. (2005). "Inside the Putin Court: A Research Note." *Europe-Asia Studies* 57(7): 1065–1075.

Kubicek, P. (2000). "Post-Communist Political Studies: Ten Years Later, Twenty Years Behind?" *Communist and Post-Communist Studies* 33: 295–309.

Kubik, J. (2005). "How to Study Civil Society: The State of the Art and What to Do Next." *East European Politics and Societies* 19(1): 105–121.

Kulikov, V. (2007). "Proizvol—za schet kazny. Vladimir Lukin predlagaet programmu zashchity prav poterpevshego." *Rossiiskaia Gazeta*, Moscow, April 24.

Kumar, K. (1993). "Civil Society: An Inquiry into the Usefulness of an Historical Term." *British Journal of Sociology* 44(3): 375–395.

Kurzman, C. (2004). "Can Understanding Undermine Explanation? The Confused Experience of Revolution." *Philosophy of the Social Sciences* 34(3): 382–351.

Lane, D., and C. Ross. (1998). "The Russian Political Elites, 1991–95: Recruitment and Renewal." In *Postcommunist Elites and Democracy in Eastern Europe*, J. Higley, J. Pakulski, and W. Wesolowski, eds. London: Macmillan Press.

Lebedeva, A. (2006a). "Ne v sluzhbu, a v 'druzhbu.'" *Novaia Gazeta*, Moscow, July 31: 13.

———. (2006b). "OMONovtsev pereveli iz lageria v SIZO." *Novaia Gazeta*, Moscow, August 10: 7.

———. (2000). "Continuity and Change of *Blat* Practices in Soviet and Post-Soviet Russia." In *Bribery and Blat in Russia: Negotiating Reciprocity from the Middle Ages to the 1990s*, S. Lovell, A. Ledeneva, and A. Rogachevskii, eds. Houndsmills, Basingstoke, UK: Macmillan Press.

Ledeneva, A. V. (2006). *How Russia Really Works. The Informal Practices That Shaped Post-Soviet Politics and Business*. Ithaca, NY: Cornell University Press.

Ledyaev, V. (2008). "Domination, Power and Authority in Russia: Basic Characteristics and Forms." *Journal of Communist Studies and Transition Politics* 24(1): 17–36.

Lee, C. K., and Y. Zhang. (2013). "The Power of Instability: Unraveling the Microfoundations of Bargained Authoritarianism in China." *American Journal of Sociology* 118(6): 1475–1508.

Lemaitre, R. (2006). "The Rollback of Democracy in Russia after Beslan." *Review of Central and East European Law* 31: 369–411.

Lenin, V. I. ([1917] 1962). Gosudarstvo i revoliutsiia. Vol. 33, *Polnoe sobranie sochinenii: V. I. Lenin*. Moscow: Gosudarstvennoe izdatel'stvo politicheskoi literatury.

Lermontov, M. Iu. (1983). "Borodino." In *Sobranie sochinenii*, M. Iu. Lermontov. Moscow: Khudozhestvennaia literatura.

Levitsky, S., and L. Way (2010). *Competitive Authoritarianism: Hybrid Regimes after the Cold War*. New York: Cambridge University Press.

Liikanen, I. (2008). "Civil Society and the Reconstitution of Russian Political Space: The Case of the Republic of Karelia." In *Media, Culture and Society in Putin's Russia*, S. White, ed. Houndsmills, UK: Palgrave.

Linz, J. J. (1990). "The Perils of Presidentialism." *Journal of Democracy* 1(1): 51–69.

Linz, J. J., and A. Stepan. (1996). *Problems of Democratic Transition and Consolidation: Southern Europe, South America and Post-Communist Europe*. Baltimore, MD: Johns Hopkins University Press.

Lipman, M. (2006). "Svoboda pressy v usloviiakh upravliaemoi demokratii." *Carnegie Moscow Center Briefings*. Moscow: Carnegie Moscow Center.

Lipman, M., and N. Petrov. (2007). "Vzaimodesitvie vlasti i obshchestva." In *Puti rossiiskogo postkommunizma*, M. Lipman and A. Riabov, eds. Moscow: Carnegie Moscow Center.

Lipset, S. M. (1994). "The Social Requisites of Democracy Revisited: 1993 Presidential Address." *American Sociological Review* 59(1): 1–22.

Liubarskaia, E. (2004). "Putin poluchil pervoe preduprezhdenie." *Lenta.ru*.

Locke, J. ([1667] 1993). "An Essay Concerning Toleration." In *Political Writings*, D. Wootton, ed. London: Penguin.

———. ([1681] 1993). "The Second Treatise of Government: An Essay Concerning the True Origins, Extent, and End of Civil Government." In *Political Writings*, D. Wootton, ed. London: Penguin.

Lokotetskaia, M. (2006). "Militsionerov sudiat za izbienie 12-letnego shkol'nika." *Gazeta*, Moscow, October 13: 8.

Lovell, D. W. (2001). "Trust and the Politics of Postcommunism." *Communist and Post-Communist Studies* 34: 27–38.

Luong, P. J., and E. Weinthal. (2001). "Prelude to the Resource Curse: Explaining Oil and Gas Development Strategies in the Soviet Successor States and Beyond." *Comparative Political Studies* 34(4): 367–399.

———. (2004). "Contra Coercion: Russian Tax Reform, Exogenous Shocks, and Negotiated Institutional Change." *American Political Science Review* 98(1): 139–152.

Machleder, J., and G. Asmolov. (2011). *Social Change and the Russian Network Society*. Washington, DC: Internews Center for Innovation and Learning.

Madureira, N. L. (2007). "Cartelization and Corporatism: Bureaucratic Rule in Authoritarian Portugal, 1926–45." *Journal of Contemporary History* 42(1): 79–96.

Mandrik, I. (2005). "Narkozachistka." *Russkii kur'er*, Moscow, March 16: 1.

March, L. (2009). "Managing Opposition in a Hybrid Regime: Just Russia and Parastatal Opposition." *Slavic Review* 68(3): 504–527.

Martovalieva, I. (2005a). "Politika/Rassledovaniia. 'My prosto khotim svobodno vybirat' vse—ot mashiny do prezidenta.'" *Novaia Gazeta*, Moscow, July 25.

————. (2005b). "Politika/Rassledovaniia. I lentochki 'oranzhevykh' v glazakh." *Novaia Gazeta*, Moscow, May 26.

Marx, K. ([1844] 1970). "Critique of Hegel's Philosophy of Right." In *Marx's Critique of Hegel's Philosophy of Right*, J. O'Malley, ed. Cambridge, UK: Cambridge University Press.

Mawdsley, E., and S. White. (2000). *The Soviet Elite from Lenin to Gorbachev.* Oxford, UK: Oxford University Press.

May, R. A., and A. K. Milton, eds. (2005). *(Un)Civil Societies. Human Rights and Democratic Transitions in Eastern Europe and Latin America.* Lanham, MD: Lexington Books.

McAdam, D. (1986). "Recruitment to High-Risk Activism: The Case of Freedom Summer." *American Journal of Sociology* 92(1): 64–90.

McAuley, M. (1997). *Russia's Politics of Uncertainty.* Cambridge, UK: Cambridge University Press.

McCarthy, J. D., and M. N. Zald. (1977). "Resource Mobilization and Social Movements: A Partial Theory." *American Journal of Sociology* 82(6): 1212–1241.

McFaul, M. (1995). "State Power, Institutional Change, and the Politics of Privatization in Russia." *World Politics* 47(2): 210–243.

————. (2002). "The Fourth Wave of Democracy and Dictatorship: Noncooperative Transitions in the Postcommunist World." *World Politics* 54: 212–244.

————. (2005). "Transitions from Postcommunism." *Journal of Democracy* 16(3): 5–19.

McFaul, M., and E. Treyger. (2004). "Civil Society." In *Between Dictatorship and Democracy: Russian Post-Communist Political Reform*, ed. M. McFaul, N. Petrov, and A. Riabov. Washington, DC: Carnegie.

McMann, K. M. (2006). *Economic Autonomy and Democracy: Hybrid Regimes in Russia and Kyrgyzstan.* Cambridge, UK: Cambridge University Press.

Merkel, W. (2004). "Embedded and Defective Democracies." *Democratization* 11(5): 33–58.

Mersiianova, I. (2008). "Sotsial'naia baza rossiiskogo grazhdanskogo obshchestva." In *Grazhdanskoe obshchestvo sovremennoi Rossii. Sotsiologicheskie zarisovki s natury*, E. S. Petrenko. ed. Moscow: Institut Fonda "Obshchestvennoe Mnenie."

"Mesto Sobytii. Militsiia poshla v zaboi." *Novaia Gazeta*, Moscow, April 21, 2005: 4

Mickiewicz, E. (1999). *Changing Channels: Television and the Struggle for Power in Russia.* Durham, NC: Duke University Press.

————. (2008). *Television, Power, and the Public in Russia.* Cambridge, UK: Cambridge University Press.

Migalin, S., and N. i. Zhukova. (2005). "Stariki napugali chinovnikov. Permskie pensionery shturmuiut mestye administratsii." *Nezavisimaia Gazeta*, Moscow, February 2.

"Militsionery, izbivshie 12-letnego shkol'nika, poluchili po tri goda." (2006). *Sovetskaia Rossiia*, Moscow, November 2: 2.

"Militsionerov posadili za izbienie shkol'nika." (2006). *Moskovskii Komsomolets*, Moscow, November 1: 2.

"Militsionery, sdelavshie zaderzhannogo invalidom, poluchili uslovnye sroki." (2004). *Novye Izvestiia*, Moscow, August 24: 6.

Mill, J. S. ([1848] 1970). *Principles of Political Economy: With Some of Their Applications to Social Philosophy. Books IV & V*. Harmondsworth, UK: Penguin.

Minkoff, D. C. (1997). "Producing Social Capital." *American Behavioral Scientist* 40(5): 606–619.

Mishler, W. and R. Rose. (1997). "Trust, Distrust and Skepticism: Popular Evaluations of Civil and Political Institutions in Post-Communist Societies." *The Journal of Politics* 59(2): 418–451.

Mohsin Hashim, S. (2005). "Putin's *Etatization* Project and Limits to Democratic Reforms in Russia." *Communist and Post-Communist Studies* 38: 25–48.

Moore, B. Jr. (1967). *Social Origins of Dictatorship and Democracy. Lord and Peasant in the Making of the Modern World*. Boston: Beacon.

———. (1978). *Injustice. The Social Bases of Obedience and Revolt*. London: Macmillan.

Morochenko, I. (2005). "Zhilishchnyi vopros. Osen' obmanutykh dol'shchikov." *Parlamentskaia Gazeta*, Moscow, November 8.

Morshchakova, T. (2003). "Na polputi k pravosudiiu." *Otechestvennye Zapiski* 2003(2); available at www.strana-oz.ru/?numid=11&article=438.

Moshkin, M., and D. Mel'man. (2006). "Sego Dnia. Altaiskii Krainii." *Moskovskii Komsomolets*, Moscow, February 4.

Moskovkin, L. (2006). "Obshchestvennikov zakopaiut v bukhgalterii." *Moskovskaia pravda*, Moscow, October 25: 1.

Nagornykh, I., I. Buranov, et al. (2006). "Polittekhnologii. Spasti voditelia Shcherbinskogo." *Kommersant*, Moscow, March 16.

Nikitinskii, L. (2007). "Tikho: Slushaetsia Rossiia." *Novaia Gazeta*, Moscow, May 10.

Novikova, A. (2005). "Portrety riadovykh militsionerov v sovremennoi pravookhranitel'noi sisteme." *Neprikosnovennyi Zapas* 2005(4); available at http://magazines.russ.ru/nz/2005/2042/nov2014.html.

"Novosti. Proisshestviia." (2003). *Vremia Novostei*, Moscow, June 9: 3

Offe, C. (1996). *Modernity and the State: East, West*. Cambridge, UK: Polity Press.

———. (2004). "Political Corruption: Conceptual and Practical Issues." In *Building a Trustworthy State in Post-Socialist Transition*, J. Kornai and S. Rose-Ackermann, eds. London: Palgrave.

"Okkupai Abai prodolzhaetsia." (2012). *RFI*, May 10.

Oleinik, A. (2008). "Existing and Potential Constraints Limiting State Servants' Opportunism: The Russian Case." *Journal of Communist Studies and Transition Politics* 24(1): 156–189.

———. (2011). "'Ofisnyi plankton' kak resurs sushchestvuiushchego politicheskogo rezhima?" *Vestnik obshchestennogo mneniia* 2(108): 47–52.

Oliver, P. E., and D. J. Myers. (2003). "The Coevolution of Social Movements." *Mobilization* 8(1): 1–25.

Olson, M. (1982). *The Rise and Decline of Nations. Economic Growth, Stagflation, and Social Rigidities*. New Haven, CT: Yale University Press.

"ONK: nachato rassledovanie po delu o pokhishchenii na Ukraine oppozitsionera Razvozzhaeva." (2012). *Gazeta.ru*, October 31.

Opros na prospekte Sakharova 24 dekabria. (2011). Moscow: Levada-Center.

Ottaway, M. (2003). *Democracy Challenged. The Rise of Semi-Authoritarianism*. Washington, DC: Carnegie Endowment for International Peace.

Ottaway, M., and T. Carothers, eds. (2000). *Funding Virtue. Civil Society Aid and Democracy Promotion*. Washington, DC: Carnegie Endowment for International Peace.

Parkhomenko, S. (2010). "Obshchestvo sinikh vederok." *Snob.ru*, April 13.

Parsons, T. (1947). "Introduction." In *The Theory of Social and Economic Organization*, by M. Weber. New York: Free Press.

Pastukhov, V. (2002). "Law under Administrative Pressure in Post-Soviet Russia." *East European Constitutional Review* 11(3).

Pavlikova, O. g., L. Mukhamed'iarova, et al. (2006). "Nekommercheskie organizatsii na zametke u prokurorov." *Gazeta*, Moscow, January 18: 3.

Pelczynski, Z. A. (1988). "Solidarity and 'The Rebirth of Civil Society' in Poland, 1967–81." In *Civil Society and the State. New European Perspectives*, J. Keane, ed. London: Verso.

Perova, A. (2007). "Sochinskii OMON zachistil detskii sanatorii ot otdykhaiushchikh i mestnykh zhitelei." *Kommersant*, Moscow, January 22: 6.

Petrenko, V., and A. Stenin. (2006). Iz KPZ v Dumu. *Gazeta.ru*.

Petrov, N., and A. Riabov. (2007). Vnutrennie problemy vlasti. In *Puti rossiiskogo postkommunizma*, M. Lipman and A. Riabov, eds. Moscow: Carnegie Moscow Center.

Pfaff, S. (1996). "Collective Identity and Informal Groups in Revolutionary Mobilization: East Germany in 1989." *Social Forces* 75(1): 91–117.

Pfaff, S., and H. Kim. (2003). "Exit-Voice Dynamics in Collective Action: An Analysis of Emigration and Protest in East German Revolution." *American Journal of Sociology* 109(2): 401–444.

Pipes, R. (2005). *Russian Conservatism and Its Critics: A Study in Political Culture*. New Haven, CT: Yale University Press.

Polanyi, K. ([1944] 2001). *The Great Transformation: The Political and Economic Origins of Our Time.* Boston: Beacon Press.

"Politika-Ekonomika. Ofitsial'no." (2005). *Vremia Novostei,* Moscow, April 14: 4.

Polletta, F., and J. M. Jasper (2001). "Collective Identity and Social Movements." *Annual Review of Sociology* 27: 283–305.

Pomorski, S. (2002). "In a Siberian Criminal Court." *East European Constitutional Review* 11(1/2).

"Pomoshchnik prezidenta Dvorkovich o vozvrashchenii Putina v Kreml': net povodov dlia radosti." (2011). *Gazeta.ru,* September 24.

"Po vsei Rossii proshli massovye aktsii protiv otmeny l'got." (2005). *Lenta.ru.*

"Priamaia liniia s Prezidentom Rossii Vladimirom Putinym." (2007). *Telekanal Rossia.* Retrieved on March 1, 2014, from www.president-line.ru.

Progonova, E., O. g. Gorbunova, et al. (2005). "Aktsiia. Oranzhevaia revoliutsiia avtomobilistov ne dala pravitel'stvu vvesti zapret na 'pravorukie' mashiny." *Gazeta,* Moscow, May 20.

Prokhorov, G., A. Irdullin, et al. (2005). "Na uglu Gagarina i Revoliutsionnoi." *Gazeta.ru.*

"Protsessy." (2003). *Kommersant,* Moscow, May 29: 4.

Przeworski, A. (1986). "Some Problems in the Study of Transition to Democracy." In *Transitions from Authoritarian Rule. Comparative Perspectives,* G. O'Donnell, P. C. Schmitter, and L. Whitehead, eds. Baltimore, MD: Johns Hopkins University Press.

———. (1991). *Democracy and the Market: Political and Economic Reforms in Eastern Europe and Latin America.* Cambridge, UK: Cambridge University Press.

Public Verdict. (2006). *Pytki v Rossii: Spravochnaia informatsiia po delam o pytkakh v proizvodstve rossiiskikh pravozashchitnykh organizatsii.* Moscow: Obshchestvennyi Verdikt.

———. (2007). *Deiatel'nost' Fonda 'Obshchestvennyi Verdikt' v 2006 godu.* Moscow: Obshchestvennyi Verdikt.

Putnam, R. D. (1976). *The Comparative Study of Political Elites.* Englewood Cliffs, NJ: Prentice-Hall.

Putnam, R. D., R. Leonardi, et al. (1993). *Making Democracy Work: Civic Traditions in Modern Italy.* Princeton, NJ: Princeton University Press.

Quigley, K. F. F. (2000). "Lofty Goals, Modest Results; Assisting Civil Society in Eastern Europe." In *Funding Virtue. Civil Society Aid and Democracy Promotion,* M. Ottaway and T. Carothers, eds. Washington, DC: Carnegie Endowment for International Peace.

Reddaway, P., and D. Glinski. (2001). *The Tragedy of Russia's Reforms: Market Bolshevism against Democracy.* Washington, DC: United States Institute of Peace Press.

Redichkina, O. g. (2005). "NKO budut zhit' po-novomu." *Gazeta*, Moscow, December 26: 2.

Riskin, A., and B. Pipiia. (2005). "Organizatorov mitingov podvodiat pod stat'iu. V regionakh nachalis' presledovaniia initsiatorov aktsii protesta." *Nezavisimaia gazeta*, Moscow, January 19: 1.

Robertson, G. B. (2009). "Managing Society: Protest, Civil Society, and Regime in Putin's Russia." *Slavic Review* 68(3): 528–547.

———. (2011). *The Politics of Protest in Hybrid Regimes: Managing Dissent in Post-Communist Russia*. Cambridge, UK: Cambridge University Press.

Robinson, J. A., R. Torvik, et al. (2003). Political Foundations of the Resource Curse. Working Paper. Paris: Departement et Laboratoire d'Economie Theorique et Appliquee.

Rogacheva, M. (2006). "Militsionery poluchili srok za izbitogo podrostka." *Izvestiia*, Moscow, November 1: 3.

Roniger, L. (1994). "The Comparative Study of Clientelism and the Changing Nature of Civil Society in the Contemporary World." In *Democracy, Clientelism, and Civil Society*, L. Roniger and A. Günes-Ayata, eds. Boulder, CO: Lynne Reinner Publishers.

Rose, R. (1994). "Rethinking Civil Society: Postcommunism and the Problem of Trust." *Journal of Democracy* 5(3): 18–30.

———. (1999a). "Modern, Pre-Modern and Anti-Modern Social Capital in Russia." In *Studies in Public Policy*. Glasgow, UK: Centre for the Study of Public Policy, University of Strathclyde.

———. (1999b). "What Does Social Capital Add to Individual Welfare? An Empirical Analysis of Russia." In *Studies in Public Policy*. Glasgow, UK: Centre for the Study of Public Policy, University of Strathclyde.

Rose, R., and W. Mishler. (1994). "Mass Reaction to Regime Change in Eastern Europe: Polarization or Leaders and Laggards?" *British Journal of Political Science* 24(2): 159–182.

Ross, C. (2000). "Federalism and Democratization in Russia." *Communist and Post-Communist Studies* 33: 403–420.

Ross, M. L. (1999). "The Political Economy of the Resource Curse." *World Politics* 51(2): 297–322.

———. (2001). "Does Oil Hinder Democracy?" *World Politics* 53: 325–361.

Rosser, J. B. Jr., and M. V. Rosser. (1997). "Schumpeterian Evolutionary Dynamics and the Collapse of Soviet-Bloc Socialism." *Review of Political Economy* 9(2): 211–223.

Rousseau, J.-J. ([1762] 1968). *The Social Contract*. M. Cranston, translator. London: Penguin.

Rudneva, E. (2004). "Putin: protestovat' mozhno, no tikho." *Gazeta.ru*, April 12.

Rueschemeyer, D., E. H. Stephens, et al. (1992). *Capitalist Development and Democracy.* Cambridge, UK: Polity Press.

Rustow, D. A. (1970). "Transitions to Democracy: Toward a Dynamic Model." *Comparative Politics* 2(3): 337–363.

Ryabov, A. (2008). Vozrozhdenie "feodal'noi" arkhaiki v sovremennoi Rossii: Praktika i idei. *Working Papers.* Moscow: Carnegie Moscow Center.

Sadchikov, A. (2004). "'Nezorovykh ogranichenii' nam ne nado. Putin zapretil zakon o zaprete mitingov." *Izvestiia,* Moscow, April 14: 3.

Samarina, A. (2011). "Nevostrebovannaia vera v politicheskoe chudo." *Nezavisimaia Gazeta,* July 14.

Sampson, R. J., D. McAdam, et al. (2005). "Civil Society Reconsidered: The Durable Nature and Community Structure of Collective Civic Action." *American Journal of Political Science* 111(3): 673–714.

Sandler, T., and J. Tschirhart. (1997). "Club Theory: Thirty Years Later." *Public Choice* 93: 335–355.

Sapozhnikova, G. (2005). "Bitie opredeliaet soznanie?" *Komsomol'skaia Pravda,* Moscow, May 11: 8.

Sas, I., and R. Ukolov. (2005). "Pravozashchitniki nashli 'Blagoveshchensk-2.' Sotrudniki Gosnarkokontrolia ne ponimaiut metanii Tverskoi oblprokuratury." *Nezavisimaia Gazeta,* Moscow, March 25: 7.

Savina, E., S. Smirnov, et al. (2011). "Vlastiam dali dve nedeli." *Gazeta.ru,* December 10.

Schmidt-Pfister, D. (2008). "What Kind of Civil Society in Russia?" In *Media, Culture and Society in Putin's Russia,* S. White, ed. Houndsmills, UK: Palgrave.

Schumpeter, J. A. (1942). *Capitalism, Socialism and Democracy.* New York: Harper & Brothers.

Sedel'nikov, P. (2006). "Avtomobilistam prostiat krasnye povorotniki." *Gazeta,* Moscow, January 27.

Sedel'nikov, P., M. Marchuk, et al. (2006). "Vlast' poluchila spetssignal." *Gazeta,* Moscow, February 13.

Selina, M., and A. Riskin. (2006). "Kommunalka zamedlennogo deistviia. V regionakh nachalis' massovye aktsii protesta v sviazi s rostom tsen na uslugi ZhKKh." *Nezavisimaia Gazeta,* Moscow, January 23.

Sergeev, N. (2005). "Pravozashchita. Bit' nuzhno v kaif." *Kommersant,* Moscow, March 25: 5.

Sestanovich, S. (2007). "Putin's Invented Opposition." *Journal of Democracy* 18(2): 122–124.

Shamburova, A. (2004). "Opyt chastnogo soprotivleniia. Bityi chas." *Novaia Gazeta,* Moscow, 27 September 27: 6–7.

Sharafutdinova, G. (2013). "Gestalt Switch in Russian Federalism: The Decline in Regional Power under Putin." *Comparative Politics* 45(3): 357–376.

Shaver, K. G. (1985). *The Attribution of Blame. Causality, Responsibility, and Blameworthiness*. New York: Springer-Verlag.

Shelley, L. I. (1996). *Policing Soviet Society: The Evolution of State Control*. London: Routledge.

Shepeleva, O. g. (2005). "Pravookhranitel'nye organy—naseleniiu: chego grazhdane zhdut i ne mogut poluchit' ot militsii." *Neprikosnovennyi Zapas* 2005(4); available at http://magazines.russ.ru/nz/2005/2042/sh2015.html.

Shevtsova, L. (2004). "The Limits of Bureaucratic Authoritarianism." *Journal of Democracy* 15(3): 67–77.

———. (2007). *Russia, Lost in Transition: The Yeltsin and Putin Legacies*. Washington, DC: Carnegie Endowment for International Peace.

Shleifer, A., and R. W. Vishny. (1994). "Politicians and Firms." *Quarterly Journal of Economics* 109(4): 995–1025.

Shramenko, M. (2006). "Voditeli—za Shcherbinskogo." *Cheliabinskii rabochii*, Cheliabinsk, February 14.

Shugart, M., and J. Carey. (1992). *Presidents and Assemblies: Constitutional Design and Electoral Dynamics*. Cambridge, UK: Cambridge University Press.

Sidorenko, A. (2011). "Rossiia: vosstanie 'setevykh khomiachkov'." *Global Voices*, December 8.

Simonia, N. (2001). "Economic Interests and Political Power in Post-Soviet Russia." In *Contemporary Russian Politics*, A. Brown, ed. Oxford, UK: Oxford University Press.

Slezkine, Y. (2000). "The Soviet Union as a Communal Apartment, or How a Socialist State Promoted Ethnic Particularism." In *Stalinism. New Directions*, S. Fitspatrick, ed. London: Routledge.

Smith, A. ([1776] 1970). *An Inquiry into the Nature and Causes of the Wealth of Nations. Books I-III*. Harmondsworth, UK: Penguin.

Smith, B. (2004). "Oil Wealth and Regime Survival in the Developing World, 1960–1999." *American Journal of Political Science* 48(2): 232–246.

Snow, D. A., and E. B. Rochford Jr. (1986). "Frame Alignment Processes, Micromobilization, and Movement Participation." *American Sociological Review* 51(4): 464–481.

Snow, D. A., E. B. Rochford Jr., et al. (1986). "Frame Alignment Processes, Micromobilization, and Movement Participation." *American Sociological Review* 51(4): 464–481.

Sokolov, S. (2011). "Kontsy priatali s nachala." *Novaia Gazeta*, November 16.

Solomon, P. H. Jr. (2008). "Law in Public Administration: How Russia Differs." *Journal of Communist Studies and Transition Politics* 24(1): 115–135.

Solomon, P. H. Jr., and T. S. Foglesong. (2000). "The Procuracy and the Courts in Russia: A New Relationship?" *East European Constitutional Review* 9(4).

Solovykh, P. (2006). "Samopiarom—po spetssignalam!" *Izvestiia*, Moscow, May 29.

Sonin, K. (2003). "Why the Rich May Favor Poor Protection of Property Rights." *Journal of Comparative Economics* 31: 715–731.

"Sotsial'no-politicheskaia situatsiia v Rossii v marte 2006 goda." (2006). *Press-vypusk*, April 11. Moscow: Levada-Center.

Sperling, V. (1999). *Organizing Women in Contemporary Russia: Engendering Transition*. New York: Cambridge University Press.

Splichal, S. (2001). "Journalism and Journalists." In *International Encyclopedia of the Social and Behavioral Sciences*, N. J. Smelser and P. B. Baltes, eds. London: Elsevier.

Stepan, A. (1986). "Paths toward Redemocratization: Theoretical and Comparative Considerations." In *Transitions from Authoritarian Rule: Comparative Perspectives*, G. O'Donnell, P. C. Schmitter, and L. Whitehead, eds. Baltimore, MD: Johns Hopkins University Press.

Stepan, A., and J. J. Linz. (2013). "Democratization Theory and the 'Arab Spring.'" *Journal of Democracy* 24(2): 15–30.

Stepovoi, B. (2007). "Mitingovat' pridetsia po novym pravilam." *Izvestiia*, Moscow, April 5: 2.

Subramaniam, V. (2000). "Comparative Public Administration: From Failed Universal Theory to Raw Empiricism—A Frank Analysis and Guidelines towards a Realistic Perspective." *International Review of Administrative Sciences* 66(4): 557–572.

Sundstrom, L. M. (2006a). *Funding Civil Society: NGO Development in Russia*. Stanford, CA: Stanford University Press.

———. (2006b). Soldiers' Rights Groups in Russia: Civil Society through Russian and Western Eyes. In *Russian Civil Society: A Critical Assessment*, A. B. Evans Jr., L. A. Henry, and L. M. Sundstrom, eds. Armonk, NY: M. E. Sharpe.

Svetova, Z. (2010). "Zhanna d'Ark Khimkinskogo lesa." *The New Times*. December 27.

Sztompka, P. (1998). Mistrusting Civility: Predicament of a Post-Communist Society. In *Real Civil Societies. Dilemmas of Institutionalization*, ed. J. C. Alexander. London: Sage.

Tarrow, S. (1998). *Power in Movement: Social Movements and Contentious Politics*. Cambridge, UK: Cambridge University Press.

Taylor, C. (1990). "Modes of Civil Society." *Public Culture* 3(1): 95–118.

Tepliakov, S. (2006). "Avtomobilisty Rossii podderzhat Olega Shcherbinskogo." *Altaiskaia Pravda*, Barnaul, March 21.

Tepliakov, S., and A. Kaspirshin. (2006). "Oleg Shcherbinskii ne vinovat." *Altaiskaia Pravda*, Barnaul, March 25.

"30 natsional-bol'shevikov vorvalis' v zdanie Minzdrava." (2004). *Lenta.ru*.

Tiazhlov, I. (2006). "Polittekhnologii. 'Edinoi Rossii' ne udalas' avtomobilizatsiia." *Kommersant*, Moscow, March 23.

Tilly, C. (1984). "Social Movements and National Politics." In *Statemaking and Social Movements. Essays in History and Theory*, C. Bright and S. Harding, eds. Ann Arbor: University of Michigan Press.

Timofeev, I. (2010). "V podderzhku Khimkinskogo lesa: speto!" *Radio Svoboda*, August 22.

Titov, E. (2007). "V bor'be s OMONom pobedila 'Druzhba.'" *Novaia Gazeta*, Moscow, March 15: 7.

Toepfl, F. (2013). "Making Sense of the News in a Hybrid Regime: How Young Russians Decode State TV and an Oppositional Blog." *Journal of Communication* 63(2): 244–265.

"Torfianye pozhary v Podmoskov'e letom 2010 goda." (2010). *RIA Novosti*, February 4.

Torstendahl, R. (2001). "Bureaucratization and Bureaucracy, History of," in *International Encyclopedia of the Social and Behavioral Sciences*, N. J. Smelser and P. B. Baltes, eds. London: Elsevier.

Tucker, R. C. (1987). *Political Culture and Leadership in Soviet Russia: From Lenin to Gorbachev*. Brighton, UK: Wheatsheaf Books.

"2010 Disasters in Numbers." (2010). Louvain, Belgium: Centre for Research on the Epidemiology of Disasters (CRED), Université Catholique de Louvain.

USAID. (1999). *Lessons in Implementation: The NGO Story. Building Civil Society in Central and Eastern Europe and the New Independent States*. Washington, DC: U.S. Agency for International Development.

Utkin, S. (2006). "Pod oblomkami stroitel'nykh piramid okazalis' tysiachi peterburzhtsev, stavshikh uchastnikami dolevogo stroitel'stva." *Sankt-Peterburgskie Vedomosti*, St. Petersburg, January 26.

"V Iuzhnom Butovo vozvodiat barrikady." (2008). *Lenta.ru*, July 31.

Visloguzov, V. (2005). "Bor'ba s monetizatsiei. Pravitel'stvo soglasilos' na 'podstavu.'" *Kommersant*, Moscow, January 22.

Volkov, V., E. Paneiakh, et al. (2010). "Proizvol'naia aktivnost' pravookhranitel'nykh organov v sfere bor'by s ekonomicheskoi prestupnost'iu. Analiz statistiki." *Annalytical Reports*, 2. St. Petersburg: Institute for the Study of the Rule of Law, European University.

Vorozheikina, T. (1994). "Clientelism and the Process of Political Democratization in Russia." In *Democracy, Clientelism, and Civil Society*, L. Roniger, and A. Günes-Ayata, eds. Boulder, CO: Lynne Reinner Publishers.

Voslenskii, M. ([1990] 2005). *Nomenklatura*. Moscow: Zakharov.

"Vse varianty dorogi do Petersburga prokhodiat cherez Khimkinskii les." (2010). *RIA Novosti*, February 4.

"Vystuplenie Vladimira Putina na mitinga v Luzhnikakh." (2012). *RIA Novosti*, February 23.

Wampler, Brian, and Leonardo Avritzer. (2004). "Participatory Publics: Civil Society and New Institutions in Democratic Brazil." *Comparative Politics* 36, 3: 291–312.

Way, L. (2008). "The Real Causes of the Color Revolutions." *Journal of Democracy* 19(3): 55–69.

Weber, M. (1947). *The Theory of Social and Economic Organization*. New York: Free Press.

———. (1962). *Basic Concepts in Sociology*. New York: Philosophical Library.

Wegren, S. K. (2003). "The Rise, Fall, and Transformation of the Rural Social Contract in Russia." *Communist and Post-Communist Studies* 36: 1–27.

Weigle, M. A., and J. Butterfield. (1992). "Civil Society in Reforming Communist Regimes: The Logic of Emergence." *Comparative Politics* 25(1): 1–23.

Weinthal, E., and P. J. Luong. (2001). "Energy Wealth and Tax Reform in Russia and Kazakhstan." *Resources Policy* 27: 215–223.

Wilson, A. (2005). *Virtual Politics: Faking Democracy in the Post-Soviet World*. New Haven, CT: Yale University Press.

Woodruff, D. M. (2000). "Rules for Followers: Institutional Theory and the New Politics of Economic Backwardness in Russia." *Politics and Society* 28(4): 437–482.

World Bank. (2004). *From Transition to Development: A Country Economic Memorandum for the Russian Federation*. Washington, DC: World Bank.

———. (2013). *Russian Federation. Export Diversification through Competition and Innovation: A Policy Agenda*. Washington, DC: World Bank.

———. (2013b). *World Development Indicators*. Washington, DC: World Bank.

Yakovlev, E., and E. Zhuravskaya. (2004). *State Capture and Controlling Owners of Firms*. Moscow: Center for Economic and Financial Research.

Zakatnova, A. (2006). "Politika: Buket oppozitsii." *Rossiiskaia Gazeta*, Moscow, April 5.

Zielonka, J., ed. (2001). *Democratic Consolidation in Eastern Europe. Volume 1: Institutional Engineering*. Oxford, UK: Oxford University Press.

Zorin, I. (2006). "'Budesh' soprotivliat'sia—pridushim i zakopaem.'" *Gazeta*, Moscow, April 13: 8.

Zvonovskii, V. (2008). "Indeks doveritel'noi strategii." In *Grazhdanskoe obshchestvo sovremennoi Rossii. Sotsiologicheskie zarisovki s natury*, E. S. Petrenko, ed. Moscow: Institut Fonda "Obshchestvennoe mnenie."

Index

Adjani, M., 112
administrative market, 66–67, 70, 77, 84, 90
administrative resources, 81–82, 84–85, 90
Afanas'ev, Iurii: on Russian power and the people, 94–95
Afanasiev, M. N., 78
Afisha, 211
Akunin, Boris, 210, 211
Al'bats, Evgeniia, 79, 163, 197
Alekseeva, Liudmila, 53, 141, 164, 192, 197, 199, 208
Alekseeva, N., 147
Alekseev, I., 85
All-Russian Popular Front, 199
Almond, Gabriel: on civic culture, 40–41, 47; on participant culture in democracy, 40–41; on state input and output mechanisms, 40–41, 60; on trust, 41, 47–48
Anderson, R. D., Jr., 5
Anheier, Helmut: on social capital and civil society, 16
Anisimov, S., 114, 125
Aptekar', P., 85
Arab Spring, 225, 226
Arato, A., 45, 47
Arrow, Kenneth: on trust as public good, 42
Ashwin, Sarah, 89, 99; on Russian patience, 10, 20
Asmolov, Grigorii, 204
Astrakhan', 107, 109, 215
authoritarianism, 6–7, 9, 61–62, 92; and democracy, 12–15, 219, 225–26;

Levitsky and Way on, 4, 60, 225–26; semiauthoritarianism, 4, 7, 13, 14, 127
Auyero, J., 89
Averkiev, I., 46
Avritzer, Leonardo, 229n4

Bakhmina, Svetlana, 140
Bargin, Pavel, 211
Barnaul, 178, 187, 193
Barnes, A., 73
Beketov, Mikhail, 162, 163
Belanovskii, Sergei, 205, 206, 209
Belin, L., 82
Belyaeva, Nina, 97, 99
Berezovsky, Boris, 77, 82, 90
Berglas, Eitan, 82–83
Berkowitz, D., 79
Beshlei, O., 141
Bezhetsk pogrom case, 121, 122, 132, 138; media coverage of, 113, 123, 124–25, 126–27, 129–30, 139; *volokita* in, 126, 129–30
Biznes Solidarnost', 141, 142
black market, 70, 71
Blagoveschchensk, 119, 129
blat, 65, 70–71, 179, 230n4
Blue Bucket Society, 198–200
Bobbio, N., 12
Bondarenko, A., 147
Borooah, V. K., 5
Borzykin, Mikhail, 164
Brezhnev, Leonid, 64, 65, 69–70
Brigada, 124, 232n29
Broadway, Robin: on club goods, 83
Browder, William, 140

co-optation, 16, 84–85, 102, 103, 160, 167, 199, 219
Crozier, M., 38
Curkowski, J., 73
Czechoslovakia, 54, 71; Charter 77, 44; Prague Spring, 226
Czech Republic: public services in, 80; taxation in, 81

Dahl, Robert, 60
Darwin's *Origin of Species*, 30
Davydov, O. B., 77, 78
democratization, 4–5, 6, 12–15, 91, 106, 225–28; Linz and Stepan on, 11, 13, 46–47, 61, 224, 226; relationship to civil society, 44–48, 54, 61; relationship to culture and history, 93–96, 100; relationship to natural resources, 73–74; relationship to social capital, 100; Robertson on, 227–28
Denisenko, M., 206
Diamond, Larry: definition of civil society, 39
Dickens, Charles: *Hard Times*, 32
dignity, 226
distributed denial of service (DDoS) attacks, 207
Dmitriev, Mikhail, 205, 206, 209
document checks, 112
Dogan, M., 16
dol'shchiki protests, 145, 156–59, 160, 161–62, 232n2, 233n16
Domrin, A. N., 3
Dozhd, 215
Drankina, E., 85
Drivers' Movement of Russia, 172
Dubin, B., 131, 134, 137
Durkheim, Emile: on civil society and positivistic law, 36
Duverger, Maurice, 12, 56; on liberal democracy, 40
Dvorkovich, Arkadii, 206
Dziadko, Tikhon, Filipp, and Timofei, 211

Easter, Gerald, 81
economic crimes, 139–42
Edinaia Rossiia. *See* United Russia

Egypt, 225
Ehrenberg, J., 11
Ekaterinburg, 174, 178, 217
Ekho Moskvy, 141, 197
Elifanova, M., 215
enabling actors, 37, 43, 56
environmentalists, 8; Khimki protests, 146–47, 162–63
equality, 30, 31, 95–96, 180, 181, 192, 201
Estonia: public services in, 80; taxation in, 81
Etzioni-Halevy, E., 77
European Commission, 112
European Court of Human Rights (ECHR), 127–28, 135–36, 164, 189
European Union, 13
Evans, A. B., Jr., 103
Evdokimov, Mikhail, 177, 178–79, 200

Facebook, 208, 211
Faibisovich, Il'ia, 211
family, 7, 8
Fatherland bloc, 84–85
Federation of Car-Owners of Russia (FAR), 198–99, 200
Fedorin, V., 141
Feldbrugge, F. J. M.: on samizdat, 53
Feldman, E., 214, 217
Ferguson, Adam, 11, 27, 29, 30; on civil society, 28, 36; on liberty, 28; on specialization, 28, 29, 34
feudalism, 23
Finaeva, K., 157
financial crisis of 1998, 72, 79, 82, 156
Fishman, M., 207
Fish, M. Stephen, 3, 4, 6, 102
Flynn, Moya, 8, 100
Foglesong, T. S., 135
Folger, R., 112
Fradkov, Mikhail, 157–58, 170
framing, 17, 96; frame bridging, 181; injustice frames, 106–7, 109, 118, 122–26, 130, 160, 162, 164, 165, 168–71, 177, 178–79, 181, 189, 200, 217, 220, 223
Frolov, Mikhail, 114, 115, 116
Fromm, E., 12, 35

Ross, Cameron, 13, 77, 78, 81
Ross, Michael: on natural resources and democracy, 73–74
Rosser, J. B., Jr., 65
Rosser, M. V., 65
Rossiiskaia Gazeta, 125, 136
Rousseau, Jean-Jacques, 30, 31, 33; on bureaucracy, 26, 27, 28; on citizens vs. subjects, 25, 26, 40; on civil society, 11, 25–26, 35, 54, 55; on general will, 25–26, 29; on justice and liberty, 25; *The Social Contract*, 25
Rozhdestvenskii, Robert, 202
Rudneva, E., 86
Rueschemeyer, Dietrich, 15–16
rule of law, 11, 44, 100, 136, 201
Russia: vs. China, 226–27; Congress of People's Deputies, 79; Constitution of 1993, 79; culture and history of, 92, 93–96, 97, 101; democratic legitimacy in, 87, 88, 89–90; economic conditions, 3, 6, 13, 72–76, 78–79, 82–84, 156–57; elections in, 1, 3, 9–10, 14, 15, 69, 85, 86, 87, 89, 90, 100, 104, 146, 154, 163, 199, 202, 205, 207–13, 214–15, 216, 219–20, 222; Emergency Situations Ministry, 204; Federal Guard Service (FSO), 170, 234n8; Federal Property Agency, 164; Federal Security Service (FSB), 170, 194, 202, 234n8; Federation Council, 139; financial-industrial groups (FIGs) in, 73, 79; gross domestic product (GDP), 72, 80; ideology in, 87–88, 91; legal and criminal justice system, 110–44, 145, 177–82, 185–86, 187, 189, 190–91, 192, 216, 221, 222, 224, 235nn45,50; Ministry of Economic Development, 205; Ministry of Health Care and Social Development, 146, 147; Ministry of Internal Affairs, 134; policies regarding imported automobiles, 167, 168–71, 173–74, 178, 186–87, 200–201; political repression in, 3, 13, 30, 73–74, 82, 91, 92, 102, 201, 216; public services in, 80–81; vs. Soviet Union, 4, 7, 8, 60, 72, 77–79, 81,

82, 84, 87–88, 90, 91, 112, 131, 134, 135, 136, 141, 154–55, 168, 188–89, 219, 222, 223, 234n8; State Duma, 146, 147, 172, 190, 205, 216; state-owned companies in, 73; Supreme Court, 141, 164; taxation in, 77, 79, 81, 82; virtual politics in, 9, 10, 86, 88
Russian Jewish Congress, 82
Russia Without Narcotics, 193
Rus Sidiashchaia (Imprisoned Rus), 141, 142, 210
Rustow, Dankwart: on democratization, 46, 61
Ryabov, Andrey, 95
Ryzhkov, Vladimir, 141, 187, 194, 208, 209, 210, 211

Sadchikov, A., 86
Samara, 146, 147
Samarina, A., 206
samizdat, 47, 53, 189
Sampson, Robert: on Putnam and civil society, 49; on social movements, 49
Samsonova, Antonina, 207–8
Sandler, Todd: on clubs, 67–68
Sapozhnikova, G., 124–25
Saprykin, Iurii, 211
Saratov, 147
Satarov, Goergii, 195, 197
Savina, E., 210
Schankerman, M., 76
Scheinkman, J., 76
Schmidt-Pfister, Diana, 102
Schmitter, P. C., 79
Schumpeter, Joseph: on elites seeking votes, 38, 40
Sedel'nikov, P., 173–74, 177
Selina, M., 147, 148
Serbia, 14–15
Sergeyev, Victor: on social networks, 100–101
Sestanovich, S., 86
Setevizor, 211
Shakhovalov, Nikolai, 120
Sharafutdinova, G., 228
Shats, Mikhail, 211
Shaver, K. G., 112